MALRAUX
An Essay in Political Criticism

MALRAUX - An Essay in Political Criticism

by David Wilkinson

HARVARD UNIVERSITY PRESS
CAMBRIDGE, MASSACHUSETTS

1967

PREFACE

POLITICAL BIOGRAPHY ATTEMPTS to understand and to explain the life of action while historical analysis of political thought strives to explain that thought through concrete reference to its time and context. The political criticism of thought, as I understand it, is neither of these; it is not an elucidation of and accounting for what is important, but an elucidation and appraisal of what is valuable.

This essay in political criticism is an attempt to present the principal political themes in the development of the thought of André Malraux; to tease out of his works his philosophy of life in its evolution, in its final and complete form, and in comparison as well as in isolation. For in all its forms it is worth contemplation at least.

1.

CRITICISM AND NONSCIENTIFIC POLITICAL THOUGHT

Political theory is neither science nor logic, although it has been suggested that political theory ought to be scientific in its methodology and logical in its presentation, that science and logic are good tools for the political thinker and good grounds for his critics. Some theorists go further, to suggest that no political thinker can be important unless he is striving to create a science of politics. Such an attitude may not affect today's view of the philosophers of the distant past, whose enterprise is of greater interest than is the mental discipline they brought to it. But applied to the present, the approach tends to obscure the very existence of most political thinkers of our times. These are not political scientists in any sense, nor do they intend to be. Like André Malraux, they are often "existential": they try to lay hold of the problems they see confronting man and his time. They are often symbolic and expressive in their attack on those problems, as Malraux is, and not scientific or logical.[1] Because their attack is existential and expressive, they come closer than objective science can to the roots of political experience.

Malraux is not an existentialist by the credos of that school; he is nevertheless an existential thinker, and not a classical rationalist or empiricist. His forebears are Nietzsche and Dostoevsky. Among his literary "descendants," if not his successors, are his younger contemporaries, Albert Camus and Jean-Paul Sartre. His concern is not with the essence of being or the nature of the universe, but with the position of man in time and among men, with man in history, with man in the social order. One minor problem of this particular concern is that it has associated with it a special vocabulary, a group of terms whose repeated use, philosophical implications, and palpable ambiguity have caused much consternation at the mere mention of the word "existentialism." Such words as "anguish," "absurdity," "destiny," "history," "the human condition," which Malraux and his critics use again and again, will be particularly offensive to philosophers of language, who are committed to the view that such terms are either too vague or entirely meaningless. Meaningless they are not; but they are so bound up with a particular world-view that they can bear meaning only to those who are willing at least to suspend judgment and not to reject that view out of hand. It is not necessary to define them each time they occur. Their origins are not in analytic philosophy; they are terms in a special and nonanalytic philosophical language, and

---

[1] In Malraux's case, the choice is a deliberate one: he does not acknowledge the objective validity of science and strongly denies its value for human life.

at some point it will become more convenient to learn the language, unfamiliar and unsatisfying as it may seem, than to continue to depend upon "translation." A failure to communicate may hide failures on both ends of the communication.

There may be reasons today which make the novel a prime vehicle for the expression of political ideas, even of traditional types of political ideas. The scholarly movement to make political theory into a "value-free" social science may or may not eventually succeed in creating a science of politics. Meanwhile it has led, if not to the total excision of values from contemporary specialized political thought—which is impossible—at least to the inhibition of the expression, exploration, overt creation, and judgment of values. There are plausible enough reasons for this movement. Sociologies of knowledge and value have shown how arbitrary and how irrationally rooted human values can be. Ideologies have proven to be deceptive, political beliefs have revealed their occasionally monstrous consequences. Traditional political faiths, meeting a changed reality, no longer seem to correspond to its problems, no longer evoke any real experience.

Values nevertheless remain and cannot be evaded. Politics and political experience remain, along with whatever needs create political beliefs. Therefore the abdicated value-carrying function is taken up by novelists, artists, journalists, theologians, by whatever groups of unspecialized political thinkers are willing to absorb it. The political thinker is, among other things, the creator of political values; and Malraux is nothing if he is not that.

Actually, then, it may appear that any reference to "criticism" here will be faulty because, with respect to Malraux, there is more exposition than hostile evaluation, and the element of judgment is confined as stringently as possible to certain discussions where it is most appropriate. In fact, criticism is a word which cuts two ways—only apparently two very different ways.

If the character of contemporary ways of thought, if the circumstances of today's political life are to be questioned, one method is through the light thrown upon them by the exposition of some thinker's insights—insights which are peculiar to his thought and which may seem sterile and merely formal. An enormous prolixity of this kind of thought exists, of course, "critical" even if it does not mean to be. It is all occasionally useful to the man of firm belief who would reestablish his perspective.

In the West, especially among its intellectuals, criticism has its other function because no set of beliefs can claim now to be firmly established. This is, rather, a time of general theoretical disestablishment; a skeptical rather than a theorizing or ideological spirit prevails. Perspective rather than attachment to ideas is the common element, except among a minority who pursue in isolation from the majority and from one another what are generally regarded as eccentricities. In this study the infusion of the same alien thoughts, the same light, may be used to provide an ultimate perspective on and against the habit of detached perspective. The extraction of political ideas from literature and their application in opposition to two sterilized traditions—one in the realm of thought, one in the world of activity—mark an attempt to reestablish a connection between an altered "theory" and an altered "practice."

I have suggested that values are still being carried and created, but outside the ranks of the discipline to which they ought to belong, into which at least they ought to penetrate. There is, then, a need for a "political criticism" prepared to act as a vehicle for the explication (sometimes the discovery) of these values, perhaps for their transmission. At a time when the chief currents in contemporary literary criticism are willfully and for their own good reasons apolitical or antipolitical, this need in turn, like the need for thought itself, becomes susceptible of fulfillment by nonspecialists.

2.

ORDERS AND APPROACHES

Malraux's thought is not simple; his writing is unsystematic; and his politics has at all times to be disentangled from the intricacies of a genre other than political thought. Malraux has never written a *Politics*: his politics must therefore be extracted from his novels, his philosophy of artistic creation, and his rhetoric. A critical work may therefore have reason to be comparably complex. The reader should be warned, however, that this work contains several additional and necessary layers of complication. Certain assumptions and theses lie beneath the surface, accounting for some superficial discontinuities in my orders and methods of approach.

The first of these assumptions and theses is that Malraux's thought is a developing unity, neither static nor radically disconnected. His political alliances have changed from left to right, his activity from violent to parliamentary; during the same time he ceased writing novels and began writing of art. His thought remains consistent with itself, broadening rather than violently shifting: this proposition is explicitly presented in one chapter; elsewhere it is an assumption that justifies the use of his prewar work to explain his postwar endeavor, and the reverse.

The development of Malraux's thought reached a completion, or at least an equilibrium, at about 1948. Thus there is a period in his evolution that demands chronological treatment and another that tolerates a more static analytical approach.

Malraux's ideas are seldom empirical, even when they appear to be: they are ethical—that is to say, in his case at least, emotive. It is, then, both correct and spurious to point out that such theses as "art is a conquest" are largely devoid of empirical meaning. It must be understood from the outset that Malraux the art critic, precisely like Malraux the novelist, has no independent (scientific or journalistic) interest in telling us facts or giving value-free historical explanations even when he may seem to be doing so. As with all his ideas, the core content of "art is a conquest" is an identical pair of sentiments, one which Malraux feels in contemplating a work of art, and another which he would have others feel. Because his work is honest, the two emotions are the same; otherwise he would be merely a propagandist, instead of a philosopher-propagandist. These sentiments and the appeal Malraux is making are the proper foci of analysis: if the reader forgets to look for them, Malraux appears to him as an intoxicated rhetorician.[2]

There is an appeal and an argument in almost every one of Malraux's works, but they are deeply embedded. Simply to summarize these "messages" would be unacceptable, since critics have employed literary evidence to argue for the presence of other, often contrary, appeals. A certain reprise of plots and "exclusively" esthetic assertions is inescapable simply to support assertions made.

I have included two segments, one biographical[3] and one comparative, before and after the main analysis, one for the conventional reason that Malraux's life (the little that is known of it) illuminates his thought, the other to suggest his proper place among kindred thinkers.

All the above explains the order of this essay. After a biographical summary, there is a chronological treatment of the period 1920-1945. Malraux's early works are significant for the several permanent themes there established; the novels explore

---

[2] At some points the dual sentiments vanish and Malraux becomes merely a rhetorician. This has led to more critical impatience than seems appropriate.

[3] Incorporating known material for the benefit of those who have not yet encountered it.

the same problems—primarily those of the totally "uprooted" individual ego. Gradually Malraux becomes more sanguine about the potentialities for "defense" of that ego by political and cultural means, through action by extant political forces. The transition period marks a shift of political stances, a further optimism about the prospects of political changes that will "defend" the individual, and a plunge into exploration of the intricate utilities of culture for the maintenance of the ego. This last is Malraux's "esthetics": but in its complete form it contains his politics. For to him art and style are social and psychological phenomena that minister, or fail to minister, to human needs; and just political action consists in the distribution of those means of cultural "defense" which he had much earlier discovered. This last phase, containing an expansion of the political concept "democracy" to the cultural level, is as interesting as, and a legitimate rival or supplement to, the earlier extension of democratic ideals to the social and economic spheres. For this thought and for others, it is not unjust to think of Malraux as a political educator, as Nietzsche was.

ACKNOWLEDGMENTS

THIS ESSAY IN POLITICAL CRITICISM could not have been completed in its present form without the prior analyses of W. M. Frohock and other American critics of Malraux. Their work gave shape to this treatment by providing points of view which often commanded acceptance and always required careful consideration. Those familiar with the Malraux literature will observe that many discussions in this essay begin with a set of statements that comment on and take a position within established arguments so extensive that citation of every component sentence in the literature would be pointless. It is therefore proper to note my general debt to the many writers who have established these arguments, and who are cited in part II of the bibliography.

I owe much gratitude to Henry Kariel, whose lectures first drew my attention to the unique career and thought of Malraux, and to the kind criticism of Leon S. Roudiez. I owe even more to Stanley Hoffmann, who has patiently read this manuscript almost as often as I have written it. All opinions and any errors herein are, of course, my own.

Permission to quote has been granted as follows: the *Journal of Contemporary History,* in which portions of this book first appeared; Random House, Inc. and Curtis Brown Ltd. for excerpts from *Man's Fate;* Random House, Inc. and Routledge & Kegan Paul Ltd. for excerpts from *Man's Hope;* Doubleday & Company and Martin Secker and Warburg Limited, for excerpts from *The Voices of Silence* translated by Stuart Gilbert; André Malraux for *The Walnut Trees of Altenburg.*

CONTENTS

Introduction 1

PART I THE DEVELOPMENT OF MALRAUX'S THOUGHT

One The Early Years: Alienation and the Absurd 15

Two The Early Years: The Conqueror, the Defeated Hero 31

Three The Bolshevik Hero 44

Four *Man's Hope; Altenburg* 76

Five Transition and Unity 116

PART II MALRAUX'S POLITICS AS A WHOLE

Six Esthetics and Politics: The Liberal Hero 137

Seven Malraux in Perspective 167

Bibliography 203

Appendix: Systematic Table of Ideas (with page references to the text) 217

Index 221

ABBREVIATIONS

L.P.	*Lunes en papier*
T.O.	*The Temptation of the West*
R.F.	*Royaume farfelu*
C.	*The Conquerors*
V.R.	*The Royal Way*
C.H.	*Man's Fate*
T.M.	*Days of Wrath*
E.	*Man's Hope*
N.A.	*The Walnut Trees of Altenburg*
V.S.	*The Voices of Silence*
Sat.	*Saturn*
M.D.	*The Metamorphosis of the Gods*
"N'était-ce"	"N'était-ce donc que ça?"
J.E.	"D'une jeunesse européenne"
H.U.	"Une humanisme universelle"

The English titles of different translations of the same work may vary. All the above abbreviations are, therefore, abbreviations of a French title. Wherever possible, however, citations have been made from an English translation published in New York. Where that is the case, the title of the English translation (e.g. *Man's Fate*) stands next to the abbreviation of the French title of the same work (e.g. C. H. for *La condition humaine*).

N.R.F.	*La Nouvelle Revue Française*
Y.F.S.	*Yale French Studies*

MALRAUX

AUTHOR'S NOTE

The reader will find a compact systematic table of Malraux's ideas, with page references to the text, in the Appendix on page 217. This presumptuous novelty is a purposeful experiment born of the author's extended frustrations with the insufficiency of alphabetical indexes as instruments of reference to theories with a complex internal structure, and is offered to other essayers of political criticism for whatever it may be worth to them.

INTRODUCTION

MALRAUX AND THE LEGEND OF ACTION

"WHO IS ANDRÉ MALRAUX?" The question is a proper one in America today, although it would seem foolish if asked in France and would have been superfluous here twenty or twenty-five years ago. At that time Malraux was well known as an adventurer about whose life a cloud of legend had grown, a novelist whose treatment of action and tragedy, heroism, violence, and revolution had a strong appeal for Americans, an intellectual who brilliantly criticized the values of a culture which then seemed to many to be in its death throes, a man deeply committed to politics—*engagé*, in his own language—who had moved away from individualist liberal democracy toward the revolutionary socialist left for reasons which had no discernible connection with the dogmas of leftist ideology. After the Second World War his reputation in France and America waned, partly because of the rise of Sartre and Camus, partly because he wrote no more fiction and his own fabulous character seemed to have grown tamer, but largely because of new political associations, which angered many of his fellow intellectuals (even those who had found equal reason for disillusion with the political far left) and led to such extreme appellations for him as "the only authentic French fascist."[1]

[1] Albert Beguin, in *Esprit*, October 1948, p. 451. In this article (one in a symposium on Malraux) Beguin notes that Malraux's fascism, so-called, was

Although his series of vast works of art history and esthetics has since restored his place in France, American interest in Malraux has remained for the most part the prerogative of students of French literature.

Malraux, for his own reasons, has never written anything explicitly autobiographical, nor has he tried to clear away the many apocryphal stories which have sprung up to fill the gap his silence leaves; some of these are seemingly spontaneous, others are plainly taken from passages in his novels which appear particularly personal in tone or reference.[2] From 1920 to 1945 the facts of his life, whatever they are, can be traced and documented only in spots. Known facts are everywhere interwoven with "the Malraux legend."

Despite the legend much can be pieced out about Malraux's actual career, and it is enlightening. André Malraux was born in Paris on November 3, 1901. Thus he was barely too young to take part in the First World War without being so young as to escape its influence. In 1919 he was working for a Parisian dealer in rare books, at the same time studying art, anthropology, and archeology. The following year he began to write as a contributor to small, obscure, and evanescent publications. His first book, a short fantasy with the title *Lunes en papier,* was published in 1921.[3]

neither reactionary nor power-mad and meant merely a loss of faith in mass-revolutionary means. In the same issue Pierre Debray sees Malraux as a "fascist of the left," inheriting the Blanquist and Leninist tradition of agitation and violence which the Communists, by "vegetating" into parliamentarism and bureaucracy, had let slip. Except for Communist literary-critical efforts (such as that in Roger Garaudy, *Literature of the Graveyard,* New York, International Publishers, 1948), such labeling died rather quickly, less because of its strained and often contradictory character than because the RPF did not last and because De Gaulle simply was not Mussolini.

[2] Not an unreasonable source, since so much in these novels corresponds to what is known of his life. It is commonplace to point out that all Malraux's major characters are cast in his own image—or in one or another of his many possible images.

[3] *Lunes en papier,* Paris, Simon, 1921 (hereinafter cited as L.P.). Untranslated. Any quotations herein cited from works without a published translation

Through his studies in Oriental art and archeology he had become interested in the ruined Buddhist temples lining the ancient and abandoned Cambodian Royal Way, and he was convinced that they could provide a treasury of valuable remnants of Khmer sculpture. At the age of twenty-two he requested and was given official permission to make a search. He set out in 1923; after ten months in the jungle and a bout with fever, he appeared in Pnom-Penh with a train of oxcarts loaded with statuary. He was arrested and charged with stealing the property of the French government. A colonial court sentenced him to three years' imprisonment. Then it was discovered that the French government had no title to the statuary. The case died, the statuary was nonetheless seized (later to be put back in place), and Malraux returned to France in the autumn of 1924.

The experience of this first Indochinese journey was by all accounts a crucial one for him. It provided the material for a later novel, *The Royal Way;* more important, it was Malraux's occasion for breaking with the life he had been leading among the haute bourgeoisie. Pierre Garine, hero of *The Conquerors,* undergoes in a Genevan court a similar experience, a serious trial on charges which seem to him trivial and incredible. Though later reprieved, he finds his treatment at the hands of the most revered agents of society both absurd and humiliating and reacts with a total rejection of the social order itself:

I do not consider society bad . . . but I consider it absurd . . . . The possibility of reforming society is a question which does not interest me. It is not the absence of justice from society that strikes me, but something deeper; my incapacity for adhering to any social order whatever. I am a-social, just as I am a-theist . . . . I know that I shall have society by my side all my life, and that I shall never be able to enter it without renouncing all that I am.[4]

are the responsibility of the author, as are certain revisions of published versions, as indicated in each instance.

[4] André Malraux, *The Conquerors*, trans. by Winifred Stephens Whale, Boston, Beacon, 1956, p. 56 (cited as C.).

It is following this episode that Garine becomes an active revolutionary; it was only a few months following his own trial that
Malraux began his own international-revolutionary career.
Garine's ideas as well as his actions parallel Malraux's at this
point. Immediately after his return Malraux, joining a whole
generation of younger French writers consciously estranged from
their own society, completed his first open literary attack on the
social values which he now rejected, a long and critical essay
comparing European with Chinese civilization.[5] Early in 1925
he set out once more for Indochina, his destination Saigon.
Though he returned to France physically in 1927, he did not
return to the roots from which he had cut himself off until the
Second World War.

For this second journey there was no such ostensible reason
as a quest for statuary, but the real motive is not hidden. Europe
("vast graveyard wherein only dead conquerors rest")[6] repelled
Malraux; Asia, with its embryonic political struggle against
Europe's domination, drew him to the first centers of that rising
conflict. In Indochina there was agitation against colonial rule,
in China wholesale revolution; Malraux was to become deeply
entangled with both. If the Cambodian episode had titillated the
imagination of the Paris press, this venture was to establish
Malraux as the outstanding inhabitant of its dream world. He
arrived in Saigon in January 1925 and at once contacted a local
nationalist movement, Jeune-Annam. Until August he worked
to organize the group, founding in the process a polemical news-
paper, *L'Indochine*; then he dropped out of sight, moving northward along the coast to Canton.

There Sun Yat-sen's nationalist movement, the Kuomintang
(with Communist-International support and the counsel of
Mikhail Borodin) was beginning its revolutionary campaign to

---

[5] *La tentation de l'occident,* Paris, Grasset, 1926 (cited as T.O.). Translated
as *The Temptation of the West* by Robert Hollander, New York, Vintage,
1961. All citations to T.O. herein are the author's translations.
[6] T.O., p. 204.

drive out European influence along the coast of China and to establish itself as the sole government in a unified Chinese state. Borodin, opposed by the Kuomintang military leader Chiang Kai-shek, was attempting to turn the Nationalist movement into a Communist one. In June 1925 the Kuomintang seized power in Canton. In March 1927 Chiang broke with the Communists and drove them out of their centers of power by force.

In the interim Malraux was deeply involved with the Kuomintang. His association with Jeune-Annam had led to his taking charge, apparently at the behest of Borodin, of Kuomintang propaganda in Indochina. After the coup he took over information and propaganda work in Canton. Then—the unconfirmed legend adds—he rose to be secretary of the Kuomintang Committee of Twelve. At the least he was an observer and an active participant until the break with Chiang, when he returned to Paris.

There he once more took to writing. Immediately after his return he published an essay[7] justifying his estrangement (and that of his generation) from the old Europe and barely suggesting that European youth might welcome an attempt at the violent remolding of the world in which they lived. In 1928, after finishing a work[8] begun much earlier in the fantastic vein of *Lunes en papier,* Malraux published his first novel, *The Conquerors,*[9] based upon the Cantonese strike and uprising of 1925. The novel was immediately successful and established Malraux's reputation as a writer; also established was the Malraux legend, since the experiences of the hero of *The Conquerors,* a revolutionary adventurer whose life is immersed in violence, bear so close a resemblance to Malraux's own that it is impossible to say which are remembered and which imagined.

As editor of art books for the publisher Gallimard (a career

---

7 "D'une jeunesse européenne," in *Ecrits,* vol. 70 of *Les Cahiers Verts,* Paris, Grasset, 1927, pp. 129-153 (cited as J.E.).

8 *Royaume farfelu,* Paris, Gallimard, 1928 (cited as R.F.).

9 *Les conquérants,* Paris, Grasset, 1928.

to which he is constantly returning, as if homeward, from ventures and adventures), Malraux continued his excursions, now archeological rather than revolutionary. In 1930 he published a second novel, *The Royal Way*,[10] based upon his first Indochinese expedition along the Royal Road. In 1933 he brought out the novel which made him world-famous and won him the Goncourt Prize, *Man's Fate*,[11] a story of the rise and destruction of the Communist Kuomintang of Shanghai in 1927. It was translated into sixteen languages, and its French title, "la condition humaine," entered the literary and philosophical idiom of France at once.

The rise of Nazism to power in Germany in 1933 prompted a large-scale swing to the left among French intellectuals, along a path Malraux had already marked out with his revolutionary novels and Communist associations. Although he never joined the party, and was distrusted by it for some of his writings, he was accepted as chief of the literary spokesmen on the far left because of his violent antifascism. In 1933 he and André Gide went to Berlin bearing a petition on behalf of imprisoned Communists; in 1934 he spoke as a "Marxist humanist" at the Soviet Writers' Congress in Moscow. He developed an oratorical talent and style, which he used at leftist mass meetings as he was later to use it at Gaullist rallies—brilliantly. In 1935 he published his fourth novel, *Days of Wrath*,[12] which was widely regarded as straight Communist propaganda.

When the Spanish Civil War broke out in July 1936, Malraux returned immediately to the life of action. He organized a foreign volunteer air force for the Loyalists and himself flew sixty-five

[10] *La voie royale*, Paris, Grasset, 1930. Translated as *The Royal Way* by Harrison Smith and Robert Haas, New York, Random House, 1935 (cited as V.R.).

[11] *La condition humaine*, Paris, Gallimard, 1933. Translated as *Man's Fate* by Smith and Haas, New York, Random House, 1934 (cited as C.H.).

[12] *Le temps du mépris*, Paris, Gallimard, 1935. Translated as *Days of Wrath* by Haakon M. Chevalier, New York, Random House, 1936 (cited as T.M.).

missions. By November, when his "Escadre" had been put out
of action by Franco's far superior air power, Malraux traveled
to America to secure funds for the Republicans and then returned to France in 1937 to publish a reportorial novel about
the war, *Man's Hope*,[13] which he himself then filmed in Spain a
year later.[14]

Still he had not ceased to live a journalist's dream life. After
the declaration of war he volunteered for the French army's
tank corps. In the fall of France, in June 1940, he was wounded,
captured, and sent to a prisoner-of-war camp, from which he
escaped in November. The next two years were a lull in opera-
tions, which he spent moving from place to place and writing
the first volume of a projected trilogy (the remainder of which
was destroyed by the Germans during the war), *The Walnut
Trees of Altenburg*.[15] In 1942 he came in touch with the Gaullist
Resistance apparatus, and in 1943 he was carrying out organization and liaison work in southern France. By 1944 he had become a commander in the maquis under the name of "Colonel
Berger"; he was engaged in harrying the Germans when he was
once again wounded and captured in June. He was freed by the
FFI in August and took command of the volunteer Alsace-
Lorraine Brigade, which participated in the liberation of Stras-
bourg and the capture of Stuttgart.

Malraux was now forty-three years old. His novels were
written, his career as an adventurer and fighter was over. But he
was not finished with writing, and he was just beginning a new

13 *L'espoir*, Paris, Gallimard, 1937. Translated as *Man's Hope* by Stuart
Gilbert and Alastair Macdonald, New York, Random House, 1938 (cited as E.).

14 Any of Malraux's novels would lend themselves, in the hands of a master
director, to a rendering on film. *Man's Hope* is perhaps the most explicitly
dramatic in form and would therefore be the most obvious choice, but all the
rest, even *Days of Wrath*—whose "action" is largely contained in a darkened
prison cell—seem to cry out for a visual medium.

15 *Les noyers de l'Altenburg*, vol. 1 of *La lutte avec l'ange*, Lausanne-
Yverdon, Editions du haut pays, 1943. Translated as *The Walnut Trees of
Altenburg* by A. W. Fielding, London, Lehmann, 1952 (cited as N.A.).

career in politics. In January 1945 he gave the first evidence of the direction this new career would take when he fought at a Resistance congress against any association with the Communists. In November of the same year he joined the Provisional Government of General De Gaulle in the capacity of Minister of Information. When De Gaulle left office in January 1946, Malraux left also; but his association with the General did not end and continues to this day. When De Gaulle returned to the political arena in 1947 to inveigh against the politicians of the Fourth Republic, Malraux was at his side; he was one of five charter signers who in April of that year formed the Rassemblement du Peuple Français (RPF), a political party whose sole objective was to return De Gaulle to power. Malraux brought his talents to the new party as its Director of Culture and National Propaganda and gave fervent and flashing examples of brilliant campaign oratory in his own addresses to mass meetings.[16]

In this campaign, which was at its height from April 1947 to April 1948, the speeches of both De Gaulle and Malraux were bitterly anti-Communist. They condemned the Soviet Union so strongly that both were denounced as fascists, a denunciation which became louder when De Gaulle, after a sweeping victory for the RPF in municipal elections in 1947, demanded a general election and a reform of the constitution and Malraux called for a plebiscite. The democratic left detected the scent of revolution in Malraux's speeches and in his few criticisms of De Gaulle's self-restraint; in fact, he had almost certainly abandoned any

[16] Up to this period the (secondary) sources on Malraux's career are W. M. Frohock, *André Malraux and the Tragic Imagination*, Stanford, Stanford University Press, 1952; Janet Flanner, *Men and Monuments*, New York, Harper, 1957; and Walter G. Langlois, *André Malraux: The Indochina Adventure*, New York, Praeger, 1966. For his political activity in France see Flanner; T. H. White, "The Three Lives of André Malraux," *The New York Times Magazine*, February 15, 1953; Alexander Werth, *France 1940-1955*, New York, Holt, 1956; Claude Mauriac, "Malraux: Again From Letters to Action," *The New York Times Magazine*, July 6, 1958; and Curtis Cate, "Malraux at the Bastilles of Culture," *The New York Times Magazine*, May 6, 1962.

and all revolutionary expectations by this time, and probably had done so some ten years before. In the elections of 1951 Malraux reappeared to speak on behalf of De Gaulle, then dropped out of the RPF as it began to disintegrate.

On the whole this period in Malraux's career cannot be counted as a successful one for him, nor as one which merits too much study. Of course the outcome of many of his previous political involvements had been spectacular failure, the collapse of a cause combined with bare physical escape; compared to this, the RPF episode might appear close to an enormous victory, if simply because of the nonviolent and relatively smooth character of the end of the RPF. The party failed at the polls, could not attract parliamentary allies, began to be troubled by factions, entered into a phase of decay, was abandoned by De Gaulle, and finally split apart.

Malraux's ties with it had begun to break quite early, when his speaking and poster campaigns proved unfruitful. All had been admittedly colorful, but they were also, as far as the voting public was concerned, unconvincing: superior as endeavors in the field of political art and showmanship, but useless as elements in the technique of power politics. They suffered, ironically, from that same weakness which Malraux was soon to ascribe correctly to the whole of modern art—an inability to reach out to the populace, to conduct a dialogue that would provoke the responses of the "masses."

Malraux was, simply enough, not suited to normal political life. What he called "la politique politicienne" (as opposed to "la politique de l'histoire") did not attract him and had no real room for him. Neither did it for the RPF, which was as out of place in the internal politics of the back-to-normalcy Fourth Republic as Malraux was out of place in the internal roilings of the RPF.

Perhaps Malraux's first plunge into French politics would bear more interest if the failure had been more spectacular.

A real and violent debacle might at least have driven him into writing a seventh novel. As it was, he found nothing there worth setting on paper. He was still writing; but now he had turned to take up an old interest in art.

From 1947 to 1950 there appeared the three volumes of his psychology of art, later revised extensively and titled *The Voices of Silence*.[17] In 1950 he published a long study of Goya,[18] and from 1953 to 1957 he produced four more volumes[19]—a complete series embodying Malraux's work in esthetics and in the philosophy of history over a span of some twenty years.

After 1951 his political activity ceased temporarily, to his satisfaction. "Write it down," he said, "the art excites me five hundred times more than the politics."[20] He appeared in print once again, briefly, in the period just before the fall of Pierre Mendès-France in 1955, with a proposal for a "New Left" in which Mendès and De Gaulle might join forces to take leadership of the left away from the Communists. The proposal caused a considerable if momentary stir, but eventually the idea proved to be only an idea and not a plan; its chief figures, De Gaulle and Mendès, had not been parties to it.[21] When the Fourth Republic final collapsed, it fell before De Gaulle and De Gaulle alone; Mendès was on the other side. Malraux had long since returned to his books on art.

[17] *La psychologie de l'art,* Geneva, Skira, 1947-50. Revised and published as *Les voix du silence,* Paris, Gallimard, 1951. Translated by Stuart Gilbert as *The Voices of Silence,* New York, Doubleday, 1953 (cited as V.S.).
[18] *Saturne,* Paris, Gallimard, 1950. Translated by C. W. Chilton as *Saturn: An Essay on Goya,* New York, Phaidon, 1957 (cited as Sat.).
[19] *Le musée imaginaire de la sculpture mondiale:* v. i, *La statuaire;* v. ii, *Des bas-reliefs aux grottes sacrées;* v. iii, *Le monde chrétien;* Paris, Gallimard, 1953-54. *La métamorphose des dieux,* Paris, Gallimard, 1957. Translated by Stuart Gilbert as *The Metamorphosis of the Gods,* Garden City, Doubleday, 1960 (cited as M.D.).
[20] Quoted in T. H. White.
[21] Regarding this episode, see the "Nouvelle Gauche" articles in *L'Express,* Dec. 25, 1954, p. 10; Jan. 29, 1955, pp. 8-10. Also "The 'New Left' Can Succeed!" *Yale French Studies* 15, pp. 49-60.

He left his books again in June 1958, with the return of De Gaulle, for a new appearance on the political stage. After serving as Minister of Information again for a few weeks, he moved to the post he still holds, Minister of State for Cultural Affairs,[22] charged with reorganizing and domesticating the French theater and film.

By 1967 De Gaulle after nine years as chief of the Fifth Republic was no less controversial than before. He had liquidated French Algeria and an African colonial empire. He had proclaimed French grandeur and bolstered it with atomic weapons. He had shaken the Atlantic Alliance and the European Economic Community by the scruff and had come close to destroying both. He had defied the Americans. He remained, in short, a current event and a focus for talk.

Malraux had become much less controversial. His purview in the Ministry of Culture included the Comédie Française, the Beaux Arts, the Villa Medicis, and the Louvre, each of which received at least one radical innovation, most innovations involving conflicts and several conflicts—notably over the management of the Comédie Française—ending in classic fiascos. The democratization of culture had shrunk slightly, into a "decentralization" of culture, with cultural centers of various sorts to be created in cities other than Paris. The conception of innovation was gradually replaced at the Ministry by the administration of innovation; neither conception nor administration left time for novels or art.[23]

A French contemporary of Malraux said of him, even before De Gaulle's return to power: "He has had so far the most successful life of any intellectual of our epoch."[24] This peculiar comment can be taken in two ways. Malraux has been able to

22 His title—Ministre d'Etat, chargé des affaires culturelles—may also be translated as Minister of Culture.
23 Curtis Cate, "Malraux at the Bastilles of Culture," *The New York Times Magazine*, May 6, 1962.
24 Quoted in Flanner, pp. 59-60.

make his life the expression of his ideas; and he has, in this, succeeded where his contemporaries have not. He has preached engagement and political action. He is a member of an intelligentsia notorious for its reticence about political commitment and of a generation notable for preaching engagement and finding nowhere to practice it. Nevertheless he, an intellectual, found ennobling virtues in revolution and became a revolutionary; found the same virtues in two wars and became a military leader; preached cultural democracy and became its administrator. The modern world knows few men whose words match their deeds. The few are consistently fascinating. Sometimes they are exemplary.

PART I
THE DEVELOPMENT OF MALRAUX'S THOUGHT

1. THE EARLY YEARS: ALIENATION AND THE ABSURD

IN MALRAUX'S EARLY WORKS an individual set of ideas emerges out of a style that expresses an attitude common to a literary generation. The notion of a style that contains and gives birth to ideas must be emphasized: a form of expression hides an esthetic intention. But that intention, which was or seemed merely esthetic, becomes in Malraux by degrees explicitly political. What are initially the themes to which he obsessively recurs become as well the thoughts he consciously explores. Several of the themes that one by one appear in these years become permanent centers around which his thought moves in ever more complex evolutions. Malraux's language in these years is already elliptical, as it remained, but it is cold, in total contrast to the later perfervid rhetoric. The sentiments, already present, are utterly cerebral; there is lacking the will to communicate and convince, the self-conscious appeal. Individuality is rising out of a literary consensus, politics out of esthetics, thought out of art: a mind trying its wings.

French surrealism was a cult of chaos among survivors of the First World War. The coherent prewar world of conventional objects and rational men had spawned pointless mass death; such a world concealed its bashful lunacy beneath stultifying categories of thought. Surrealists mimicked this world and exposed it to itself by creating equally fantastic worlds of art in which conventional objects possessed incredible or monstrous properties. With the help of the psychology of dreams and of the unconscious, conventional meanings and categories of thought were assaulted to show the incongruity behind apparent coherence; new shocking meanings, revelations of irrationality and violence, were generated to reveal the repulsive coherence behind apparent incongruity. The intention was to "capsize the mind," to do violence to and even destroy a meaningless "world" of thought, with the weapons of art. And of art alone: esthetic rebellion was initially accompanied by political quietism.[1]

1.

Lunes en papier (1921) illustrates the surrealist manner of expression along with motifs and preoccupations which become very much Malraux's own. The whole piece is done in the style of the times: disorderly sequences of dream images, weird synesthetic metaphors, nonhuman characters, incomprehensible events, insane images. A party of strange little men journey to the Bizarre Kingdom to kill its ruler, Death, so that they can seize power from Satan, who has dethroned God. The disappearance of God from human experience, the dominion of a "demonic" within man himself, the journey into unfamiliar lands to seek power and to struggle against the very real presence of death, all subsequently became elaborate themes for Malraux.

---

[1] See Albert Camus, *The Rebel,* translated by Anthony Bower, New York, Vintage, 1956, pp. 91-99, and Jean-Paul Sartre, *What Is Literature?,* translated by Bernard Frechtman, New York, Philosophical Library, 1949, pp. 174-185. Sartre does *not* intend the analysis of surrealism to apply to Malraux; since he considers Malraux an older member of his own generation, that which succeeded the surrealists, he includes him in the analysis of the later group rather than the earlier. He "belongs to our generation. Malraux had the immense merit of recognizing as early as his first work that we were at war and of producing a war literature when the surrealists . . . were devoting themselves to a literature of peace." Actually "war" in this sense can hardly be said to appear in Malraux's work until *The Conquerors,* in 1928, and perhaps not even then. Sartre discounts the importance of all Malraux's earlier writings (as does Malraux himself), but on the basis of his work from 1920 to 1928 Malraux fits the surrealist definition and analysis very nicely indeed.

In *Lunes en papier* they are marginal to the surrealist style, which is odd but not shocking.

That style returns in its fullness only in *Royaume farfelu* (1928), another fantasy. A sailor comes to Trebizond on a ship plagued by flying devils. Thrown into prison for no apparent reason, he is released as abruptly and sent with the Trebizond army to write the history of its impending siege of Ispahan. The army reaches the suburbs of Ispahan but cannot find its way inside. Demons and starvation haunt them; an army of scorpions advances on the invaders, and they scatter into the desert. The sailor-narrator returns to Trebizond and prepares for another voyage.

In this work the characters are supposedly human, not allegorical, figures. The grotesque and fantastic perceptions are those of the narrator, not of the author, and the underlying assertion is no longer "I experience the world as insane, incoherent." Rather, *men* experience painful, grotesque, meaningless events. But the sailor-narrator is a comic robot, not a man; he preserves an emotionless objectivity amid deaths which will provoke laughter and terror when Malraux's characters become truly human.

Royaume farfelu adds to the continuing concern with death a lasting preoccupation with violent action, and with defeat in action; for the little men of *Lunes en papier* do kill Death, while the fantastic encounter of the men of Trebizond destroys them, to no apparent purpose. Defeat, pain, imprisonment, death, all without reason: the themes now dominate and use the surrealist style, which begins to yield to a detached narrative. An unpleasant manner of living is fatalistically recounted, disturbed by no sense of horror on the part of the puppets or of rejection on the part of the writer. When both appear, Malraux the surrealist taleteller becomes, at once, Malraux the political novelist.

The style of these two early works is, according to one critic, a "style of revolt," the characteristic style of a generation of literary revolutionaries. According to another, it is a style against which Malraux himself, in line with his own esthetic formulas, was later to revolt in order to replace it with a far more personal one, representative of Malraux rather than of his period.[2] Both are correct: surrealism and the fantastic were at this time very clearly the instruments of a widespread revolt against the real; but when some particular flaw in the political system is revealed, they must eventually appear to be inadequate instruments. Malraux "revolts" against the limitations placed upon him by the surrealist style of revolt and casts it off for what is in his eyes a more effective one. If a date is needed, 1924 serves: the high point of European surrealism, the time of Malraux's trial in Pnom-Penh.[3]

After this breach the surrealist grotesque crops up twice more in Malraux's work. Kassner, isolated in prison in *Days of Wrath,* is made the prey of phantoms and hallucinatory memories, demons which he fights and to which he is forced to yield against his will; his own unconscious mind rises up and overwhelms him despite himself. And Baron Clappique in *Man's Fate* is himself the grotesque personified, delighting in a sort of surrealistic mythomania, combatting the absurd world with his own absurdity: "the Baron de Clappique does not exist." But he is the exact antithesis of Malraux's heroes; not only is he pictured as a member of a group of escapists who have surrendered themselves to conditions they ought to fight, but of all Malraux's characters no one, not even the banker-capitalist-counterrevolutionary Ferral, is so discredited in the end.[4]

Add to the stylistic and thematic elements already named a vivid imagery, especially of the menacing aspects of an unfamiliar land: that is what survives of Malraux's surrealist fiction. There is no political thought there: when the cold-eyed neutrality of

2 See Frohock, *André Malraux and the Tragic Imagination,* p. 21.

3 *Royaume farfelu,* published in 1928, was virtually completed by 1924.

4 See Nicola Chiaromonte, "Malraux and the Demons of Action," *Partisan Review,* July 1948, pp. 776-789, Aug. 1948, pp. 912-923; quoted p. 777. And Frohock, pp. 21-26.

author and narrators vanishes and reflection begins to compete with narrative, these survivals turn into ideas.

Malraux continues to ponder meaningless—surreal—experience long after he stops rendering it. After these works, however, all experience is not presented as equally and universally empty. Another manner of living exists, at least as a possibility. But this possibility at once justifies affirmative and negative judgments and action, a seeking of the meaningful and a rejection of the meaningless. If all is not uniformly, necessarily sterile, the question may be posed of what, concretely, is responsible for empty lives. Malraux begins to ask and to answer in *The Temptation of the West*.

2.

In *The Temptation of the West* (*La tentation de l'occident*, 1926), Malraux reveals a hostile separation rather than a neutral detachment and fixes provisionally upon the culture of "Europe" as the repulsive source of sterility. This identification of the enemy lasts, at best, only through *The Conquerors,* but other features of the work provide better clues to the direction of his future thought. The diagnosis of a cultural disease provides Malraux with a negative pole, but not a positive one; he finds something to reject, nothing to espouse. Again his prose is cold even when brilliant. Even though his characters now have and express emotions, they are private men. Two men, a young Chinese in Europe and a young Frenchman in China, reveal their separate estrangements from the West in an exchange of letters in which they analyze and respond to Western and Oriental culture. They communicate little to each other, for both are as isolated as they are uprooted.

Through the mind of Ling, the Chinese traveler, Malraux analyzes Western culture; through the Frenchman, A.D., he judges it. The young Chinese, fully aware of the disintegration of the old China, is both hostile toward and curious about the alien civilization which has been invading his own; he seeks to defend China and to understand the power of Europe by grasping the ideas basic to both as cultures and by contrasting them.

The West is to Ling a land consumed by geometry: planned streets, the cut of clothes, carpentry, architecture—all bear the geometrical imprint and denote a barbarism so tightly organized as to have been confused with true civilization. Behind the geometric construction lies the desire to impose upon the world an order created by the mind of man. And this desire rests upon an idea, the key to the culture: there exists, for the West, a total separation, a bridgeless gap, between something called "man" and something else called "the world." Man is a thing in himself, the most important thing in the universe, because he is no part of it. Therefore he is a value in himself: and before he can be at home in the universe he must bend it to his will, make it conform to his plan.

The idea of man as a thing in himself is the source of the sickness of the West. The Chinese see in man one animal among many, not an incomparable; not the shaper of the world, but one part in an unbroken universe; therefore not a value in himself. To this polar duality of conceptions of man all the clashes between Occidental and Eastern world views may be traced.

Which is correct? The question is unanswerable. To every culture there corresponds some world-view, and each is based upon an irrational and impenetrable choice, an unjustifiable and irrefutable act of faith. The West arbitrarily postulates divisions in experience, contemplates them with anguish, and devotes itself to their transcendence. Not content with severing man from the world, it uses the belief in personal identity to sever the individual from the world and from other men. China rejects the seductive illusion of the self, reasoning from the fragmentary and inconstant character of experience to the denial of personality as real or ideal. But the European, loaded down by private suffering and by an anguish born of self-imposed isolation, responds by grasping power to bend the world to his own tortured and overgrown will. The Western will confronts history in order to overcome it, the Western mind analyzes the world in order to subject it to categories. China knows that to exist it is necessary not to act but to experience, not to analyze but to acquire an intense consciousness of life. History cannot be mastered, but it can be illuminated and understood as a rhythm of permanence and transformation.

Western culture combines the heavy legacies of Greece, Christendom, and Rome. Greece created the myth of man, separated from the gods, measure of all things: a man doomed to struggle with the inhuman forces of the world upon which he must impose his own orders, doomed to self-destruction in this struggle for the very pride that motivated it. Christendom bound man to God, but that tie is gone: all that is left is the anguish of man alone, his unending quest, his separate existence, and his frenzied belief in the importance of his own acts. Rome left behind the bitter virtue of violence, the memory of power, the enduring ideal of conquest and empire without joy or contentment. The product is a desperate race, which has vowed to conquer: to conquer the world, to conquer the idea of the world, to conquer nations, one another, oneself. But the victories are petty, and at the last the individual comes only to death. The West begins with a perception of the world and of man's distinctness from it, an inescapable heritage, consecrating action, violence, power. But action ends in disaster; inevitably and predictably Western man fails to reconquer the world so gratuitously lost. The mad dilemma of the West leads to a conclusion whose phrasing by Malraux influenced a generation of French speculative philosophers: "At the center of European man, ruling the great movements of his life, there exists an essential absurdity" (p. 72).

For Ling, Western culture is something to contemplate; for A.D. it is something he rejects even while he cannot escape its influence—he accepts the Western dichotomy of man and world.

Cultural values are not arbitrary, then: they are a means of "defense of the spirit" against "the unceasing solicitations of the world" (p. 85). Minds and groups create "realities," world images, as a means of defense against those "solicitations" (p. 94). A. D. does not explain what these may be; Malraux will do so, elaborately.

For A.D., then, the absurdity that has captured Europe is not the Western idea of man to which Ling objects. What A.D. sees and Ling does not is the decline, the decay of that idea. The European, instead of living the life of action, dreams of it, reads a novel, sees a movie. His character has decayed because the West's old conception of man, the rationalistic doctrine of individualism, has collapsed. This doctrine, this myth, made each responsible for his own acts and demanded reasonable grounds for them. When the Europeans began to search for the rational basis of action, they discovered only a highly irrational psychology, in which the will to act was grounded only upon itself. This was too much self-knowledge, a truth that could neither be hidden nor assimilated. Repelled by the irrationality and meaninglessness they found in their lives, Westerners fled from action, became inert dreamers, took refuge in fantasy, eroticism, or passive enjoyment of artistic pleasures. As for their culture, it will be annihilated through abandonment by its members, or it will be reborn in a new form: it cannot remain indefinitely in this state of inward contradiction.

A.D. himself is unable to hold any convictions or to find any cause for which he might immolate himself, because his analytical European mind has shown all beliefs to be illusions or lies. Since potential for heroism and sacrifice (those Western virtues) remains within him, as within all his kind, he consciously incorporates the weakness of European culture, the will to act and the belief that no action is justifiable. He has therefore abandoned Europe—"great cemetery where only dead conquerors sleep"

(p. 121)—and resolves to remain devoted at least to the bitter half-pleasure that comes from lucid awareness of an absurd reality.

In *The Temptation* are planted many more of the seminal ideas which grew and were developed far more fully in the rest of Malraux's work. The call of other cultures and other lands, the corruption and at the same time the half-hidden prospects of one's own, the analysis of experience as absurd and the attempt to isolate the origins of the Absurd, the overthrow of rationalistic individual psychology by unconscious motives and groundless values, even the entry of Oriental ideas that ironically balance and question Western notions of individualism and freedom—all are anticipated at some point, however fleetingly.

The indications here are all against one future commitment, to politics. The illusions behind cultures and causes, the myths that the mind must create and miscall realities, are perceived but not accepted; engagement cannot therefore be accepted. Malraux refuses to hold to the beliefs of a society and culture that begin to seem strangely out of order. He abandons Europe for Asia, not because of a positive faith, but because of a denial.

3.

In the essay "D'une jeunesse européenne" (1927), Malraux elaborates the autopsy on Western culture of *The Temptation*, probing ideas like a spiritual Marxist in search of fatal inner contradictions. At the same time that he finds old Western myths intolerable, however, Malraux asserts that some myth is necessary if men are not to abandon themselves to despair. This position leads him to anticipate the creation of some new, regenerating myth; but the anticipation is vague, and it is not clear whether the new, fruitful illusion will be general or particular, cultural or political, leading to words or to action.

He begins, again, by examining the inner weaknesses of Western culture.[5] "European thought is breeding a strange crystallization, like hoarfrost, the whole length of its constructions"—an oracular phrasing, indeed, but one that is at once reminiscent of Spengler and of the similar crystallization that afflicts the thought and mind of a culture that becomes sterile and turns into a "civilization." All through the continent of Europe "I see weakening that movement *without end* that is the master of our race." But now there are men, members of this dying culture, who are attempting to deliver themselves from its weight. Once before, a burdensome old civilization had been thrown off, the Christian civilization of faith, which fell before the assault of rationalism and individualism; these too, having become predominant, have now run their course and provide the precedent for their own overthrow.

Each great culture or race obliges its members to create for themselves a distinct and particular reality. This statement is an extension of the formulations of *The Temptation,* now plainly resting on the basic influence of a philosophical idealism which places the social context of the knowing subject before that subject, in time and causality, and the subject itself before the world of appearance as that is manifested to the perceiving and ideating individual. A culture, which exists historically because it contains human persons, is still something beyond its members, prior to them, an influence upon them, because of its past history or present extent; the individual culture directs the individual person into certain ways of understanding and interpreting the world of

[5] For the benefit of those who have not engaged in the peculiarly difficult sport of finding the coherencies under thought so elliptically, discursively, and unsystematically expressed as Malraux's, a warning and an apology are in order. An interpretation, really an exegesis, of Malraux looks deceptively like paraphrase. But paraphrase is also necessary and justified, for Malraux avoids logical order and exposition. The critic's problem increases as Malraux's career progresses. An elliptical thought of 1961 will be incomprehensible unless its logical context is presented, and that logical context will be found, not twenty pages before, but twenty years in the past.

things and appearances, phenomena and events, time and space, that surround him; this translation is for him reality, a reality he is able to share with those who are also members of his culture. The notion of a "particular reality," suggesting the plurality of interpretations of whatever the real may be, implies the nonexistence of any *one* supreme or correct reality. A reality, tool of human minds, exists only as it is created by a subject, given him outright by his culture, or partly made and partly imposed. This sort of "reality" is certainly not an empiricist's, certainly not what common sense and everyday usage mean by "reality." It has been known under many names; it is reality, the only reality known to man, and at the same time "myth" and illusion; the forms, ideas, values, images, beliefs that make up the sensibility, order of the mind, concept of man, world-view, style of thought, consciousness, mode, or "soul" of a culture; the result of the psychological need to apprehend the world, of the defense of the spirit. "The world we have inherited touches us less by its images than by a *secret* hierarchy, which rules the mind." Philosophical systems are "only the ornaments, and sometimes the veils" of the different times, and conflicts of cultures are able to exist only because there are differences among cultures in the "fashions by which the real penetrates them" (p. 137).

Evidently "the real" is not directly accessible to minds. "The real" can be reached only through the intermediacy of a "particular reality." The individual mind most often receives that "particular reality" from a preexisting culture; what is received is, necessarily, partial and incomplete, as its conflict with other partial views reveals. As the inaccessibility of "the real" to direct experience becomes clearer to him, Malraux appears to become more reconciled than was A.D. both to the inescapable requirement that his mind will work along the lines of some already created illusion and to the fact that any "particular reality" in whose creation he may participate will also be illusion—a reconciliation peculiarly related to the realm of propaganda and to the propagandist's relation with himself. Without a myth man cannot live: so to seek or to create myth becomes a legitimate and vital enterprise. Why not, then, accept the dominant myth of one's own culture?

The most important element of the metaphysic specific to a culture is its notion of man and of the place of man. The epoch of Western individualism sought to found its "reality" upon the notion of the liberty and primacy of the human mind. The individualist epoch based its concept of man on the consciousness each man has of himself, with the implication that a man may know himself, that he may properly be his own judge and interpreter, and that he is capable of establishing the relation between his own principles and actions. But a man does not evaluate himself in the same way as he does another. Here the Absurd first makes its appearance, because Western man is well aware that his subjectivity is limited and his self-consciousness conditioned by elements outside his own being. He sees his memories most blatantly conditioned, not by any order of their rational importance, but by the amount of passion attached to each: facts are real only if they are "bound to an intensity . . . a particular possibility of moving us"; when intensity is lost, they are not real, they are mere lifeless names whose presentation evokes nothing. And passion, besides afflicting memories, does not absent itself from daily life: feelings, sentiments, emotions are effortlessly able to make the would-be rational will into their tool, able to condition idea, experience, imagination. Physiology, an irrational psychological nature, and cultural values, all create their own particular realities to compete with and drown out "the real"; rational capacity to evaluate is absent for the knowledge of the self as for all else. What, then, is to become of that self, upon which an idea of man was to be built? Modern man cannot accept—meaning that Malraux cannot accept—his subjective vision of the world as valid, and yet, because of the individualist ethos of his culture, he can do nothing else.

Individualism and subjectivism have destroyed the world by making it equal to each person's own private perception (special deformation) of it. In the private world real facts are mingled in a hodgepodge with imaginary and future actions, and all that is not perceived with a particular intensity is excluded. The self is a palace of silence which each penetrates alone, filled with the mingled rubble of lucid and demented ideas; and the picture each man draws of himself, the self-knowledge which he thinks he has, is dissected into a mélange of hopes and dreams and vain desires. These last are his most intense perceptions: how, then, can there be hope for a correspondence between them and others, how hope for a rational world view? There is no shared rational world, only the common stamp of individualism. Malraux's generation, he holds, expected to develop and enrich the particular and shared reality myth, of which individualism was only the doctrine and starting point, possibly into such a high synthesis as other cultural mythologies have reached. But the nature of this type of illusion bars its own fulfillment, stunts its growth: rather than sharing his mythical ideas of the real with all his culture, he is moved to develop purely personal myths.

The sensation of being *one,* of being distinct and set apart from all others in the instant of experience, is strong enough in Western man at the outset, an intangible given (perhaps the only one) of human existence alongside the tangible givens of being flesh and blood (or matter and energy). Doctrines of personality do not generally express personality, but are legends, mythologies woven about this *one* with its successive madnesses, nets in which to contain it. But to add to the natural sensation of oneness a doctrine—no less than the basic legend of our culture—that in its mythology also expresses the self is to move inevitably toward the acceptance of those successive madnesses and distortions on an equal basis with what would otherwise constitute the real, because they *are* real. All perception of the formerly shared world, even all perception of others, is lost in the exaltation of

the self by the self (love, for example, presumably a bond between two beings, is revealed as the constant fantasying of the
partner's sensations). "To push to the extreme the searching of
oneself, *accepting from it its own world,* is to tend to the Absurd"
—or drive fast to madness; that is, the "real," the social madness
(p. 144).

To deny that the self is as one perceives it drives equally to
absurdity. We wish, then, to study the self as we would study
other selves, to divorce a concept of selfhood from our own self-
consciousness. But we cannot reach others, and the legend of
personality, whose necessity we have accepted and which we
would reconstruct, therefore becomes baseless or dissolves in a
soup of probabilities.

Certainly, we can make the idea of personality enter the system of
allegories which is our thought; but if no one can grasp himself, what
importance has a notion of the self? . . . After having affirmed his
existence and his rights, man begins his proper quest, like those
knights whose victories permitted them to penetrate the palace, object
of their dreams, where they found only deep perspectives of shadow.
[Pp. 146-47]

Absurdity and disillusion: such a civilization as this has neither
a common goal nor a common ground; it supplies its members
only with tools to destroy themselves. The result is those members' despair and violence, for which the prophet is Nietzsche,
and the detachment from world, self, and culture that penetrates
Europe. The younger generation of Europe in the years just
following the war is united by a strange fraternity: the brotherhood of despair. And beside the despair rises a certain violence
which ought to be surprising because it veils a renewed power
that will manifest itself as destruction, as a negative thought, a
nihilism: instead of the dubious affirmations of late individualism,
a rejection of "reality." It is too early to say what will become
of this tide.

A great movement of the mind, when it begins, only makes known its direction and its will to destruction; one only divines its existence by the wounds it bears. We know then our wounds, not our destiny. [P. 147]

It seems that an appropriate future direction would be the creation of a new reality. One reality or another there must be— the needs of the soul demand it. One can point specifically to men's need for certain ideas as a defense against the slow and irreducible transformation that time imposes on all flesh. This is a tragic situation, since age itself imposes a hierarchy that no hierarchy of values seems capable of overcoming, that no man is able to escape. "Against this eternal order, what revolts are possible?" And yet revolts and new realities there must also be, even if all crumble away as men do, and this latest revolt takes its place in the disintegrating chain of them. Still there has arisen no new doctrine, only as yet the lucid and resolute determination to revolt, to do battle with a cultural myth grown destructive and worthless.

It is proper to call this essay, curtly, an examination of myth. Men suffer and die. There is no inherent reason for or purpose to their anguishing experiences. Their minds in self-defense need, seek, and create myths that invest their lives with meaning. But the myths are artificial and somewhat fragile: at times they wither and die. Then the absurdity and meaninglessness of their lives becomes apparent to the defenseless, and they display symptoms of their disease: Angst, estrangement, despair, violence. To live, they must and will raise new defenses, create—perhaps consciously create—new myths.

Malraux has gone one step beyond A.D., who could not accept any belief because all beliefs were lies. Myths are not truths or lies, they are conditions and instruments of life that either serve it or do not. He is, therefore, prepared in principle to accept or create a myth, provided that it works. This must be one of the strangest, most coolly conscious approaches to a political theory on public record. But it is by now clear that Malraux is working in that direction, for according to him the next myth will be founded on the rejection of individualist metaphysics and ethics, and myth itself is a property of social groups. To defend oneself, then, others must be made able to defend themselves. The scope of the new illusion is not yet fixed: the essay proposes that a whole culture's "reality" must be changed; *The Temptation* seemed to suggest that a political cause to which an individual could attach himself would do. In fact, Malraux never firmly and finally defines this scope: it turns out to be a matter of circumstance.

Later Malraux embroidered the key concept of myth and approached more closely to the theories of Georges Sorel. At this point they are far enough apart to seem entirely distinct. Malraux proposes to manipulate cultural world-views in order to relieve men's mental agonies; Sorel proposed to teach some men in a culture to believe in a future apocalypse (the General Strike), so that they might in the present become ethically superior men. The difference turns out not to be so great.

Malraux has come far since the fantasies. Meaningless experience is no longer a constant to be exposed without emotion but the contingent product of variable circumstances; it is a function of the sickness or health of the culture to which one belongs, a function of the decadence or living presence of myth. Human lives require that man not be neutral toward the shattering of an old illusion: he must find a faith, or create it. This is what Malraux proceeds to do. To the rest of European youth, in search of a belief that will relate to action, he presents a number of possible commitments and at last chooses and defines one of his own.

2. THE EARLY YEARS: THE CONQUEROR, THE DEFEATED HERO

THE FIFTEEN YEARS from 1928 to 1943, in which Malraux published six novels, mark a movement in his thought from directionless political revolt through a form of Marxism to a humanistic political philosophy. Metaphysical criticism and speculation give way to the representation of a concrete reality that recreates this abstract speculation and examines its political implications. Malraux turns from the essay to the novel, from consideration of the Absurd as a feature of a culture to expression of the Absurd as a feature of individual experience. The leading figures of all Malraux's novels are alike in that they perceive and respond to the Absurd in some shape and under some name. Through the examination of the success or failure of their lives Malraux passes judgment on the validity of these particular responses. Thus he presents to that European youth in search of a belief that will relate to action a number of possible commitments, of possible lives (and so of possible vivifying myths). Among the heroes who lead those lives, three types stand out: we may call them the Conqueror, the Bolshevik hero, and the liberal hero. Malraux's first two novels are devoted to a study of the Conqueror-type, the epitome of the "Western man" dissected in abstracto by Ling in *The Temptation*. The conclusion of the analysis is mainly negative: the Conqueror figures are failures, the Conqueror-type is not made into an exalted myth. But certain elements of this type—notably the element of political engagement and violent action—are preserved and are integrated with emergent minor themes to form the next hero type and main object of scrutiny.

Malraux's characters, especially the early ones, are highly self-conscious figures. They are tortured, they are aware of it, they have a name for the causes of their malaise and a program for overcoming it. Their careers, their lives, are their programs; they have made a deliberate choice, an existential if not a moral decision. Since they are products of will rather than of drift, it is legitimate to treat them as moral prototypes, as they treat themselves and in certain cases treat one another.

What is new in the first two novels, *The Royal Way* and *The Conquerors*, is the serious examination of such prototypes: their special perceptions of the Absurd, their methods of defense against it, and their almost total defeat at its "hands." Otherwise the themes are familiar: the static predicament of Western man in *The Temptation* is dynamically rendered; the plot of *Royaume farfelu* (journey, action, death) is repeated, though without the ironic detachment of the earlier work. This persistence and reappearance of earlier motifs in new forms remains a feature of Malraux's novels, accounting for the need to view this period of his work in chronological terms of succession and metamorphosis.

1.

The Royal Way (1930) is logically the first (though actually the second to be published) of Malraux's major novels. It is founded on Malraux's experiences previous to his entry into revolutionary politics; unlike *The Conquerors* and the later novels, it is not rooted in current political struggles. Though the place is fixed and the time must be not long after the First World War, the action takes place beyond the familiar stream of history. Its central character, Perken, an explorer-adventurer, does not act within society or with reference to particular social forms. Divorced from society, he lives by preference among the unconquered frontier tribes on the borders of Cambodia and Siam. He lacks even a native country: a Schleswig German by birth, the settlement of the First World War has denationalized him. Chance, which has left areas of the world still uncivilized and un-Westernized, has given Perken the power to become an adventurer rather than a criminal or a revolutionary.

But Perken is a highly conscious adventurer, obsessed by the notions of defeat and death. Life to him is ultimately fruitless, a series of baffled hopes, the decline into old age and into the certainty that "what you haven't had already you never will have"— and, at the end, death, astounding proof of the futility of life. Life is the net in which men are snared for slaughter by destiny; everywhere it is dominated by the Absurd, man's "human lot" which he cannot escape. Aging and death are only two reflections of the subjection of men to the power of destiny.

The established order of society is another such reflection, but against this one, revolt is possible. The object of the social order is the reduction of man to the level of a termite. History bids the individual to truckle to order, customs, rulers—to obey, in short, the law of the ant-heap. "I will not obey." Instead Perken revolts against his human lot. He repudiates society and resolves to live his life and die his death according to a plan of his own. In preference to a submission to destiny, a constant perception of its dominance, and an increasing despair in the face of its power, he chooses to make his life as much his own creation as he can. Though all come to the same end, men are free to choose the lives they will lead. Perken chooses a life of action on the frontiers of Western civilization and a conquest of absolute power in opposition to it. The life of the adventurer can be "turned to account"; violent action can strike a blow at destiny by tearing a rent in the established order, destiny's creature. The ultimate human achievement, for Perken and his nihilist philosophy, is to force one's way into history, "to leave a scar on the map."

His one goal on the frontier had been to create an independent power of his own. "Just to *be* a king means nothing; it's the building-up of a kingdom that's worth while" (p. 73); and for fifteen years he had laid the groundwork by establishing close and dominant relations with the Moi and Lao tribes. Now he joins a young archeologist, Claude, in a search for valuable sculptures to be found along the ancient Khmer Royal Way, presumably so as to secure money for buying arms. In fact he is seeking not money but a man, a legend—Grabot, an adventurer whose myth Perken would like to emulate and whose power he fears. The explorers find the sculptures; then, among the savages, they find Grabot. He has not raised a kingdom of his own, as Perken had feared. The tribes have blinded him and leashed him to a grindstone. Perken rescues this wreck of a hero and of his own hopes at the cost of a minor wound whose infection means death. Then he rushes back to the tribes to save his power; instead, dying, he is able to watch the civilization he loathes, using Grabot's case as pretext, relentlessly swallow up his tribes and his kingdom.

Perken's dreams are broken apart, and his character disintegrates into that of a frightened, weak, wretched, and dying man. His plan for life vanishes, and he is unable even to choose a hero's death; the wound that poisons him is a mere accident. He has sought and found action, but even that proves degraded and absurd. His isolated quest, his revolt against his lot ends, like Grabot's, in self-annihilation, in an involuntary dehumanization and an unsought defeat. By the end of the novel Malraux has turned against the individualist, antisocial, nihilist escape from the human predicament.[1] The hero-character he has introduced remains a part of Malraux's philosophy; but the implications of that figure which Malraux now begins to explore are those to be found beneath the surface of the least "heroic" figure of *The Royal Way*, Claude Vannec.

[1] Perhaps he had intended to accept the possibility when he began the novel (finished after *The Conquerors,* but apparently started before it); but in the course of writing, Malraux's attitude toward Perken apparently shifted unfavorably; like Claude (perhaps), he came to think of Perken's quest as nothing more than a search for self-destruction.

Claude is equally obsessed with the Absurd. Finding it in society, he chooses to wrench free of the inert world. But he also finds it in the jungle, in the mass of inhuman life where man has no place and where his will and act have neither sense nor power. At last he finds it in the life and death of Perken, whose compulsive will to power in any form, combined with the legends of greatness that are circulated about him, had initially made him appear to Claude as nothing less than a superman. To Perken, Grabot is the superman whose life, or myth, he takes as exemplary and strives to imitate; Claude resolves, in turn, to live his life like Perken. But the myths surrounding these supermen-presumptive prove greater than the men themselves, and they meet defeat and degradation.

Perken learns nothing from the collapse of his idol. But Claude comes to understand the depths of Perken's failure, a failure which derives from his complete isolation from other men. That isolation, which leaves his life and death meaningless and absurd, is tragically a creation only of Perken's own belief. Perken is set apart because he considers himself set apart: he never becomes conscious of the real significance of the act that freed Grabot and destroyed himself. That was clearly no act of personal power seeking; if it had any essential nature, it was one of sacrifice, but Perken never sees it as such. He contrives to remain alone in his life, and he is never more so than at his death.

But Claude, who feels the impact of the world even more deeply than does Perken, is not totally and permanently fixed in his human isolation. From the beginning of his companionship with Perken, at first because of their common obsession with death, a relation of comradeship, implicitly giving the lie to isolation, has sprung up between them. At the moment when Claude decides to accompany Perken on the death-run northward, there is a moment of complete communion between them strong enough to bring immediate constraint. But after that, Perken becomes lost in the contemplation of the frustration of his life, while Claude, "confronted by the vanity of human life, sickened by silence and the irrefutable arraignment of the universe that is the death of one we love," watching the eternal conclusion of the eternal combat between death and life, is wrenched out of himself, out of his incomplete isolation, by the "desperate fraternity" that he feels for the dying man.

This first appearance in Malraux's work of the themes of isolation and fraternity is of marginal significance. The whole movement of *The Royal Way* is from a struggle to an apparent victory (when Perken goes out to the Mois, choosing his death) to an absurd defeat. The burden of the book is the review of the Conqueror-type, of his method of defense against absurdity, and of its failure. But it is Malraux's constant preoccupation to discover new manifestations of the Absurd, further causes of the feeling of meaninglessness in the face of one's life and of the world: isolation became one of the many aspects of the Absurd, along with aging, death, the failure of action, and helplessness in the face of nature or of the social order. But some of these manifestations are contingent rather than necessary: fraternity overcomes isolation. Whatever constitutes a triumph over one form of the Absurd becomes, sooner or later, a good and a goal for Malraux. Perken's illusory target is a social relation—independence and absolute power—as is Claude's momentary discovery—a sentimental unity between man and isolated man. The former, the illusion, is the goal of the Conqueror; the real reward is a chance byproduct of his action and struggle, when that is not undertaken in self-imposed isolation. The next Conqueror discovers other byproducts of the doomed struggle for power. When the byproducts become more important than the power, Malraux's hero ceases to be of the Conqueror-type.

2.

The Conquerors (1928), with a similarly defeated hero, is based on the 1925 Cantonese uprising. Both novels have for their chief figures Westerners who, having discovered the extent of the alienation of their real lives from Western society and culture, have replied by leaving for the Orient to strike out against the influence of the West, carrying with them only the visions of power which their cultural origin has implanted in them. But Perken goes to the Cambodian jungle to fight a delaying action on the fringes of an advancing, encroaching, colonizing West; the Orient which Pierre Garine, the hero of *The Conquerors,* seeks out has already felt the hand of the West and is rising in revolt against it. For Garine, the East is not Cambodia but the new revolutionary China, formerly a civilization existing side by side with that of the West, then shattered and remolded by it, and now struggling to cast out its influence entirely.

The Conquerors is built on the same model as *The Royal Way.* An intelligent man is tortured by obsessive anxieties and by feelings of isolation in a meaningless world. Ordinary experiences take on an appearance of terrible gravity, yet make no sense. He applies his intellect to his experiences and supplies an abstract causal diagnosis of the causes of his ailment: they are to be found primarily in the external world—this diagnosis being his own special vision of the Absurd. The next step is coldly rational: he "revolts"; that is to say, he takes measures designed to change the external world so that he may be at home in it. But his revolt fails. Either he has miscalculated his power or, if his struggle seems outwardly successful, he does not achieve serenity because he has made a wrong or incomplete diagnosis. But in his failure there are unplanned and unsought moments of inner peace that suggest the true solution, the true curative, which he does not comprehend. Perken's intention is to allay his obsessions by single-handedly carving out a kingdom, but he reaches harmonious consciousness only at the moment of his unpredictable sacrifice for another man. Garine seeks his cure by wagering his life in a revolutionary enterprise, and finds it only in the fleeting consciousness of communion in that enterprise.

For this general form of personal encounter the plot is not subordinated but exploited. The novel deals with a general strike at Canton, a political struggle that pits the Chinese against the British in Hong Kong, the Kuomintang against the military bosses allied to the British, the violent wing of the Kuomintang against the Gandhians, and the Communists in the KMT against the less restrained terrorist element. Garine is fully allied with, but not under the discipline of, the first parties in each of these struggles; by his decisive acts, all his allies win striking political victories. It is he who takes over and reorganizes the bankrupt KMT Propaganda Department, who attaches all the police forces in Canton to it, who utilizes the proffered collaboration of the agents of the Communist International. It is Garine and these agents who have driven the Kuomintang and the Cantonese government to declare a strike for the expulsion of British influence. In the period of action—a little over a month and a half—Garine defeats his rightist opponents and keeps the strike alive, defeats his terrorist opponents and keeps the wealthy Nationalist sympathizers alive, and is responsible for the destruction of two marauding hostile armies. At the end, as he leaves Canton, he forces the Cantonese government to issue a boycott decree which will bring the British to terms. Truly, he seems a conqueror, and in this respect his life seems different from Perken's, because his enterprise is a success.

But the workings of his mind reveal that he feels otherwise. It is not the material condition or public character of their lives of which Malraux's heroes are sharply aware. As with Perken, the Absurd dominates Garine's perception: to him, his life and all lives are meaningless and futile. His capacity for sympathy is stunted by the sense of the Absurd, since suffering only makes the sufferer's powerlessness more public and thereby turns him into an object of contempt and laughter for those who can only respond to their own emptiness in the same way. This is a classical configuration of comic perceptions: an intelligent, insightful, but pitiless observer views the empty struggles of those who believe (falsely, as the reader knows) their lives to have a possible meaning, in quest of which they suffer; he feels contempt for them—amused contempt the more he senses his distance from them, hysterical contempt the more he senses their nearness. Now, however, only Malraux's heroes have this comic character, where previously Malraux's work was comic also in form and in the relation of author to work. As Malraux's heroes follow his own emotional and intellectual evolution, break down the walls around their insulated selves, and create a community of will and dreams, they lose the comic view of the impact of the Absurd.

To Garine, the Absurd appears in many shapes. His vision, if not his revolt, is also Malraux's. Garine is man alone in a strange world—and physical nature and other men are equally strangers to him, equally parts of this world—to which he is bound, from which he cannot escape, which he can neither rule nor fully understand, against which he briefly struggles, and which finally imposes its dominion on him. It is "the world of tragedy, the ancient world" of the preface to Days of Wrath: "man, the crowd, the elements, woman, destiny"; only woman is missing from that ancient world here. There are many masks under which the incomprehensible, half-mad, half-invisible world around Garine travels. The first: in the absence of men, both natural and human works become foreign, dangerous, awesome: the man who sees them feels, more than ever, anguish at his aloneness, despair at his powerlessness. The second mask: the monstrous but enormously moving visions which the world thrusts on men in dreams, in insane carnivals, in waking delirium. The third mask: the crowd, which Garine can manipulate, but whose emotions are as far beyond understanding as those of a pack of animals. All these are violent perceptions for moments of Garine's life: they deepen or renew his alienation, but are of passing importance. But two more masks of destiny dominate his life: the social order, against which alone he revolts; and the inexorable order of disease and death, against which no revolt is possible for him.

Every social order, present and future, seems to him a form of absurdity: it will try to strait-jacket him, to reduce him to ant level, to impose surplus humiliation on him. "There is one thing that matters in life: not to be conquered." One may conquer, or one may be conquered. Therefore, Garine is possessed with a lust for power. "To direct, to determine, to constrain—that is life"; at least, it is the opposite of being humiliated.[2] He sees politics as an area of great conflicting forces whose struggles determine the flow of power; any idealism or doctrine beyond this vision is trash. The only question is, to what violent movement should he attach himself? The World War is of no use to Garine; he is inspired by the Russian Revolution, though repelled by its ideology; luck presents him with a chance to join the Chinese Revolution, and he snatches it.

Garine, while seeking power, also strives to throw down the ruling classes, who are detestable because they are on the side of absurdity. This is not so contradictory as it seems: those who hold power provide themselves thereby with a shield against the Absurd in their lives;[3] but at the same time, as far as everyone else is concerned, they are the instruments of the Absurd. Garine knows that once the strike is won his fellow revolutionaries, in power, will become contemptible in his eyes: he will have no alternative but to continue his quest by destroying them and becoming a dictator or by breaking with them and organizing the counterrevolution on behalf of England. (And indeed, at the end of the novel the latter is the course he is considering.)

The victory of the revolution can therefore bring Garine no solace, for he has no interest in the revolution as such, its success is not his victory. At the end Garine is losing a personal battle with the fifth mask of the Absurd, disease. Malaria and dysentery are destroying him: ordered to leave the tropics, he cannot resist

---

[2] Kyo Gisors in *Man's Fate* has another idea of what is meant by the opposite of humiliation.

[3] They are no longer the *victims* of humiliation.

the appeal of the power struggle, for he knows that without him the revolution will collapse. Disease hollows him out: at last only its movement distinguishes his face from that of a corpse, and he becomes aware of his own defeat in the midst of victory. The only value in his life was not to be conquered, and he is conquered.

What cripples Garine and makes him a defeated hero is one of the distinguishing attributes of the Conqueror-type—his solitude. It is the lack of shared feeling that makes the carnivals and the crowds meaningless and monstrous. For the isolated individual the world is the multiple mask of destiny with which he cannot cope. Even if he conquers the social order, what of it? He will still die; the world will still subjugate and overwhelm him. Yet there are three fragments of Garine's life which are not consistent with this totally hopeless vision. His own propaganda has convinced thousands who had no aspirations that their lives, their individual identities, were important: in them he has created a dream of victory, a hope for a future when they will live in dignity—and "it is hope that makes men live and die." They are defended by the hope, the myth, that he has created. He himself is briefly defended by the consciousness that he has created souls: "This is my work." And Garine finds to his surprise that in the struggle and the desire for a common victory he is bound more strongly to certain of his comrades than he would have believed; indeed, it is the death of one such man that precipitates his final decline into despair. Garine is barely conscious of the immense possibilities, the potential victories, which the sentiments of the believer, the creator, the fellow fighter contain. But when Malraux at last turns to examine the lives of revolutionaries who hold and believe in a myth of a good future and a comradeship in the present, he simultaneously begins to work out his ideas of the creative art.

The Conqueror-type cannot sufficiently defend himself against the Absurd; his life cannot constitute a fruitful myth. Perken was deceived by the myth of Grabot, Garine was deceived when he read the lives of men of great power and decided to imitate them; the would-be imitators of Perken and Garine (Claude in *The Royal Way,* the narrator in *The Conquerors*) are drawn to them by their myths and educated by the reality of their lives. Henceforth the Conqueror becomes a character of the second rank. There are many such figures of the second rank in Malraux, and most of them are also clearly types—the Policeman, the Organization Man, the Terrorist—who serve to set off the hero by displaying different responses to the same dilemma. Normally they lack the intense consciousness of the hero; normally they share his failure. *The Conquerors* contains a little picture gallery of such types, but they are so much less important than Garine that little can be said about them. In Malraux's next work that is not the case. The Conqueror steps down, and a variety of solutions, a variety of defenses, is considered. But there is a main figure, a hero. Retaining the immense energy and the political activism of the Conqueror-type, he adds to them the ability to believe in a myth (rather than to manipulate it) and to love those beside whom he fights (rather than to use them as instruments of his own craving for power). He is, unlike Garine, a Communist; but he is, like Garine, not a Marxist. The Bolshevik hero comes on stage because his predecessor died of internal contradictions; he departs when he dies of his own.

The departure of the Conqueror-types from center stage in Malraux's novels symbolizes their double failure in Malraux's eyes. Such men do not solve for themselves the psychological problem postulated in *The Temptation* as imposed upon Westerners by the collapse of the Western myth of personality. Like all the rest—all the rest of the intellectuals, at any rate—they fail to attain a serene confidence in the value and meaning of their own lives. Their lives cannot therefore be the source of new political faiths and cultural myths of personality, such as would solve for all Westerners the problem that a harmonious life can solve for the one who lives it (and such as are demanded in the essay "D'une jeunesse européenne"). For these two reasons the Conquerors lose their fascination for Malraux.

But something of them remains in the Bolshevik hero. Malraux's new attempt at depicting a human type whose life solves its own problems and therefore stands as a fruitful myth discards the lasting solitude of the Conqueror but retains his politicization, his will to combat, and his revolutionary hostility to the social order, conceived as the systematic humiliation of the ruled by the rulers. And this new type raises to a higher estate the Conqueror's untypical moments of fraternal sentiments, and the unintended or manipulative myth of a good life which his activities generated in those around him. And this new balance of attributes outlasts the Bolshevik type as it survives the Conqueror.

3. THE BOLSHEVIK HERO

MALRAUX'S NEXT TWO NOVELS, completed in 1933 and 1935 (at the height of his own period of cooperation with the Communists), represent a distinct phase in his development. Not a party member, he rejects both the organizational methods of the party and a key aspect of Marxist dogma. But the central figures of *Man's Fate* and *Days of Wrath* are Communists because in this period Malraux has accepted without any reluctance the value of fighting the same fight as that of the Communists. *Man's Fate* arrives at this conclusion by debating what Malraux sees as the alternative ways to lead one's life at a moment of revolutionary crisis. *Days of Wrath* dispenses with the debate entirely. Both works present mythic, exemplary heroes—figures not to be rejected, like those of the preceding works, but worthy of imitation. Malraux has reached his first resting point here, his first partly stable notion of what is man's political good. This abstract idea of the good life is rendered concrete in the successful lives of Kyo Gisors and Kassner, in the successful figure of the Bolshevik hero.

Man's Fate (1933) appears to employ a plot structure familiar to Malraux: action, apparent success, failure. But at the opening of *Man's Fate,* as if to differentiate it from the works that come before, stands not a journey but a murder. At the end, there is not death or departure but a succession, a new and yet renewed debate, a continuation into the future. If the future has ever until now had any meaning or real existence for Malraux, his readers have not been made aware of it. With all its similarities, real and apparent, to its predecessors, *Man's Fate* is a different book. Still an enormous exploration and lesson in the tragic shape of human destiny, it constitutes a new lesson, breaking new ground.

The plot is more complex than earlier ones (though this point is not significant for the present investigation), and the action will demand and accept the summary of "success and later failure." The greater complexity simply consists of the larger involvement of those characters other than the central figure in the movement of the novel; more attention must be directed to them; and this orientation becomes the ostensible reason for a more basic search into these other figures than the highly concentrated focus of *The Conquerors* permitted. The time is March 1927, the place Shanghai. The Kuomintang, which now holds Hankow as well as Canton, is moving northward over the hopeless opposition of various forces; those that matter briefly in the novel are the "White" forces associated with the Shanghai government. The immediate issue is over the seizure of Shanghai—will it fall to the organized Communist groups within or to the "Blue" Nationalist army of Chiang Kai-shek? For Chiang is on the verge of splitting with the Communists, until now his allies in the Kuomintang, and the question of who takes Shanghai points beyond itself to the question of which will be victorious in China in the struggle which both know must come. More to the reader's interest are the problematic relation between the hierarchical Communist party (centered now in Hankow) and the Shanghai revolutionaries (who are still psychological individualists, if individualist in no other way) and the general relation between order and the person in a situation of revolt. And, inevitably, the destiny of men, taken one after the other, as a clue to the destiny of man.

A Communist insurrection, led by Kyo Gisors and the Russian Katov, captures Shanghai in about a day and a half. The Communists divert a government arms shipment to themselves and by distributing the weapons turn a general strike into a revolution. The Shanghai Communists have won, Chiang is fore-stalled. But already in the first day of the uprising preparations are being made by the President of the French Chamber of Commerce, Ferral, to deal with Chiang Kai-shek and to turn him against the Communists. As the city falls, the deal is closed; and one portion of the action ends with the presentation to the Communists of a Blue order to surrender their arms and leave themselves helpless. Kyo and his friend Ch'en, a terrorist, make a journey to Hankow, trying and failing to receive the support of the International in a refusal to give up their weapons and an immediate break with Chiang. Ch'en returns, to be killed in an unsuccessful attempt on Chiang's life. Kyo also returns, to organize combat groups and await the inevitable repression. When it comes, he is arrested and later commits suicide; Katov is taken and executed, along with all the other revolutionaries except for a few who escape to continue the fight or to muse upon it. The plot itself, like that of *The Royal Way,* ends in a defeat. But an analysis of the characters individually leads to a different "conclusion."

The apparently stable plot is dominated by the new method of constructing the actual argument. Instead of examining the life of one moral prototype, finding the elements of strength and weakness in that type, the reader is exposed to a large set of important characters. Each of them displays a certain perception of the Absurd and a certain reaction to it: all are figures searching for some enduring value in the face of isolation, defeat, and death. Though they do not argue the case for the lives they lead with as many words as do the figures of *Man's Hope, Man's Fate* is nevertheless a debate among many possible responses to the Absurd—a debate in which the characters argue with their lives.

The point at issue is the response of the hero to his predicament. Each character becomes aware of a particular mask of the Absurd, a manifestation of destiny which stands in his path.

How does he react to it? Does he attempt to blind himself to its
existence? Does he submit to it and become an instrument? Does
he revolt against it, attempt to conquer it, and turn it to use?
And is his conquest merely a pretense, the verbal screen for a
hidden surrender or a real failure? To this interrogation the
figures of this political novel must be subjected, to discover which
of them, if any, is indeed its hero.

Each key figure has his own special ordeal. König, Chiang
Kai-shek's police chief, cannot forget that once, when he was
captured and tortured by the Reds in Russia, he wept before
them; now he is forever obsessed by that memory, driven literally
to lose himself, unable to forget his disgust with himself and his
humiliation, unable ever to recapture what he was. The Baron
de Clappique has fallen out of his social place into a sordid subterranean life on the fringes of the night world of Shanghai; he
cannot think of his degradation without renewed anguish. Old
Gisors, Kyo's father, is an intellectual, anguished for a more
Malrauvian reason: the constant perception of his own solitude,
the fear of death. Ferral, President of the Franco-Asiatic consortium and the French Chamber of Commerce, in terror of being dependent upon the will of another, is beset by the craving
for power and the fear that it will escape him. The phonograph
seller Hemmelrich, who has lived an atrocious life of poverty
and wretchedness for thirty-seven years, writhes at the thought
of a future like his past, in which he cannot afford to die because
he has a family but cannot alleviate the misery of his wife or the
constant pain of his sick child. The young Westernized Chinese,
Ch'en, has received from a Lutheran pastor a deep religious
anxiety, an agony of sin and shame, a consciousness of isolation
from the world, a need to fulfill an apostleship—but no love, no
religious vocation, no faith. This variety of human torment is in
sharp contrast to the morbid unity of Perken's obsession: some
of these maladies look superficially more curable than the con-

sciousness of death. But in fact it is mainly those who are doomed to die who make the best of life, those who want something from life who live on contemptibly and in despair.

The responses to the human lot in *Man's Fate* fall into three broad groups: some men, like the Conquerors, seek their defense in power and violence; others seek to escape by transforming their consciousness, overcoming their perceptions of the world; still others are revolutionaries who find the causes of their condition in the social order and attempt to amend it.

König, Ch'en, and Ferral belong to the first group. König's memory of humiliation by torture can be wiped away, for a moment only, by torture and murder, by the killing of a whole class of men whom he holds responsible. He was tortured by the Reds: now "*my* dignity is to kill them"; he believes that he can live the life of a man again only when he feeds his solitude with blood. And even to kill is not enough—first he must degrade and humiliate the victim just as he has been degraded. He is exacting retribution, but not retribution alone. König denies that he is a free man, free to choose his own way of living. Because the Reds drove nails into his shoulders, and because he wept before them, he lives by punishing them; because he insists on blood, he must not admit to himself that he could have lived otherwise. Only if he can persuade his victim to degrade himself—as had König— during the ordeal can he prove—as he must prove again and again—that men with a dignity of their own do not exist. If no one can withstand his torture, then dignity consists merely in being torturer rather than victim, and König possesses all that life can afford a man; if no one can withstand his torture, then the humil- iated cannot choose their lives, and König could not have chosen to become anything but what he is. His justification of and satis- faction from his life require a certain submission from all his prisoners. König captures the revolutionary Kyo Gisors, con- verses with him humanely, hears him talk of his decision for the revolution as the product of "a will to dignity." König determines to pull him down, as he must. He interrogates Kyo; he cajoles him, threatens him, tempts him to change sides and save his life; "only I will know it"—know again, that is, that men in torment are *all* without dignity. Kyo refuses and is sent to be killed. König has not had his full measure of satisfaction: his solution to the problem of his own pain has been violated, for he has only captured the body of his victim. Worse still than this outrage is the fact that a man should have endured the same atrocious condition that distorted and destroyed König: for now König can know that it was not his condition but his choice of a cure for it that deformed him as a man and made his loss of dignity permanent. He might have recovered himself, but his defense was both unworthy and unsuccessful.

By the time König comes onstage, the independent elements of his personality have long since vanished and he has been swallowed up by his role: counterrevolutionary in politics, policeman in society, killer in existential reality. Ch'en Ta-erh is swallowed up before our eyes by the role of anarchist assassin, terrorist, Conqueror and murderer. He appears first as a revolutionary conspirator who stabs a sleeping man as a matter of duty; he dies in political and actual solitude as a man who has parted with revolution in order to make terrorism into the meaning of his life. To possess himself he must become a lonely executioner. Killing—political killing of certain men, as for König—is what will free him from his absurd burden.

The Absurd presents itself to Ch'en as religious Angst without the comforts of religion. Like the pastor, his teacher, Ch'en is driven to forget himself in action, to justify his life by making a sacrifice of it. But Ch'en's religious version of the unhappy consciousness lacks the charity that might direct him to sacrifice for others, and it lacks the inner life and sense of the presence of the divine that might permit a religious renunciation: since he has no faith, religion cannot be his defense. He is seduced away from Pastor Smithson by an intellectual recruiter for the revolution, who plays on his illusion of heroism to bring him into political activity.

In the course of this activity Ch'en becomes a decisive influence, setting off both the revolt and the repression. To him this is only by the way, for he is entirely involved with the meaning of his acts for himself, for his own life. He begins by murdering a man so as to steal a paper which will get the insurrection the arms it must have to start. But for him the political meaning of the act vanishes as it is performed and is replaced by an entirely personal, religious one. He feels that the murder has thrown him into a world from which there will be no escape. By his bloody act he is in his own mind set apart from "men who do not kill," cut off from the realm of the living, absorbed into a world of murder, of imprisoning solitude and increasing anguish. He struggles to return, but he cannot. Neither in conversation nor in action can he convey what he has felt, his sudden familiarity with death. As his combat group attacks a police station, they link arms in a chain on its roof (the top man holding to a roof ornament so that the bottom man can hurl grenades through a window): "In spite of the intimacy of death, in spite of that fraternal weight which was pulling him apart, he was not one of them." The murder means, to him, the revelation and the seal on his utter solitude.

But this world of solitude that he has discovered is created by a specific act and can only enfold him completely when he repeats that act. Ch'en becomes obsessed with the idea of terrorism. His sleep is poisoned with new anguish, with terrible monsters conjured from his memories of murder, that only a new plan and a new murder will relieve. He begins to draw away from the other revolutionaries, to defy discipline as well as doctrine, to insist upon the assassination of Chiang Kai-shek. He breaks with them and makes an attempt on Chiang's life.

Politically this is the provocation that sparks the repression. For Ch'en the decision to kill has (again) a personal meaning only. He tries to give it a political meaning as well by fabricating an ideology of terrorism: the individual without hope, says this ideology, must find an immediate meaning to his life, not through an organization, but through an idea—the idea of martyrdom; the terrorist mystique will require every man in solitude to assume a responsibility, to appoint himself the judge of an oppressor's life, to decide alone, to execute alone, and to die alone. But this mystique is without political end, is intended to achieve nothing beyond the deaths of the "accused" and his "judge." The only meaning available to the individual is, therefore, the immediate meaning: he kills; he dies. Ch'en makes no serious attempt to convey this mystique to others or to judge whether or not Chiang or some other should be killed. An ideology which cannot survive its author has a merely personal meaning. The decision to make an attempt in which he must die silences Ch'en's nagging anguish and replaces it with a "radiant exaltation," a complete possession of himself. Thus it appears that his true object is in his own death, met amid a ritual of sacrifice. He achieves his objective.

Ch'en's reaction to his "human condition" has in common with those of the other Conquerors, which otherwise it hardly resembles, that it takes the form of a sickness, and of a submersion in sickness, rather than a cure. His self-destruction does not even pretend to free him. His world, so alien to that of men, is finally dominated, not by men, but by death and by fatality. Yet on one occasion it seems to Kyo that Ch'en embodies man himself, a moth that creates the very light in which he will destroy himself. No argument in *Man's Fate* denies it: only the lives, and even more the deaths, of Katov and of Kyo himself.

The entrepreneur Ferral, the third of the Conqueror-types in *Man's Fate*, is what Garine might have become by living to associate himself with England. Ferral is an ex-intellectual and former deputy, using his enterprises in the Orient as the stairway back to power in France. The revolution menaces the Chinese portions of his empire, and he reacts vigorously even while it is in progress, routing out the money which will enable Chiang to pay his army and break at once with the Communists. He is successful in buying off Chiang, but at the moment of success his financial troubles grow; though he has beaten the nearest enemy, he is in turn vanquished in his own field, and his consortium is finally dissolved.

Ferral is thoroughly devoted to power seeking. Intelligence for him is "the possession of the means of coercing things or men," and he thinks of other men not as persons, but as part of a network of mechanisms to be operated (p. 239). " 'A man is the sum of his action, of what he has *done,* of what he can do. Nothing else. I am not what such and such an encounter with a man or woman may have done to shape my life; I am my roads' " (p. 242). Yet he vaguely suspects how thoroughly dependent he is on forces which he does not control, and it is made inescapably plain to him when, after his victory, a roomful of candy-chewing "sedentary nonentities"—the representatives of the French banks —in a long, incomprehensible ritual deny him the funds needed to save the consortium and the power for which he has fought.

Old Gisors identifies Ferral's real urge, one that is both endless and hopeless.

"Men are perhaps indifferent to real power . . . the king's power . . . the power to govern. . . . What fascinates them . . . is not real power, it's the illusion of being able to do exactly as they please. . . . Man has no urge to govern: he has an urge to compel . . . to be more than a man, in a world of men. To escape man's fate, I was saying. Not powerful: all-powerful. The visionary disease, of which the will to power is only the intellectual justification, is the will to god-head: every man dreams of being god." [P. 242]

Gisors also remarks that "there is always a need for intoxication: this country has opium . . . the West has woman. . . . Perhaps love is above all the means which the Occidental uses to free himself from man's fate" (p. 241). For Ferral, if we read "eroticism" for "love," this is true: his ideal "power" is really the

complete sexual possession of a woman, and he carries out oper-
ations in that sphere in just the same manner as in those of
counterrevolutionary and financial maneuvering, with the same
absorption—in fact, with the same ending. This will to possess
dominates his relation with his mistress, Valerie: by giving her
sexual pleasure and by humiliating her, he believes, he triumphs
over her. But this triumph is not lasting, for she responds by
making him ridiculous in public; in turn, furious with humiliation, he imagines fantastic punishments, finally fills her rooms
with animals and satisfies himself by humiliating a prostitute in
his turn. "His will to power never achieved its object"; he could
never possess another completely nor completely penetrate the
consciousness of a woman; "in reality he never went to bed with
anyone but himself." His activity is frenzied and meaningless,
and a wash-drawing he has placed on his wall is his emblem:
"on a discolored world over which travelers were wandering, two
exactly similar skeletons were embracing each other in a trance"
(pp. 245-46). And to give the lie to all the activity which is only
a disguise, there is his strange, superficially inappropriate craving
for sleep:

Sleep was peace. He had lived, fought, created; beneath all those appearances, deep down, he found this to be the only reality, the joy
of abandoning himself, of leaving upon the shore, like the body of a
drowned companion, that creature, himself, whose life it was necessary each day to invent anew. "To sleep is the only thing I have always
really wanted, for so many years. . . ." [P. 244]

Games of power which defeat him, craving for an omnipotence
which he can never reach, the need to inflict humiliations which
end in his own humiliation, the need to possess and to possess
what forever escapes him, a flight at last from himself into sleep
where he finds only nightmares and, once more, himself: all are
forms of the attempt to be released from "man's fate," and all,
equally, fail.

Ferral and König each yield to an obsession growing out of

past humiliation, Ch'en to one with which his mentor infects him. Each permits his obsession, with power or violence, to create an inner anxiety that is relieved only in the anticipation or the act of damaging, indirectly or directly, some other person. But the compulsion to rule, to torture, or to kill grows insatiable and boundless. They must fail to satisfy it sooner or later. But only Ch'en discovers the true end toward which the impossible desire points: permanent peace; self-destruction. In the earlier stages of this passage from obsession to death, Ferral and König (who leave their victims alive) no doubt transmit their disorders as Ch'en's pastor transmitted his own, for they present to others the same experience of humiliation that molded them. They are the carriers of the Absurd, as they are its victims. This latter quality at least they share with those who would defend themselves through changing their ways of looking at the world. If those who choose to be intoxicated with action destroy others as well as themselves, those who choose other forms of intoxication (that touch themselves only) are perhaps to be preferred. That they turn against themselves at least suggests that those who turned against society did so by choice rather than by necessity: that, despite the seeming logic of their lives, they could have done otherwise.

As Malraux continues to explore the question, "How can a man live?"—which is to say, how can one contend with one's human lot—he encounters answers that are as futile as they are fascinating. One answer that fascinates is the Baron de Clappique's: mythomania. Clappique is a fugitive, expatriate, penniless, fallen member of a deteriorated upper class. His normal existence is sordid: he is first found playing the fool in a jazz-hall, the Black Cat, between a pair of dance girls. He appears simply whimsical, but he is like the other denizens of that fringe world, "in the depths of an identical despair" (p. 38). He drinks, throws away all his money in one night, concocts variegated and fabulous tales about himself, with one object: the denial of his life, of his decline. Wealth does not exist, poverty does not exist; " 'Nothing exists: all is dream.' " Kyo and his father have an occasion to discuss him: " 'No man exists by denying life.' . . . 'One lives inadequately by it. . . . He feels a need to live inadequately.' 'And he is forced to.' 'He chooses a way of life that *makes* it necessary . . .' " (p. 46). Old Gisors claims that Clappique's affliction has no more depth than the man himself; but if Clappique's is not deep, it is still the same malady that belongs to all men. He cannot think of the manner of life from which he has fallen without one form of anguish, and his simple confrontation with the serenity of the Japanese painter, Kama, brings him another: "the atrocious sensation of suffering in the presence of a creature who denied suffering" (p. 202).

Like the others Clappique senses the presence of an Absurd; he tries to defend himself against it by outperforming it in absurdity, by means of his fantastic vagaries. He suffers and denies it as best he can—though absurdity personified never thoroughly outfaces the Absurd even in his normal life—by making everything into an alcoholic or outrageous dream, even his own being: " 'Baron de Clappique does not exist' " (p. 207).

Clappique becomes involved with the revolutionaries by chance, because he runs out of money and can be of some service to them in obtaining the arms shipment; the police, for whom he has usually provided information, discover this, and his connection with Kyo leads one of his contacts, on the day before the repression, to warn Clappique to leave Shanghai. Instead, Clappique warns Kyo; the latter, who has long since made up his mind to stay and fight to the end, asks Clappique to go back to try to obtain more information; Clappique arranges to meet him at the Black Cat. Before the appointment, with time to spare, Clappique is attracted to a gambling house; the information he has, vital to Kyo, is forgotten as Clappique suddenly seems to find himself in the world of true and unconcealed reality, a man confronted by destiny in the form of a roulette wheel, with the clarity of a revelation. From a man with no depth, he becomes one who seems to comprehend everything in Malraux's philosophy, in one experience.

He had the feeling of seizing his life, of holding it suspended to the whim of that absurd ball . . . the living reality . . . of everything by which men believe their destinies to be governed. . . . Through its agency he was embracing his own destiny—the only means he had ever found of possessing himself! [P. 257]

Yet a sense of wrongness, of a false twist in his revelation, seeps through to us: he is gratifying "at once the two Clappiques that composed him, the one who wanted to live and the one who wanted to be destroyed" (p. 257); he tries to win "no longer in order to take flight, but to remain, to risk more, so that the stake of his conquered liberty would render the gesture even more absurd!" He finds in gambling "a suicide without death" (p. 259). Knowing that his play will lead to his own inability to leave Shanghai and to Kyo's capture,

he threw Kyo back into a world of dreams . . . he was sustaining that ball . . . with his own life . . . and with the life of another. . . . He knew he was sacrificing Kyo; it was Kyo who was chained to that ball, to that table, and it was he, Clappique, who was that ball, which was master of everyone and of himself—of himself who was nevertheless looking at it, living as he had never lived, outside of himself, held spellbound and breathless by an overpowering shame. [P. 257]

His liberation begins to seem false to him the moment he leaves the gambling house; "anguish was returning" (p. 261); he tries to defend himself by going from prostitute to prostitute, concocting a tale of his own coming suicide, becoming drunk on his fabrications of "a world where truth no longer existed . . . neither true nor false, but real." Again his old metaphysics argues that since this new universe did not exist, "nothing existed. The world had ceased to weigh upon him. Liberated, he lived now only in the romantic universe which he had just created" (pp. 263-64).

Much later he returns to his room, trying to banish torment and solitude with whiskey. He spies a mirror and, in a weirdly terrifying scene, "as if he had found a way of expressing directly in all its intensity the torment which words were not adequate to translate, he began to make faces transforming himself . . . into all the grotesques that a human face can express," then suddenly recoils from the "frightful mirror" whose "debauchery of the grotesque . . . was assuming the atrocious and terrifying humor of madness" (p. 275).

He feels no remorse, only a fear of death; having lost his money, he destroys his identity by passing himself off as a sailor on a vessel about to depart, preferring, as a stowaway, a voyage that will probably lead to prison to his real physical annihilation; and aboard ship he returns to his continuing round of mythomania and alcohol. He stands firm on his conviction that "men do not exist" because "a costume is enough to enable one to escape from oneself" (p. 313)—even though that escape is only the construction and reconstruction of a series of prisons. Clappique might have been able to alter his life, to emerge from his self-imposed regime of degradation, if he had cared to notice the chance and to will the change. Instead, and despite a series of insights into the sources of his anguish, he has chosen—and knows he would choose again—one more, and the grandest, of a series of abject illusions of liberation, "the most dazzling success of his life" (p. 313), since he is no longer telling a lie but existing as one. He is a figure out of surrealist quietism, and his nonviolent confrontation with destiny, his absurd reaction to absurdity, is a form of subjection and submission that scarcely pretends to be anything else.

Another character who follows an escapist road away from his own overwhelming Angst is Kyo's father, Old Gisors. An intellectual, he has organized revolutionary cadres but avoids action himself. Quite unlike his son (or Garine), he is a contemplative, interested in what is deepest or most singular in men rather than in what can be used to make them act, in individual men rather than in the moving forces of the world of flux. His meeting with other major characters—Clappique, Ch'en, Kyo, Ferral—all turn into analyses which the reader may accept as true but which lead to no conclusions. And these disjoined analyses are but one step away from a total lack of contact; it is only his son who binds him to the world of men and makes them matter at all, and after Kyo's death human individuals no longer exist for him at all.

At the outset Old Gisors is a Marxist for reasons precisely opposed to those of Kyo, for a fear of death brings to him a consciousness of fatality; rather than revolt against this fatality, he wishes to bring himself into harmony with it; while Kyo lives and men still count for something to him, Gisors is therefore attracted to Marxism, not by the will it contains, but by its element of fatality. As for the men he scrutinizes, however much he knows or deduces about them, he does not know them. He begins with the abstract cognition of the distance lying between himself and others. As the revolution begins, he comes to apply this realization, to feel the gap, to understand that he does not know his own son, that there is no point of contact between them even though they are on the same side of a political contest. As a former professor, he can be sure only of what he has taught or given to a man, and it is not he who has taught Kyo to follow the life of action. He loves his son ("One never knows a human being, but one occasionally ceases to feel that one does not know him"—p. 239), he teaches his students to give themselves wholly to the *willing* side of Marxism, solely to give Kyo allies; but his love cannot overcome the separation he perceives between them, his own consequent solitude, anguish, and obsession with death.

A photograph of Kyo lies under the tray which holds Gisors' real escape: opium. Since he cannot escape his total solitude, since he can neither reach nor be reached by another consciousness, he chooses to plumb the depths of his own "furious subterranean imagination" clothed in the benign indifference of the drug. The oppressive world loses its bitterness to his perceptions: "His eyes shut, carried by great motionless wings, Gisors contemplated his solitude: a desolation that joined the divine, while at the same time the wave of serenity that gently covered the depths of death widened to infinity" (p. 74). When Kyo is captured, Gisors makes hopeless attempts to secure his release; after Kyo's death he is plunged into grief but refuses at first to smother it with opium. He watches near his son's body and allows the meaninglessness of the world to burn out and destroy all the bonds which had linked it to him; "he felt the basic suffering trembling within him, not that which comes from creatures or from things, but that which gushes forth from man himself and from which life attempts to tear us away" (pp. 332-33).

But at the last he flees to Japan and to opium again; he abandons his Marxism and becomes indifferent finally to life and death. " 'Men should be able to learn that there is no reality, that there are worlds of contemplation—with or without opium— where all is vain . . . !' 'Where one contemplates what?' 'Perhaps nothing other than this vanity. . . . That's a great deal.' . . . 'All suffer, and each one suffers because he thinks. At bottom, the mind conceives man only in the eternal, and the consciousness of life can be nothing but anguish. One must not think of life with the mind, but with opium' " (p. 356-57). He becomes able to view Kyo's death without torture. " 'It takes fifty years to make a man, fifty years of sacrifice, of will. . . . And when this man is complete, when there is nothing left in him of childhood . . . when he is really a man—he is good for nothing but to die' " (pp. 359-60). He contemplates men whom he no longer resembles and achieves an understanding from his distance of

all those unknown creatures who were marching toward death in the dazzling sunlight, each one nursing his deadly parasite in a secret recess of his being. "Every man is a madman . . . but what is human destiny if not a life of effort to unite this madman and the universe. . . . Every man dreams of being god." . . . Humanity was dense and heavy,

heavy with flesh, with blood, with suffering, eternally clinging to itself like all that dies, but even blood, even flesh, even suffering, even death was being absorbed up there in the light like music in the silent night . . . human grief seemed to him to rise and to lose itself in the very song of earth; upon the quivering release hidden within him like his heart, the grief which he had mastered—slowly closed its inhuman arms. [Pp. 357-58]

He sees men, but he has lost them; his escape has cut him off from all that is human in them: "for the first time the idea that the time which was bringing him closer to death was flowing through him did not isolate him from the world, but joined him to it in a serene accord. . . . Liberated from everything, even from being a man, he caressed the stem of his pipe. . . ." Like his son's dead body, he is "already something other than a man" (p. 358).

Clappique and Old Gisors seek to escape by transforming their awareness of the world. Clappique's weapons are alcohol and lies, Gisors' are drugs. Clappique concocts fabulous tales about himself to deny life, to support his principle that "nothing exists: all is dream." He drinks to create a dream, he gambles to achieve the sense of victory and liberation. By mythomania and alcohol he constructs a series of spurious illusions of freedom—a series of degradations and submissions and self-imposed humiliations, lies which at last he can neither believe nor escape. Gisors, like Clappique, resolves the struggle between man and the world, between self and otherness, by merging man with world, self with otherness. Like Clappique, he escapes by a voluntary destruction of himself, akin to suicide: he is finished with the struggle and pain of being a man. Men must strive and suffer always, if not the one then the other; those who leave off doing either become foreign to mankind. And whether the escape is effected by self-brutalization or self-transcendence makes no difference, for a completely successful escape, like a death, closes the books on a human existence.

Power, violence, lies, and dreams do not escape the judgment of destiny. The third group of characters, the true revolutionaries, even in the face of their own humiliations and deaths grasp human and permanent values. Malraux, with a new "social" consciousness, discovers a human type for whom human isolation is neither necessary nor eternal: in the present it can be broken in a common struggle, even in a common defeat; in the future, toward which that struggle is directed, it may be withered by the transformation of civilization.

In his life Kyo Gisors fights for a value that will outlive him— the "human dignity" that is the just common property of all man. He conceives of dignity primarily as a negation, the absence of the humiliation of man by man, the end of the absurd cycle of being humiliated and of humiliating, of being tortured and torturing, that describes the life of König or of Ferral, or of Garine. The implication of a struggle for "human dignity" instead of for "my dignity" (which for König lies in "humiliating them") is a utopian anarchism, an opposition, not to government, but to the urge of the powerful to compel. Garine knows of only one way not to be beaten—to conquer. Kyo subscribes to a third path. He does not elaborate on the changes that would have to be made in the social order or in the psyches of individuals of the conquering and escapist types before the utopia of dignity could come to be. But he cannot take the problem of the future as seriously as he might because physical victory in the present is not achieved in the novel. Therefore the utopia of human dignity remains at the level of a Sorelian myth, emphasizing and driving a will to act in the present rather than describing in detail the future brought by victorious action.

Yet the hopeful future is not left so vague as this. Malraux himself reveals a subdued utopianism, introducing hope, not only through Kyo, but also through Old Gisors and Hemmelrich. In one of his detached analyses Gisors declares that a civilization becomes transformed when its most oppressed element suddenly becomes a *value* and that for modern civilization this will occur when the worker ceases to attempt to escape his work and finds in it his reason for being—when the factory becomes what the cathedral was, and men see in it, not gods, but human power struggling against the earth. And Hemmelrich, driven into Russia after the suppression of the Shanghai uprising, fulfills Old Gisors' prophetic words by discovering his own dignity in the work that had previously crushed him—because for the first time "I work and know why I work." The inference is that the transformed future will involve not merely sociopolitical transformations of an anarchist sort (the abolition of the institutionalized opportunity to dominate) and psychological changes (the healing of the Conquerors), but new cultural myths as well.

Myths appear in many forms in Malraux's work. Myths about the heroic life of an individual inspire initiates to imitate him; such myths, thus far, have only appeared as damaging, since they have attached themselves only to Conquerors (as in the Grabot-Perken-Claude chain). Myths about a new future and a good life therein have been manipulated by psychotechnicians to procure them power (Garine). Such myths, of a future in which the content of the good life is absolute personal power, accepted by the Conquerors, have stirred them to action and struggle but have always yielded defeat, though at moments the presence of the other men whom he is using in the fight has broken through to the Conqueror and has revealed to him some real value, which he normally passes by. Myths about men and the world dominate whole cultures: the Western myth leads to anguish and despair for those who believe it (according to Ling) and for those who do not (according to A.D.). But Malraux, perhaps because of his early anthropological training, cannot espouse the impossible —a civilization without myths. Instead he has begun the search for new, potentially creative myths (in J. E.), at all three levels: hero myths, political-utopia myths, and cultural myths. The first possible hero myth (the Conqueror-type) has been tried and found wanting; Malraux is now examining the second type. He has only just begun a reflection on a political utopia of dignity: one feature of that utopia will be a cultural myth that destroys the alienation of the worker from his work by explaining it, not as something he must do to keep alive and get cash, but as a role in a common struggle. Since this is a peaceable utopia, the worker is to be animated not by a class-struggle myth (as with Sorel and Stalinism) nor by one of national struggle, but by a myth of the struggle of man against the earth—a humanist myth. Gisors' lecture on the transformation of a civilization is the first sign of what is to become Malraux's humanist position, in which the Western cultural myth described by Ling ("men" as separate from and in conflict with "the world," and the "individual" as separate from and in conflict with all other "individuals") is to be supplanted by a myth of "man" as a naturally harmonious unity separate from, and as a whole in conflict with, "the world."

But, because the political order of the moment offers no immediate chance to bring about the better world, the mythic heroes of *Man's Fate* do not conduct a revolution to victory and build a new order: they follow it to defeat and find a new value. The political utopia they seek is not within sight: but, in making them struggle for a good future, it yields them part of its values in the present. This situation is partly exemplified by Hemmelrich and by the Russian Organization Man, Katov, and fully by the death of the Franco-Japanese intellectual, Kyo Gisors.

The shopkeeper and phonograph seller Hemmelrich is an ambiguous character: almost the counterpart of König, through half-ironic and uncontrollable, half-unexplained means he has managed to hold back and win over the dehumanizing forces around him. For thirty-seven years he has lived unable to rise above wretchedness, "a blind and persecuted dog" (p. 191). If he could, he would "offset by violence—any kind of violence . . . this atrocious life that has poisoned him since he was born, that would poison his children in the same way" (p. 190). But he cannot join the revolution and die, because of his wife—whom he married because she was as wretched as he—and their child, sick with mastoiditis and in constant pain. He cannot strike back; out of fear for them he cannot even give shelter to his friends.

If he had had money, if he could have left it to them, he would have been free to go and get killed. As if the universe had not treated him all his life with kicks in the belly, it now despoiled him of the only dignity he could ever possess—his death. [P. 192]

But when the repression begins, his shop is "cleaned out" by grenades in his absence, his wife and child are killed; an ironic fate has freed him. "He could not banish from his mind the atrocious, weighty, profound joy of liberation . . . now he was no longer impotent. Now, *he too could kill*" (pp. 270-71). He runs to the nearest Communist strongpoint to help in its defense. There is an explosion; he recovers consciousness to see a Blue scout coming toward him through the barbed wire, an opportunity to kill. "He was no longer a man, he was everything that Hemmelrich had suffered from until now. . . . 'They have made us starve all our lives, but this one is going to get it, he's going to get it. . . . You'll pay for it!' " He kills the man and escapes in his uniform (pp. 292-93).

Hemmelrich might now be ready to join König as a man capable of nothing but killing; yet, inexplicably, this one murder appears to bring his second, and real, liberation. His hands, covered with the blood of his family, had been horrors which could only be forgotten if he held a knife or a machine gun in them; but now two drops of blood from the man he has killed fall in turn on the victim's hands, "and as if this hand that was being spattered with blood had avenged him, Hemmelrich dared at last to look at his own, and discovered that the blood-stain had rubbed off hours before." Unlike König, Hemmelrich is able to stop at this juncture without making himself once more a subject of the Absurd. He leaves China, and the reader is told that he has finally found what becomes in this novel Malraux's foremost value— his dignity—in work.

"He is a mounter in the electric plant. He said to me: 'Before, I began to live when I left the factory; now, I begin to live when I enter it. It's the first time in my life that I work and know why I work, not merely waiting patiently to die. . . .' " [P. 352]

Hemmelrich has been freed; more importantly, he has been able to free himself.

Malraux's Organization Men (Comintern professional revolutionaries) have tended to be moral mediocrities who are skillful at explaining why revolutionaries must compromise to survive and why foreign revolutions must be subordinated to the welfare of the Soviet Union. But Katov (and Kassner of *Days of Wrath*) transcend mediocrity through suffering. By the time of the Spanish Civil War all the old questions and more arise: but in these two novels the Organization Men are permitted to surpass themselves.

Katov, unlike the other Shanghai insurrectionists, has already been freed of his burden of anguish. This burden, like that of Hemmelrich, was the suffering of others whom he could not relieve; as Hemmelrich is freed in the course of the novel, Katov had long since been liberated by death to fight. He knows what he is fighting for: every battle now recalls to him a memory from the Russian Civil War—the capture of his battalion in winter, the digging of their own graves, their taking off coats and trousers in the cold before the White firing squad, the uncontrollable sneezes "so intensely human, in that dawn of execution, that the machine-gunners waited—waited for life to become less indiscreet" (p. 76). The other Organization Men act in the name of a fatality, the inevitable Revolution; Katov acts in the name and memory of men. With his fellows, Katov is captured in the repression. Almost nothing is known about him when he finally appears in a school-yard, used to hold the wounded prisoners waiting to be shot, and is put with Kyo in a space reserved for those who are to be tortured to death by being thrown alive into the boiler of a loco-motive—their deaths signaled back to those in the schoolyard by the shriek of the locomotive whistle. It is the way of his living those last hours which says all there is to be said about him.

"Katov was lying . . . beside him, separated from him by the vast expanse of suffering" which separates all, but also "joined to him by that absolute friendship, without reticence, which death alone gives . . . among all those brothers in the mendicant order of the Revolution: each of these men had wildly seized as it stalked past him the only greatness that could be his" (p. 319). When Kyo dies beside him, Katov is thrown back into solitude, but without suffering. He too has cyanide with which to end his life; but next to him are two of his fellows without it, and in the grip of fear.

In spite of all these men who had fought as he had, Katov was alone, alone between the body of his dead friend and his two terror-stricken companions, alone between this wall and the whistle far off in the night. But a man could be stronger than this solitude and even, perhaps, than that atrocious whistle: fear struggled in him against the most terrible temptation in his life. [Pp. 325-26]

He gives them the cyanide and condemns himself. Katov is a doctrinaire among the revolutionaries, but nothing in his doctrine obliged him to make that sacrifice, and it puts him on a plane above both those who decline to act and those whose action relates to themselves alone.

His Japanese education gave Kyo Gisors the conviction that "ideas were not to be thought, but lived" (p. 69). He has taken up his manner of living through a conscious and voluntary act rather than under a compulsion (like Ch'en). "Kyo had chosen action, in a grave and premeditated way, as others choose a military career, or the sea: he left his father, lived in Canton, in Tientsin, the life of day-laborers and coolies, in order to organize the syndicates" (pp. 69-70). He is a different type from the nihilist-adventurers and terrorists. He is not restless; since he is not secretly in love with death, he does not use the idea of a heroic life to justify continuing to live; the heroic sense merely gives him a form of discipline in action. The Absurd is not his constant companion: "His life had a meaning, and he knew what it was: to give to each of those men whom famine, at this very moment, was killing off like a slow plague, a sense of his own dignity" (p. 70). Thus he rejects the most debilitating element of Western cultural consciousness and affirms its most humanistic potential values. The oppression that was grist for the propaganda mill of Garine —who only half understood the value he was communicating to the Chinese masses—becomes for Kyo the real enemy, and Old Gisors' utopian hope in a sense becomes a destination. " 'There is no possible dignity, no real life for a man who works twelve hours a day without knowing why he works.' That work would have to take on a meaning, become a faith" (p. 70). Katov co-ordinates the insurrection along with Kyo; but Kyo has more of a sense of its possible meaning: the revolt is intended "to conquer here the dignity of his people."

The author shows more of Kyo, who is the deeper character, and therefore the reader becomes aware that this new type of hero is not someone who has had a fortuitous escape from his humanity. He too can be tormented: a phonograph becomes the symbol of his transient obsession. Having made a recording of his own voice, he finds that he cannot recognize it when it is played back to him. The occurrence nags at the depth of his consciousness, and he questions his father about it. " 'It's undoubtedly a question of means: we hear the voices of others with our ears.' 'And our own?' 'With our throats: for you can hear your own voice with your ears stopped.' " And then: " 'Opium is also a world we do not hear with our ears . . .' " (p. 48). And later the event comes back to him in a moment of self-doubt:

His torment returned, and he remembered the records: "We hear the voices of others with our ears, our own voices with our throats." Yes. One hears his own life, too, with his throat, and those of others? . . . First of all there was solitude, the inescapable aloneness behind the living multitude. . . . "But I, to my throat, what am I? A kind of absolute, the affirmation of an idiot: an intensity greater than all the rest. To others, I am what I have done." [Pp. 58-59]

But there is a reason for this torment, and it passes when Kyo is able to overcome its real cause.

Kyo—the first of Malraux's heroes able to feel toward a woman more than an eroticism which is really a relation of himself to himself—is deeply in love with his wife, May. She is, like him, a revolutionary (and it is not by chance that the ability to love is combined with a commitment to revolution). "For more than a year May had freed him from all solitude, if not from all bitterness" (p. 322). His brief convulsion of despair and futility is brought on when she tells him on the morning of the insurrection that in the face of suffering and death she has just gone to bed with another man. He is consumed, not by real jealousy or hatred (since he understands her only too well), but by a feeling of being suddenly separated from her, of being unable to find her: she has returned him to solitude.

In his tormented meditation Kyo stumbles on a suggestive psychology of love: it is to May only that he exists as something more than a biographical summary of his actions; in the same way that Old Gisors is able to know in others what he has changed in them and made of them, Kyo and May are able to know each other because they love each other, and this ability has been their mutual defense against solitude.

"My kind are those who love me and do not look at me, who love me in spite of everything, degradation, baseness, treason—*me* and not what I have done or shall do—who would love me as long as I love myself—even to suicide. . . . With her alone I have this love in common. . . ." It was not happiness, certainly. It was something primitive which was at one with the darkness and caused a warmth to rise in him, resolving itself into a motionless embrace . . . the only thing in him that was as strong as death. [Pp. 59-60]

Not until the collapse of the revolt, when Kyo goes out to be captured, does he regain this relation with May: he refuses to allow her to accompany him, under the guise of protecting her; there is a moment of total separation, until she motions to him to go; finding that his torment only recurs, he returns for her, having learned "that the willingness to lead the being one loves to death itself is perhaps the complete expression of love, that which cannot be surpassed" (p. 216). Because this love is sufficient for him, before he dies—alone—he regrets only that May, who is weaker than he, must be left alone with her grief. That Kyo is able to build, and to rebuild, such a relation is enough to show his difference from those who can only suffer or "triumph" alone.

As with Katov, more is revealed about Kyo when the apparent victory of the insurrection is transformed into defeat, and he determines to die for it, than before. He is captured and faced first with humiliation—the same sort of humiliation which has brutalized his interrogator König—and then with death. The humiliation comes when he is thrown into a temporary prison: darkness, the odor of a slaughterhouse, wooden cages, and within them "men, like worms," and the warder with his whip. Because all the prisoners are utterly powerless before him, the warder takes on the shape of a bestial incarnation of fatality. Kyo witnesses the flogging of an old harmless lunatic, is helpless to prevent it, and horribly and ignominiously must struggle against a desire to watch the torture. But he is able to stop the beating, then to endure his own whipping and then to have his slashed hand shaken by the torturer. "Life had never imposed upon him anything more hideous" (p. 303); yet, simply by departing from the prison, he is able to leave behind that "loathsome part of himself" which has been created there. After this, it is not merely a pompous gesture when he tells König:

"I think that Communism will make dignity possible for those with whom I am fighting. What is against it, at any rate, forces them to have none. . . ." "What do you call dignity? It doesn't mean anything." . . . "The opposite of humiliation. . . . When one comes from where I come, that means something." [P. 306]

Like Katov, like Hemmelrich after the death of his wife and child, Kyo Gisors is a free man. He is aware of the presence of the

Absurd, but he is not obsessed by it, he is not a compulsive killer
or liar or addict or master. When he does feel anguish, it is for a
specific reason, not because he is an unhappy consciousness, and
if the reason passes, so does anguish. At the last he knows that
dying in the common fight for dignity can be an act as exalted as
any act in life and that there would have been no value in his life
had he not been ready to die for it.

He had fought for what was in his time charged with the deepest meaning and the greatest hope; he was dying among those with whom he
would have wanted to live; he was dying, like each of these men,
because he had given a meaning to his life . . . . It is easy to die when
one does not die alone. A death saturated with this brotherly quaver-
ing, an assembly of the vanquished in which multitudes will recognize
their martyrs, a bloody legend of which the golden legends are made!
[P. 323]

Kyo has made a success of his life. He cannot avoid, as no man
can avoid, the final fatality, but even that he seizes, rather than
accepting as it is thrust on him. His life, which could have been
made meaningless if he had let fatality or events, oppression or
despair or discipline, make it so, has a meaning because he has
made a meaning for it. He exists in solitude because he is an individual, but he overcomes that solitude in the company of those
who had shared first victory and then defeat and who, prisoners,
are now to share death. One bond links them in spite of all the
movements of events that tend to separate or degrade them:
"fraternity," the immediate communion among human persons
converted into a fellowship by direct confrontation with a common fate. Kyo's life is an image to others because he has not
merely had a hope, as Gisors had, but has fought for its realization, and because its realization would involve a value above
self-concern and self-love and even self-fulfillment. He has
struggled to procure for others a dignity which is native to him;
his death is as worthy of him as is his life; he is, in short, a political
hero of the highest type shown in Malraux's works.

That type may be called the Bolshevik hero.[1] His solitude is a contingent condition, with which he breaks by action. If his action is successful, it may lead to a new social order in which isolation and malaise will be contingent and conquerable for all men. Because his action is directed to that end, his will has given a meaning to his life; because his life has a meaning, he is not perpetually restless. Because he fights in common for a common hope, he can even in physical defeat breach solitude and attain fraternity, the present good that is his reward for seeking the future good. From the display of human types and ways of life a high myth, a political commitment, has emerged.

The mythic Bolshevik hero collects and reconciles fragments from Malraux's past. He captures the fraternity that Claude felt by chance and the meaning in life and death that Perken grasped for one single moment. He creates men's souls as Garine did, but he possesses the hope that Garine manipulated. He holds the values that the Conquerors overlooked. One may wonder about some of his more obscure features. Can he remain a Communist when the party is run by the Organization Men? What will really happen to a society where the Bolsheviks are victorious? On such a day, what will become of the fraternity of the elite revolutionary intellectuals? The workers will find meaningful work: what will the dignity of the few consist in, once the persecutors whose repressions aroused their fraternal sentiments are gone? But in Malraux's next novel such questions are not relevant because victory is still not in sight. His second hero-type thus attains a temporary stability, and his political thought finds a first resting place.

---

[1] Not in the historical sense of "Bolshevik," but in Malraux's later use of the term to designate a human type who combines enormous energy with a humanitarian ideal. The "Bolshevik hero" is a Malrauvian, not a Marxist, breed: Kyo Gisors suspects and rejects the doctrinaire counsel of the Organization Man Vologin to the effect that historical destiny assures the eventual victory of the revolution. Kyo accepts from the Marxists a utopia and the exaltation of the will to take, not the deification of a destiny that will deliver it.

Days of Wrath (1935) returns to the single-main-character pattern, this time with a positive figure at the center. The work deals with nine days spent by a German Communist, Kassner, in a Nazi prison cell. *Days of Wrath* is a natural successor to *Man's Fate;* it contains none of the ideological conflict of the earlier work, but it contains the resolution of that conflict. Kassner, like Katov, is a man committed without the constancy of anguished doubt that has rightly accompanied the commitments of others. Because he is not so deep a man as Kyo, his book is a lesser one; but he adds more substance to the figure of the Bolshevik hero.

The intellectual structure of *Days of Wrath* is unlike that of the previous single-hero books. Instead of an anguished vision, a revolt, and a defeat, there is a revolt, a sacrifice, an escape, and a new revolt. Kassner is an organizer of the German Communist underground. He is arrested when he deliberately springs a police trap to save his comrades. He is imprisoned, questioned, tortured, and isolated. If the insane fantasies born of his solitude do not kill him, the Nazis will. But an unknown comrade saves him from madness by establishing communication with him through the cell walls; another saves his life by assuming his identity and his place in prison. Outside Germany Kassner is reunited with his wife at a mass meeting of his comrades, and he prepares to return to Germany.

At one level this book is a work of propaganda: the brotherhood of mutual sacrifice in which the Communists are united preserves them from the impacts of life and death, permits them to overcome the fear of death, to overcome torture and solitude. The party (whether or not it ever existed on earth) makes its men into brothers and heroes. At this level *Days of Wrath* is a skillful lyric peroration to the dramatics of *Man's Fate.* The only question of special interest is why Kassner is an Organization Man, why the movement proceeds from Kyo, who rejects the dead weight of the apparatus of the International, to Kassner, a man wholly within the organization, with no sense of conflict between its objectives and his own, no qualms about his position. Malraux's heroes, like Malraux himself, seek a good in political action which they cannot secure by their own power. Repeatedly they must choose as allies political forces stronger than themselves. The force chosen is that which comes closest to providing the desired goal; the intimacy of the alliance depends upon the similarity of the goals of individual and movement. Garine wanted to overthrow an old order of power and take it for himself. He allied himself with the Kuomintang Communists because they were both passionate and competent: but after a joint success he and they would have become rivals. By 1927 and the Shanghai affair the Comintern had lost its passion, but the revolutionaries on the spot had not. And Kyo wants something different— "human dignity": he believes that the Communists may supply it while their enemies will certainly not. In 1934-35 the Comintern had a short-lived "humanist" outburst which suggested that its explicit positive goal might not be far from Malraux's (it was at this time that he was honored in Moscow); that trend was followed by the policy of the popular front, which recaptured for the Communists in the eyes of many the "will" and activism they had lost at the time of *Mans' Fate*. On the basis of the behavior and misbehavior of the Communist apparatus alone, therefore, it was valid to portray Kassner as a Communist, because at this time there existed no other political force which could or would do what Malraux wanted done. It was on the same ground that in 1948 Malraux defended his alignment with De Gaulle. In 1935 it was the Communists who, in carrying on the struggle for a valid future, permitted even such ordinary men as Kassner to live herioc lives and to enjoy the fraternity of heroes. To convey that fact is one intention of *Days of Wrath*.

But at a level less bound to current events there is a more universal intent, which can outlast the conditions of a current alliance. (Like the elements of the first two novels that are preserved and developed, this aspect is present in fragmentary form.)

At this universal level the matter of chance that Kassner is at a certain moment a Communist is unimportant. In the preface Malraux speaks of "the world of tragedy, the ancient world," composed of man, what oppresses him (the elements, isolation, destiny, death) and what defends him. Kassner is simply fundamental man: his successive trials are meant to be typical of the ordeal of men before the everyday risk of death, and his defenses —comradeship, fraternity, love—are meant to be recourses universally and eternally valid. Kassner is a worker by social origin, an intellectual only by self-education—Malraux's first such hero. Even the most oppressed of men in the most oppressive of states can have what is needful to combat his suffering; even he can choose the right life and death.

When doubts return about the virtues of the apparat, the almost serene acceptance of a conclusion to political debate will not persist. *Man's Hope* explodes the passing resolution of all political problems expressed in *Days of Wrath*. But Kassner was able to transcend his isolation outside as well as inside the frame of politics. He feels a sense of communion, not only with his fellow sufferers, but also with the woman he loves, with a crowd, with a pilot in a storm. Politics is not essential to personal "salvation" in every case: for the Absurd has many faces, as Garine knew very well. The revolutionaries in *Man's Fate* have almost forgotten this truth, for each of them is the victim of one chief form of absurdity, its political form. Kassner sees many forms again: in the face of oppression and torture, of the inhuman power of nature, of the madness of the crowds, of the certainty of death, he is able to work an inner change by reflection, to conceive in each case a different communion and a different defense. Where there are brothers, therefore, it will be possible for men to transcend their isolation by political action so long as they are subjected to a common and indiscriminate oppression; but it does not necessarily follow that where oppression is not felt in common or where isolation is not political, isolation and oppression cannot be transcended. Communion comes through politics in *Man's Fate*. Some other areas of life afford it in *Days of Wrath,* though only peripherally.

The moments of self-transcendence afforded to the insurrectionists of *Man's Fate* turn into a lifetime of such moments in the permanent underground of *Days of Wrath.* So long as a vigorous, united, and consciously repressive state machine confronts, persecutes, but cannot destroy an organized resistance, these rebels and brothers can be compelled to lead short, happy lives as individuals and a long, lyrical existence as a group. Because victory is not in sight, they need not trouble themselves with difficult political questions. Because circumstances permit them to identify a certain ruling class as oppressors, and a certain oppressed class as brothers, they have only to act, only to keep the faith, and they are healed. Their health depends on the existence of a cruel, deliberately oppressive, but inefficient regime (for so the Nazis are presented). If the revolutionaries were to win, they must needs take thought, as becomes clear in Malraux's next novel. But what if the Kassners (and the Kyos and the Katovs) had no such oppressive order, no such clear-cut enemies and comrades? Such was the situation of Garine: he traveled to find a revolution, but it was not his; he attained no lasting communion. And what if there is no "clearly" just cause, no self-evident and self-conscious community of the oppressed, no painstaking and deliberate persecution?

When the historical circumstances require it, Malraux turns to answer these questions. New means of transcending the human situation will continue to reveal themselves, far more fully than they do to Kassner. So long as a delicate balance of social forces permits it, the Bolshevik remains a hero. Either victory or tolerance would derange that balance. When they do, the Bolshevik becomes an incomplete hero, and another replaces him—a more rounded and varied human type.

4. MAN'S HOPE; ALTENBURG

WITH MALRAUX'S LAST TWO WORKS OF FICTION—the first (1937) more overtly political than any which precedes it, the second (1943) superficially as much outside politics as *The Royal Way*—there is an end to what has been shown to be a single cycle of development in his thought. *Man's Fate* was, for all purposes, a debate whose momentary resolution was later found in *Days of Wrath; Man's Hope* opens up all the closed questions under the impact of new possibilities in the European world, and *The Walnut Trees of Altenburg* reaches a new stopping point. The swarms of complex and intriguing characters are similar in *Man's Fate* and *Man's Hope* and resemble one another in their multanimity and narrative points of view. *Days of Wrath* and *The Walnut Trees of Altenburg* are both written on a smaller scale, and the single viewpoint of the former is matched against a double view which begins to take on characteristics of unity. One style puts itself at the service of differentiation and dialectical interplay, the other is suited to conveying the results of that discourse. In 1943 the synthesis rested on a tragic and humanistic idea of how man's life ought best to be conceived and lived. This tragic humanism, visibly growing underneath all the more time-bound social and political orientations of the last two novels, now evinced itself fully as these other orientations were in large measure skimmed off. The dialectic of *Man's Hope*, both slow and frenzied simultaneously, mostly involves these problems of the "surface": instead of presenting the reader with the synthesis of tragic humanism, it serves to burn off virtually everything but an underlayer of this humanism, and another of real but uncertain political hope. Events served to lay to rest the hopes events had roused, returning the action from the interior of a German prison to the interior of a German prison camp, forcing thought to cope with a new historical defeat after the interlude in Spain. And the new defense against defeat was as good as final. In all the years and through all the apparent changes of face following the publication of *The Walnut Trees of Altenburg*, there was to be no abandonment of humanism, but instead an extension and a deepening of its perspective.

What forces the renewed debate of *Man's Hope* is the menace of victory. The revolutionaries in Shanghai and Germany had no real chance of success: they could enjoy fraternity in the present and take little thought for the future for which they fought their hopeless battle. But *Man's Hope* is the story of the Civil War in Spain, where there seemed to be real prospects of winning through. For revolutionaries at such moments two questions impose themselves: How many of the genuine values of the revolution should be sacrificed in the present in order to secure victory, and with what justification? And who will be the new rulers, what guarantee is there that they will be the right type of man, what surety that they can and will turn the utopia into a program, and a program into a reality? Malraux fought with the Loyalists in Spain; reportedly he encountered Stalinism in full bloom and was unkindly treated in a few brushes with it. In any case, with the arrival of the danger of victory the Bolshevik hero's simple tactical alliance with Communism undergoes an interrogation; when he acquires the opportunity to persecute as well as to be persecuted, his simple virtue of energy and action becomes less simple and more "manichean," his easy belief in the mythic political future he has propagated becomes more difficult. He is forced to split and choose one portion of his hero myths and political myths: either he lives a life of fraternity and defeat or one of victory and solitude; either he chooses a new political order in which there will be little more human dignity than before or he gets the old order back. In the final analysis in *Man's Hope* the issues seem less stark than this; but from now on revolutionary political action is not seen as an untarnished good: the Communist alliance becomes ever more dubious; all political action, even the best (for there are still degrees), assumes an aspect of corruption and of the Absurd—as did all political orders in Perken's eyes. And the post-Bolshevik hero becomes more interested in filling out the changes in the cultural order outlined by Old Gisors and the Preface to *Days of Wrath* and in exploiting the immediate defenses which art and culture, as well as action, offer him. The pendulum does not swing away from action in *Altenburg* as far as it appears to: for by then Spain had fallen, the Nazi-Soviet Pact was signed, the menace of victory was gone, and even the chance for political action was lost in the solitude of the concentration camp.

In those works of Malraux's in which he has used many narrative voices, and thus has raised in our minds a conflict of opinions, there has always been a certain amount of really diffuse perspective and a tendency (which the author, intentionally or not, communicates to the reader) to be swayed by more than one party to the conflict. This ambiance is indispensable to the quality of the work: an artist who ventured to exclude all ambiguities when he touched on politics would sooner or later inevitably reduce himself to the status of a sound truck. Nevertheless, in *The Conquerors* and *Man's Fate,* and despite Malraux's strong affinity for most of his own characters, the reader is able to make out the heroic figure who is the center of the novel and around whom the mental debate orders itself. In *Man's Hope* (1937), a story of the first year of the Spanish Civil War, this is not so easy. The Spanish Communist military leader Manuel comes closest to being central, yet he is not so. His importance is diminished by the mere amount of attention given to others—Magnin, commander of the International Air Force; Garcia, the anthropologist turned intelligence chief; Hernandez, the idealistic captain at the siege of the Alcazar and the fall of Toledo; Scali, the Italian art historian become a bombardier; Ximenes, the devout Spanish Catholic and Loyalist. Most of the major contacts among different persons do not involve Manuel. Since he is neither dead, dying, nor self-condemned to die at the end, the reader is denied access to the whole of his life. In short, as a character he personifies only one small portion of the contending forces in *Man's Hope*, not necessarily either the most important, as with Garine, or the most in accord with Malraux's own view, as with Kyo. The majority of the characters in *Man's Hope* fail to arrive at any such resolution of their lives as death or the acceptance of defeat provided for nearly everyone in *Man's Fate*. This lack of finality with regard to each individual matches a general shift in the treatment of individuals, from a view of them as characterological types whose metaphysical innards are to be carefully and relentlessly explored and compared (and whose personal finish demonstrates something about an ideal-typical form of human being) to a view of them as actors and voices in a dialectical interchange in which nothing is finally settled for certain, for them or within the interchange. Therefore there is no single character in *Man's Hope* (nor in *Altenburg*) who embodies the human type of the liberal hero, the tragic-humanist successor to the Bolshevik figure.

The need for focusing away from a single personality is understandable. The fragile synthesis of *Days of Wrath*, which depended for its continuance on the persistence of an overwhelmingly hopeless situation, is shattered now. The condition of total oppression no longer pervades the action. An atmosphere filled with the scent of victory replaces it, for the novel was written during the lifetime and not after the fall of the Spanish Republic, and its action, beginning with the first fascist risings in July 1936, closes in March 1937, with the Republican success at

Teruel. Thus, as the prospect of victory mounts, the political questions put to silence in the earlier work again come forward, multiplied and in new forms.

Where its predecessors captured the reader's attention with a few concentrated episodes, this novel sweeps and overwhelms with a torrent—again, of episodes. There are over fifty main characters, and the action moves among numerous locales—the cities, the fronts, the aerial engagements. But action, as always, becomes significant only through reflection and sentiment—or rather, reflection, sentiment, and discourse, for in *Man's Hope* verbalizations replace for the most part detailed inner explorations of consciousness. Of confrontations of two or more characters which have the air and the implications of grave debate, there are no fewer than eighteen, with twenty-three characters taking part. The points of view once represented by the careers of the figures of *Man's Fate* are now become so complex that they must be presented by the declarations of the characters in *Man's Hope*. And their dialogues are realistically inconclusive: no one wins; no single figure monopolizes right or reason.

The lack of a single hero therefore displays the absence of a single, generally valid, emergent understanding. In the drama, as in the history, none of the points of view that create the discussion persuades; none (since in *Man's Hope* the Nationalists do not speak) conquers. Malraux seems not only to be raising all available questions, but also to be simultaneously on all sides of each and yet on none, lending himself more than ever to interpretation and to misinterpretation. It is as if the reader were compelled to view the world through one great, multifaceted compound eye that absorbs all possible angles of vision, and were then required to explain what he had "really" seen. Malraux's compound vision provides a series of apparent resolutions and at the end almost an abandonment of resolution as such. Despite the amount of literary energy expended in the dialogues examining man's place in the world, one is almost at a loss to say finally what Malraux thinks. If he had ended his work here, it would have been very easy to contend that he was no longer able to believe in thought, that he had found the dilemmas of man's political life incredibly complex, infinitely debatable, and utterly intractable and unyielding in the face of debate. And, if it were known only that he did go on, it would be out of the question to predict, or to hope to predict, where his wanderings might have taken him: there are too many values to pick, too many courses which might be chosen. If, then, the actual movement toward *The Walnut Trees of Altenburg* seems foreshadowed here, if it should begin to appear not only logical (which it is) but inevitable, the appearance should be noted for what it is—an illusion pleasantly created by critical hindsight—and checked back against the reality, which is always chastening to critics.

Nevertheless, *Man's Hope* should not appear entirely beyond analysis: it is not inscrutable, it is perplexing. The questions it takes up are at least explicit, and their substance can serve as a guide. Old problems now play rather minor parts: the basic "condition" of the impenetrable world and isolation, the quality and the impact of death, even a short vision of the human grotesque. Only two men, Hernandez and Moreno, feel anything like the full weight of the metaphysical agony which has been on the decline since the revolutionaries learned how to meet it, although a third, old Alvear, exposes himself to it by calling into question the entire revolution. Plainly unresolvable and therefore irrevocably tragic dilemmas are revealed: the intellectual and the demands of action; the effect of leadership and power upon those who must hold them. And there is the basic dialectic of the book, which absorbs the problem of the present and the future, pits anarchists against Communists, the idea of the people against that of an army, individual heroism against command hierarchy, apocalypse against organization, and hope against itself: a multiform and baffling engagement. It would be wrong to dissolve the whole pedantically into these parts or to believe that the novel exhausts itself in them; but it would be foolish to suggest that they are not there—and definitely there—or that their being there and identifiable makes *Man's Hope* a meretricious work. If they were superfluous and wrongly injected, the book would be an account of a meaningless but highly developed slaughter attended by meaningless justifications, which is some people's view of war and others' (as we are aware) of life. Even a belief as bare as this cannot minimize the impact of action and word here; and of course the majority of observers will not, or not yet, be quite so disillusioned. They will find that without insistent probing into all problems there would be little more to *Man's Hope* than just such an account of incomprehensible butchery. Its literary merit rests on its political value: it is the questioning and not the manner of representation of action that makes *Man's Hope* into art, and art which is neither sterile nor the proclamation of a universal sterility.

The structure of the novel compels analysis in terms first of theses; then of the character of those who advance these theses; then, perhaps, of the verdict that the ebb and flow of action passes upon theses and characters alike. It is convenient to approach the argument of *Man's Hope* by setting forth first of all the two theses that are rejected.

1. *The price of a victory won by violence is the present sacrifice of the values that victory is intended to bring; revolution and political violence therefore become foul precisely at the point when they begin to become successful.* Of the characters of *Man's Hope,* Alvear defends this view; Unamuno and Hernandez, Scali, Puig, and the Negus, all live it; Garcia rebuts it in words, Manuel and Magnin in their lives.

2. *The price of victory is precisely stated above; therefore the values of the present must be sacrificed in the name of victory, and that sacrifice will be repaid at the moment of victory by the reestablishment and security of those values.* Garcia argues this view and discredits it with his own words; Manuel lives it, and

by the living of it discredits it; Magnin rejects it verbally and confutes it in action.

It is in accepting the argument that the price of victory is tragically high, while rejecting both withdrawal from action and moral anesthesia as palliatives for tragedy, that Malraux divulges his own view. Politics can be made more the theater of the values he holds, can be made less the puppet show of the Absurd; but there is no hope for the elimination of absurdity and tragic contradiction from human life. The only answer, if it is an answer, is consciousness (rather than anesthesia), just action rather than mere intellection, and the will and determined effort not to coordinate the tragic but to erode it.

Let us now examine this argument, as is customary, through the interrogation of the characters who stage it. It has been shown that to Malraux a revolution that fails may be worth its price in blood. But what of a revolution that succeeds? Can values won by force survive their own victory? Alvear is the first interrogator of the Spanish revolution in *Man's Hope*. Alvear is no enemy of Malraux's ideals: he espouses "the human element . . . the quality of man" as the highest value. But he believes that it is art and not the revolution which can inculcate and preserve it: to the doubts of his fellow art historian Scali, who has become a bombardier and who says, " 'In the churches of the South where there'd been fighting, I sometimes saw great pools of blood in front of the pictures. And the pictures . . . had lost their efficacy. . . . No picture can stand up against a pool of blood— more's the pity!' " Alvear replies, " 'We've got to have new pictures, that's all' " (pp. 320, 322). He sees in the hope of the crowds for the revolution only a terrifying delusion which has replaced the earlier delusion of an eternal life, for any "economic liberation" the new order may bring will be canceled out by acts of repression, violence, and treachery; there is no reason to take sides if one form of servitude is simply to be replaced by another. The quality of man cannot be upheld by politics, and Alvear would prefer to see each man turn upon his inward self the effort he spends in action involving nothing of his real self.

The answer to his sometimes telling arguments appears in several parts. To the attack on hopeless hope, Scali replies, " 'Men who are joined together in a common hope, a common quest, have, like men whom love unites, access to regions they could never reach left to themselves. And there's more nobility in the *ensemble* of my squadron than in almost any of the individuals composing it. . . . It's just such circumstances bring out what is . . . most fundamental in men' " (p. 324). Realism might add that in fact each man will not, left to himself, make something better of himself even if he is capable of it and that, as there will always be violent struggles among men, it is within the grasp of the individual to take sides against the existing servitude and attempt to mitigate or vitiate the new. Malraux would add that art preserves the quality of man, but not for all men, and therefore that those other elements that do so are at least as effective. And Alvear himself is hardly able to meet tragedy; music gives him only a temporary relief—visual art does not— from the sight of his son Jaime, who has been blinded fighting for the ideals in whose possible realization his father does not believe; and he is left resigned to his own death, waiting in Madrid to be shot for his son's service by the fascists who do not arrive.

There is a more compelling problem for the revolution in Spain as soon as there is a chance of a thoroughgoing political victory. It is seen by an insider rather than a passive neutral, by Garcia, the robust, corpulent, smiling ex-anthropologist and chief of the Spanish Intelligence Service. Garcia is a man without any particular ideology and with an incomplete understanding of the problem of ideas: he considers that economically—that is, in his view most crucially—there is no real difference among anarchists, socialists, and Communists. His purposes are economically meliorist, to better the lot of the peasants and no more, and socially reformist, to create a social structure which will contain conditions favorable to individual intellect and nobility of character: "enlightenment in Spain." He gives an answer to Alvear's doubts about taking sides: " 'In that case, as no one can be perfectly sure of the purity of his ideals in the future, there's nothing for it but to let the fascists have their way' " (p. 397). He is a realist of sorts, understanding that to resist means to take up a program of action, with all the inevitable consequences that entails. His realism takes the form of an acceptance of the organization and acts of the Communists, together with a rejection of their ideology—and an incomplete understanding of how closely the two are linked.

But he does not lack perception and a great deal of comprehension. He sees the great internal cleavage of the revolution, which in discussion after discussion pits the idealists, the "men of fraternity"—again Magnin, Barca, Hernandez, the Negus, Mercery, Guernico, Scali—against the Communists, the "Organization Men," and the men who are *for* organization—Vargas, Pradas, Golovkin, Manuel, and Garcia himself. There is a separation and a contradiction between the idea of a " 'People—with a capital P' " and the real form which a revolution takes, the revolution which is the replacement of a destroyed regime by a new regime, of old by new political systems and elites. The revolution has indeed taken form as an attack on humiliation and on hierarchy; but no social change can do without a technical organization to enact and enforce it. Apocalyptic fraternity was enough to defeat the fascists in the local revolts, but to defeat armies, armies are needed. Just so, to carry out Garcia's program, a party—a hierarchy—will be needed; and though there are just wars, there is no just army; though there are just policies, there is no just party. A popular movement can hold power only by methods directly opposed to those sentiments that animated it in the beginning. The tragedy of the revolution, in Garcia's eyes, is that it has swept up two kinds of people, those who can accept this and those who cannot. The Communists want to get things done; the liberals and the anarchists see in the revolution only an opportunity to *be* something. Those concerned with concrete realities, with action, with systems, and with practical propositions are yoked together with those who are concerned with dreams, theories, sentiments, myths, and apocalyptic visions; but the latter are all doomed men, consecrated to something other than the revolution and to their own deaths, for they must change or die.

Up to a point Garcia's is the voice of Malraux. It is particularly his when speaking of the tragedy specific to the intellectuals, who see the clash between being and doing and are confronted by a tragic choice. They may opt out of the action, like Alvear and Miguel de Unamuno; they may enter the action as men still devoted to being something and be torn to pieces by it, like Hernandez. Garcia, however, lacks understanding (or, more likely, does not express it) of the third figure of the tragedy—the intellectual who chooses to put all ideals aside in the service of action. Garcia does not express this tragedy, but he lives it.

Unamuno is a man resolved "to live in Truth, even though it means to suffer"; his sole political desire has been for federal unity for Spain, and at the outset he defended the fascists in the belief that this was what they would accomplish. Now, toward the end of his life, he finds in fascism both centralization and lies, and on both sides violence and irrationality. Therefore he withdraws from the world and life, shuts himself up in his room, and prepares to die. He has abjured both sides because they are not completely just in their means, and in Garcia's view he is therefore "downright immoral," because the only just things which exist are just ends, and those he has also repudiated.

Captain Hernandez, a liberal Republican professional officer and in charge of the siege of the Alcazar, is an idealist, a "semi-Christian . . . for whom the revolution means a way of realizing his moral aspirations." Garcia points out how close he is to the anarchists, for whom the times in which they are living also provide a "personal apocalypse": "Between the liberal and the libertarian the difference is only one of terminology and temperament" (p. 208). Self-sacrifice and death in the name of an ideal are more important to him than the reality of a victory: in this he resembles not only the Spanish anarchists, but all of Malraux's earlier characters who pursue death in the name of something else (Kyo Gisors is not in this group because for him the question of victory does not arise); for this reason the Communists are suspicious of him. Truth to himself compels Hernandez to forward a letter sent by his direct enemy, the commandant of the surrounded Alcazar, to his wife, and leads him to argue bitterly with Garcia, who condemns him for the act. "What's the point of the revolution if it isn't to make men better?" (P. 211) Hernandez wants to make an example, to show that the revolution is in the hands of the "most humane element of mankind." But he discovers that if the war is not to be lost, all the ideals for which he has fought will have to go by the board, that he must give up what he has lived for. He comes to realize that "one expects everything all at once from 'freedom,' but for man to progress a bare half inch a great many men must die" (p. 228)—but not to accept and live with this realization. It becomes impossible for him to remain alive and be himself; he accepts the fact that he is doomed, and he chooses to remain and die with the men for whom he is fighting when Toledo falls to the fascists. He has become a victim of the conflict within his own mind, from which the only escape is death. Therefore, when he is captured and offered his freedom because of his conduct toward the officers of the Alcazar, he refuses it and refuses to take a chance to escape presented him as he is roped in a line of men on their way to the firing squad: "He was too tired, and tired of life as well" (p. 255). He wills to die, to return to the earth and its oblivion, "inert, reposeful . . . . Only living men are torn by anguish and disgust" (p. 258).

Garcia makes Unamuno and Hernandez into examples in a general theory of the tragic nature of the relation between the intellectual and action.

"The great intellectual is a man of subtleties, of fine shades, of evaluations; he's interested in absolute truth and in the complexity of things. He is—how shall I put it?—'antimanichean' by definition, by nature. But all forms of action are manichean, because all action pays a tribute to the devil; that manichean element is most intense when the masses are involved. Every true revolutionary is a born manichean. The same is true of politics, all politics." [Pp. 392-93]

"For a thinker, the revolution's a tragedy. But for such a man, life, too, is tragic. And if he is counting on the revolution to abolish his private tragedy, he's making a mistake—that's all. . . . The path that leads from moral standards to political activity is strewn with our dead selves. Always there is a conflict between the man who acts and the conditions of his action—the line of action he must follow to win . . . ." [Pp. 397-98]

But the point Garcia represses and exemplifies is that the tragedy of the man who chooses to follow action to its final implications, who consciously espouses the manichean, is equally inevitable and perhaps more pervasive still.

Garcia's own voiced sympathies are all with the organizers, because what he wants is a concrete historical triumph. The fraternal spirit is the adolescence of revolution: the apocalypse and the unreal hope are the baits with which masses of men are caught. But masses of men are one thing, and the parties and armies which organize them for common action are another. "The age of parties is beginning." To win, the armies must possess revolutionary discipline, and after them so must the parties, and this discipline has nothing to do with the spirit or the personal psychology of authoritarianism: it is simply "an organization of the factors which give an army in the field its maximum efficiency" (p. 115). " 'Our humble task, monsieur Magnin, is to *organize* the apocalypse' " (p. 118).

Yet at the same time that he agrees with the Communists that no moral code has any utility whatever for practical politics, that dreams and visions are superfluous and dangerous, he encounters and voices quite realistic truths that falsify what he is saying, although he scarcely seems to understand the paradox. It may be, as Barca says, that Garcia can talk about fraternity without grasping its meaning to those who experience it, because he has never been humiliated: in any event he does talk about it, with eloquence, and equally he is one of the few characters in the book who see fraternity only from the outside and do not feel it. He does realize that the revolution cannot get along without a moral code and that without humiliation and fraternity it could attach virtually no one to itself; but once again he fails to go on from there, to draw conclusions. At the end of the book, when the Communists have begun to come to the fore everywhere, he can repeat what Guernico has told him, "they have all the virtues of action and no others," and then go on to say, "But action is what matters just at present," with no conclusions about what happens to the values for which he fights (p. 504). As he studies atrocity reports, he thinks to himself that moral problems can never be evaded: "Whichever way the war ends . . . what sort of peace can possibly prevail after such bitter hatred? And what will the war make of me?" No answer (p. 306). Later: "One of the things that worries me most is seeing how in every war each side adopts the characteristics of the enemy, whether they wish it or not" (p. 506). The point is pursued no further. Garcia's is not a formally tragic position, because he is not completely aware of it. He is constantly on the verge of a realization and never reaches one. His maximum consciousness is a puzzled disillusionment, and even that does not last. He has sacrificed everything, every shred of intellectual integrity, in the name of victory, and he is ready to say that Teruel is the Valmy of Spain, and that all was worthwhile. The reader can only wonder what becomes of Garcia's self-awareness when this victory too (like all victories?) turns into a historical defeat.

Beyond the tragedy of the intellectuals is the tragedy of the entire enterprise. Garcia is right to see its internal division, and Malraux confirms this opinion by certain of his subtitlings in the division of the work: "The Lyric Illusion," "Operation Apocalypse," "To Be and To Do." The first tragedy is the division between the "to be" and "to do" and the conflict between them; the second is the tragic nature of each.

The major good of the apocalyptic, tragic "to be" is clear: it is the lyrical illusion, it is fraternity, developed and communicated. The reader has already seen the fraternity of the defeated, and the fraternal ecstasy of the Communists, which has been turned into a Sorelian myth. But in *Man's Hope* it is confined by no such boundaries of defeat or of myth: "the lyric illusion" is illusion because it is not functional, not because it is unreal. It appears in the union of hitherto opposing forces and parties, Liberals, Republicans, Communists, UGT, CNT-FAI, the anarchists and the civilian police "allied in an incredible fraternity!" (P. 28) It is present for the crowds of people: "Cars were racing past . . . the men in them waved their fists by way of greeting, shouting *'Salud!'* And the triumphant crowd seemed united by the cry, which rose in a never-ending chorus of fraternity" (p. 43). "The roar of half a million voices, a wild, inhuman, exultant paean, rose to the dim sky, loud with the thunder of the people's planes" (p. 420). "It seemed that everyone in the street was uttering a response which imitated the clang of funeral gongs; 'Dong-ding-a-dong.' . . . in response to words he could not hear, that human gong was beating out: *'No pasarán'* " (pp. 387-88). Fraternity appears for the fighters of the International Brigade as they march through the streets of Madrid and as they fall by the Manzanares, for the flyers as an antiaircraft shell bursts and lights up the interior of their plane. It is found most poignantly in the descent from the mountain of the wounded aviators whose plane has crashed, a procession carried and saluted in silence by the peasants of Valdelinares.

But fraternity is not a permanent condition, it is a sentiment; and Garcia is only too correct when he points out that to depend solely upon a momentary sentiment would insure defeat. The badly trained socialist militia is glorious in its successes at the start; but at Toledo, as the armies of the enemy approach, the defense degenerates into a struggle for authority, the militiamen throw away their rifles and desert their posts, and a terrified mob abandons the city. Magnin's air force, with the strongest fraternal bonds to start with but without discipline, begins to grow demoralized after a series of losses and has to be thoroughly put in order, even though Magnin does not believe in organization. The anarchists must also compromise their beliefs: Puig sees his fellows making suicidal frontal attacks, in the best tradition, on positions fortified by machineguns; despite the fact that everything in him forbids him to give orders, he cannot let them be slaughtered, and he and his fellow leader, the Negus, coordinate them and capture the positions. Puig almost at once, as if in retribution, gets himself killed in the very same kind of suicidal attack. The Negus goes on, to defend his principles eloquently in debate with the Communists, whom he considers a gang of plotting priests for a religion consisting purely of hierarchy.

"We've no use for 'dialectics' or red tape; delegates are all right, but bureaucrats never! Or an army to defeat the army, or inequality to stamp out inequality, or playing the bourgeois' game. What we are out for is to live the way men ought to live, right now and here; or else to damn well die." [Pp. 200-01]

At the end he has lost his belief in the revolution, has seen the end of the apocalypse, and continues to exist only to fight the fascists. He is not dead yet, like Puig and Hernandez, but he has taken up the sport of mine laying, "that underground warfare in which nearly all the fighters are foredoomed and know it; in which, for the most part, each plays a lone hand. When up against insoluble problems, the Negus always fell back on violence or self-sacrifice; best of all, on both together" (p. 417). And all the other partisans of the tragic "to be" are dead, out of the fight, or on their way.

The tragic "to do" almost exactly complements and reverses this situation. The runaways from Toledo are organized by the Communist Manuel at Aranjuez and turned into something like a fighting force. The Communist Fifth Regiment, slowly and painstakingly organized, becomes the backbone of the Spanish army. The equally organized International Brigade is the instrument of victory at Brihuega; Magnin's reorganized and disciplined International Air Force becomes as valuable a professionalized instrument. Garcia appears to have been proven correct: organization, efficiency, discipline—these are the means to the real victory.

But the triumph of the Organization Men has meant the slow withering away of that human quality of which Alvear spoke. The "to do" compromises those who uphold it (Garcia); dehumanizes them (Manuel); or partly or completely alienates them sooner or later from it or from the entire enterprise (Scali and Magnin).

Scali—the fuzzy-haired, thick-set, hail-fellow-well-met art historian from Italy come over to be a bomber—is brought to face all the contradictions of his position. He has no talent for commanding, he is averse to physical violence, he dislikes the sensation of judgment over others which bombing gives him; nevertheless he accepts his role because, in reaction to the fascist contempt for man, he has chosen revolution, along with its implications. But he comes in contact with entirely different psychologies in the war, particularly that of the machinegunner Karlitch, who has not chosen his enemy but hates him nevertheless and who takes a physical pleasure in his job. If the result of organizing the apocalypse is to let sadists fill the revolutionary ranks, the present is paying a heavy tribute to the future. Scali accepts without comment the need for organizing the demoralized Air

Force, but he soon has the problems of his choice brought home to him again. Alvear forces him to ask whether the revolution is not simply another form of servitude; this examination throws the future into doubt as well as the present. Garcia explains that there are no just parties; this interpretation seems to Scali to open the door to racketeers as well as to sadists. And to Garcia's thoughts about the inevitable conflict between the man who acts and the condition of his action to ensure victory—which Garcia pictures as a "rough-and-tumble"—Scali counterposes the memory of a burning plane and its struggle to the death with the fire that overpowers it. Unable to sort out the contradictions in his own mind, Scali too becomes a machinegunner, in order to silence his thoughts through the sort of action he had abhorred. But after he loses his foot from an explosive bullet, he is left without the refuge of activity; and, at the moment when the anarchists have obviously become an obsolete group, he goes over to them and into opposition to the Communist Party.

The commander of the International Air Force, Magnin, is an intellectual also, but an able judge and leader of men, and a man of great energy as well as a passionate flier. Since he has been a factory manager and the director of an airline and is a trained engineer, he might be expected to fall in easily with Garcia's arguments for expertise. But he has become a revolutionary because he wants people to know why they are working, because he wants "each individual man to have a life that isn't classified in terms of what he can extract from others" (p. 116). He is a revolutionary leftwing socialist rather than a Communist because he does not care for the CP's conspiratorial, plotting nature and self-centeredness. He replies to the arguments of Garcia and Vargas with an evocation of the apocalypse and a determination not, in any case, to enforce even the least authoritarian revolutionary discipline on those who do not want it. Garcia rejoins, " 'I doubt if you expect to keep your aviation corps up to the mark on a basis of mere fraternity' " (p. 118). He has struck

home, because Magnin is troubled about the increasing irrespon-
sibility of his people and impressed by the discipline without
coercion achieved by the commissar Enrique and his Communist
Fifth Regiment. As lack of discipline increases, Magnin happens
to find himself at Albacete, face to face with the newly formed
International Brigade, which has managed to combine discipline
with fraternity. When he returns to his aerodrome to find it in
a state of demoralization and chaos, he summarily fires the unruly
and imposes organization, discipline, and uniforms on the Air
Force. The result is a successful professionalization leading to
an efficiently working force that nevertheless is able to retain its
fraternity in action.

Magnin has solved that problem, but there is another: the
advance of the Communist Party, which he still cannot accept;
the advance of the armies to the fore, bringing an enormous
growth in the scope and extent of the war, killing or putting out
of action the majority of Magnin's comrades, forcing him to mix
his planes with those of the Spanish Air Force and to scatter the
remains of his group all over Spain. Discipline has not overcome
him, but the Organization Men and their organization war have
rendered the International Air Force as such dead to him. Yet
this situation does not overcome him either, merely sends him
back to his individual philosophy. A descending procession of
wounded Air Force volunteers at Linares brings about one meditation: he sees an apple tree surrounded by its dead fruit, and

the ring of decaying fruit seemed to typify the passage from life to
death that not only was the doom of men but was an immutable law
of the universe. Magnin's eyes wandered from the trees to the ageless
ravines . . . the deep gorges into which they were now plunging, as if
into the bowels of the earth, seemed imbued with the same agelessness
as the trees. He thought of the quarries in which prisoners were left to
die in former days. But that shattered leg which the muscles barely
held together, that sagging arm, that obliterated face, that machine-gun
on a coffin, all these were the results of risks voluntarily accepted,

sought after. The solemn, primitive march of that line of stretchers
had something as compelling about it as the pale rocks that merged
into the lowering sky, something as fundamental as the apples scattered on the ground. . . . And the steady rhythm of their tread . . .
seemed to fill the vast ravine . . . with a solemn beat like a funeral
drum. But it was not death that haunted the mountain at that moment;
it was the triumphant human will. [Pp. 482-84]

Magnin has been able to settle with his own beliefs. And still
later, as Garcia talks to him about the beginning of the age of
parties, and claims that all that is left in the conflict is the clash
of "the two real Parties," fascist and Communist, Magnin remembers that Garcia has not been infallible. Magnin has no explicit
counterargument to offer. But he can only think of the partyless
peasants who were with him everywhere before and after Linares,
one guiding him to a hidden fascist airfield, others bringing their
trucks to light up an airstrip for him, others going up to carry
down the aviators, and others along the road silently raising their
clenched fists in salute to those whom nobody had forced to fight.
Fraternity was still there; and once, as he had flown over Teruel
where an enormous war was in the process of being born, and
when his own gray and lightless world of the air seemed to be
conspiring to cut him off from victory, he saw and remembered
the new stone walls which the peasants below were struggling to
raise on the fallow lands, "the first condition of their dignity,"
and he knew that among the peasants, if not among the parties,
the values for which he had fought were being preserved.

Magnin's life as such is not tragic then, although it contributes
to the tragic contradiction of the "to do"; and the same will finally
prove surprisingly true of Manuel's. Manuel is also a man of some
culture, a talented musician who at the beginning of the rebellion
is working as a sound engineer. An active member of the Communist Party, he at once puts himself at its disposal. His first
assignment has him carrying the more or less romantic weapon
of dynamite about in his gadget-filled sports car. It is wrecked;

Manuel, unscathed, has begun to lose the things tying him to his past and to develop a distrust of the romantic style of fighting. Caught up in the sweep of events, he finds himself in the Sierra, where his Party training allows him to lead a successful assault. He begins to acquire more experience, seriousness, and responsibility: the need for a responsibility that will change his life strikes him sharply when he sees a young man writing on a wall in the blood of a dead fascist. " 'When we are building the new Spain,' he thought, 'we shall have both alike to contend with. And one will be no easier to handle than the other' " (p. 85). He is appointed a company commander in the Communist Fifth Regiment, where his Party organizational experience and a natural discipline and liking for efficiency make him successful. His superior, Ximenes, is one of those who feel it necessary to get results rather than to set an example, to institute discipline, to organize courage; and Ximenes tells him that to use his authority well he must avoid the "dangerous foible" of wanting to be loved by his men. No doubt it is hard to be a man; but it is harder to be a leader. Manuel becomes an outspoken advocate of organization, more and more so as he sees the disorder on the Tagus front; he learns to be a commander from the organizer and International Brigade commander Heinrich, and he rises steadily in the ranks of the Spanish army. He sees the militia disintegrate at Toledo and leads them into a reorganization at Aranjuez.

His own voice begins to be replaced by the loud voice of command he has learned; but in the regiment he creates he discovers a fraternity expressing itself in effective action as well as in sentiment. He leads this regiment in the Sierra and discovers after a courtmartial of deserters what is happening to him. One of the men sentenced to death clings to his leg outdoors in a downpour, on his knees in the mud, to beg for mercy. "Never had he realized so keenly the necessity of choosing between victory and compassion." He bends down to dislodge the man, who looks up at him to say: " 'So that's it? You've no voice now, as far as we're con-

cerned?' Manuel realized that he had not spoken a word"
(p. 390). And later, as he tries to announce a victory and the
executions at the same time, he loses his voice completely. His
regiment, for whom he is responsible, for whom he has had these
men killed, marches by him: "their gaze told him that today they
were pledging themselves to him in a blood-bond" (p. 406).
They pass him, and he is left alone; and then the general head-
quarters orders him to leave them to take up command of a
brigade.

He talks to Ximenes, who is struck by an almost complete
change in his appearance: Manuel has found that he is becoming
more and more alienated from himself; and "every step I've taken
towards greater efficiency, towards becoming a better officer, has
estranged me more and more from my fellow-men. Every day
I'm getting a little less human!" (Pp. 407-08) He is linked more
and more closely to the Party and estranged from those for whom
he is working. Ximenes cannot help him, for to him it is impossible to lead men and still remain their fellow, outside of "fellowship in Christ." Manuel talks to Heinrich, who tells him that he
has not yet given up enough, that to serve the proletariat he must
not waste compassion, and that to win to victory he must also
lose his soul. He does reach the victory, at Brihuega, ever more
cut off from men and from himself: to replace comradeship he
adopts a wolfhound; he ceases to carry the pine branch which
has always been in his right hand, an emblem of nerves, and of
inadequacy; he plays a Kyrie for Ximenes, and discovers that the
playing of music is finished for him, that the war has "purified"
him and pushed him over into another life. With his dehumanization, his increasing isolation rather than fraternity, he has become
another casualty of the tragic "to do."

What makes Manuel's own life something other than simply
tragic is seen in the last pages of the book, in a scene akin to
Magnin's. Stimulated by music, to which he is still able to listen,
he moves in his mind one step beyond the bounds of his present

life and is able to look back at his past and down upon himself as he is. He is a soldier now, as if he had been born to war and to the responsibility for life and death.

He felt the seething life around him charged with portents, as though some blind destiny lay in wait for him behind those lowering cloud-banks which the guns no longer racked . . . . Someday there would be peace. And he, Manuel, would become another man, someone he could not visualize as yet; just as the soldier he had become could no more visualize the Manuel who once had bought a little car to go skiing in the Sierra. . . . War may be discovered only once in a life-time; life, many times . . . . For the first time Manuel was hearing the voice of that which is more awe-inspiring even than the blood of men, more enigmatic even than their presence on the earth—the infinite possibilities of their destiny. [Pp. 510-11]

Manuel, like Magnin, unlike Garcia and the others trapped by the tragic dualisms of the revolution, has been able to move past them to a moment almost of redemption.

The issues of victory are thus raised and answered in the lives of the three major characters—Garcia, Magnin, and Manuel. Garcia is quite right to propose the manichean nature of action, and Magnin sees it: "Action, he mused, always involves injustice." But he is out of order in preaching a virtually complete submission to it; as Magnin continues, "No, it was not in the cause of injustice that he had come to Spain," and he, at least, is able to make it stick (p. 157). The intellectual's role is tragic, but not always so, nor always in the same way: if Garcia himself shows that the general tragedy cannot be escaped, the other two reveal that it does not differ sharply from the rest of the human situation and can like that in one way or another be transcended. Garcia is right once again in insisting upon the necessity for organization to achieve victory. The experiences of Manuel and Magnin both bear out the point that the fraternity of fighters is not necessarily destroyed thereby. At the same time each is an unnecessary casualty of the order which goes beyond the needs of order. Manuel is isolated by his experiences far beyond what is actually necessary, because he listens to the fanatic, self-destructive leadership mystique of his superiors. A Communist, he wishes to live his beliefs before he has found out what they are; too late he discovers that these Party beliefs (rather than anything in the nature of organization itself) commit him to this isolation. Magnin, who soon learns that Garcia is right to demand organization, succeeds in reworking his Air Force so as to absorb efficiency without denigrating humanity, not least because he comes to believe that it can be done: he is the best exemplar of the case against Communist belief, and when his work also becomes fruitless for him, it is not because of some inner flaw, but because of the activities of the "Organization Men" of whom he is not one. Everything Garcia has to say is revealed in the course of the action to be almost exactly half true. The question of organization is shown up as plaguey and dangerous to those who are forced to deal with it, but not necessarily insoluble. It is possible to make compromises, and possible (though difficult) not to be compromised in making them. Fraternity can be organized without being destroyed.

It is possible to see now in the movement of the action a triple pattern. There is the initial victory and the later movement to defeat of the lyric illusion as such. There is the rising tide of organization to a point of human defeat as it splits off, compromises, or destroys as persons those who have been its supporters and its victims. The two tragic movements seem to make clear the exclusively tragic character of human existence. But Magnin sees the peasants reclaim both fraternity and the older value in whose name Kyo Gisors fought, their own dignity as men, and he knows that neither value can be choked out of existence. And Manuel finds that those who have once been made into automaton soldiers will be able to make themselves over, and that human destiny no longer means exclusively inevitable death but has been transformed into the infinite possibilities of life.

Neither the lyric myth nor the Communist myth has survived unscathed; both have become subordinated to what now shows itself to be a philosophical humanism.

The content of this humanism is tragic rather than optimistic, accepting the inevitability of a partly unjust life and a partly unjust order. What then is its idea of justice? Justice is to be found in the "infinite possibilities" of human destiny. Of these possibilities at least two were already familiar, the two opposites of humiliation: the dignity of individuals and the fraternal bond among fellow fighters for that dignity. Now they have been amplified—fraternity, lyrical illusion or not, has been found possible in real life, and for great masses of people rather than merely for a small fighting elite; and human dignity, which had been almost as rigidly confined to a few in the representation of present time, and to a large but not clearly universal class in the prospective future, becomes an equally expanded potential. If the revolutionaries win, the novel suggests, they may restore the "quality of man" to all humanity. The implication is that eventually this concept of "all humanity" must and will be specifically applied to the momentary enemy as well as to the allies of the present. The fascists, who "pick and choose" among men, must be fought while they do so, for just that reason, and fraternity must therefore exclude them for the present; but there is no such necessity as class hatred.

It is precisely the opening up of possibilities that makes it morally incumbent upon men to act, even if action can never be pure and must always pay its tribute to the devil and even if the action itself should in the end become tragic. To the would-be supermen, what justified their quest was the prospect of their own unlimited *power*. "Every man dreams of being god." Since they could not succeed, they destroyed themselves in trying: action was only a more roundabout means of putting an end to themselves than the alternatives of mythomania, drugs, eroticism. For those who are not interested in becoming nothing, the motto must be rephrased: "Every man dreams of becoming Man." No longer can it be sufficient, either, that each as an individual should organize his struggle against destiny. The victory of each depends on his ability to make contact with others: each is thus dependent on the struggle and final victory of every other. The degree of present compromise with the dehumanizing demands of organizations is justified by a really possible future in which a universal human fraternity will be made possible by a universal freedom to pursue dignity, in which Garine's one value in life, "not to let oneself be beaten," has developed to the point that no man need be "vaincu," no one defeated, none oppressed.

That, at any rate, is the promise of *Man's Hope*. There is no program. Only Garcia and Magnin express fragmentary visions of the victorious future: all the other characters have fears and hopes, not goals. And from Garcia and Magnin, what program can be derived? Improve the economic lot of the worst off; let the workers understand why they are working; create social conditions wherein an individual's life is organized, not in terms of what he can expect from others, but of what he can expect from himself—not of humiliation, but of dignity; create conditions such that those who as persons could reach a high development of intellect and nobility, can do so. This is not too concrete or particular a program. But it will take many years for Malraux to reveal more of what he had in mind; when he does so, surprisingly, the economics will be thoroughly subdued, and another aspect will dominate.

The possibility that his political myth will become a reality has thus prompted Malraux to make it more generous and to incorporate within it some extensive reflections on the ethics of authority. The figure of the hero is submerged in *Man's Hope* and is replaced by a cast of three troubled men—none of whom is exemplary. No new hero-type emerges, while the Bolshevik is subjected to a scrutiny and an interrogation which he does not survive. Several clues to the character of his successor are passed along in the subtle conclusions to the stories of Magnin and Manuel—the most enduring, not to say the most vital, elements in the whole of *Man's Hope*. He will not rebel against organization, nor will he anesthetize himself to its consequences for him. He will not abandon fraternity; but he may well subject it to "cultivation" or "refinement," so that (as with Magnin over the fields of the peasants) it will not necessarily be born of violent conflict with other men. Such conflict will become ideologically nonessential: humanism presupposes the potential harmonious unity of mankind, while fraternity has required human enemies; in a utopia without struggle, what becomes of the sentiment for whose preservation the utopia was created? Magnin suggests one part of Malraux's answer: among the peasants, the struggle for land will be replaced by the struggle with the land.[1] Manuel suggests another: the intellectuals may be preserved through their experiences with art.

One loose strand should be considered before attention is turned to *Altenburg*: the continuing role of Communism in Malraux's politics. Kassner was a Communist and could be nothing else, because only the Communists were at that time, in that place, carrying on the struggle that Malraux thought necessary and just. The other Organization Men (offstage figures in *Days of Wrath*) were not temporizing, were not failing the revolutionary intellectuals as they had failed Kyo Gisors. The persecution of the apparat made its organization into a virtue: without the structure and discipline of the Party, Kassner would have lost both his life and his passing fraternal bonds with men who were, as persons, strangers to him. Organization and authority, though

---

[1] There is an artificiality here, as well as a resemblance to concocted ideologies, that is revealed by the fact that this idea emerges from the mind of the intellectual Magnin, not from that of a peasant. Inarticulate nonintellectuals do not fare well in Malraux's novels (at least until *Altenburg*): it is their destiny to be idealized. Malraux is concerned with the inarticulate but engaged only in the defense of those who "think their life." As such men are the likeliest victims of the maladies he has described, that seems only just.

depersonalized in *Days of Wrath,* are no longer masks of the Absurd. They resume this role in part in *Man's Hope,* where they are instruments of a tragic condition that is neither personified nor nauseating, only present and painful. Malraux has come partway to terms with authority and power in politics; he will come no further. Some leadership, some organization is justifiable. At a moment of opportunity those who organize fraternity without nullifying it in order to extend it, are those whose leadership is justified. The Communists in *Man's Hope* do not meet this test. But since no other party or political force has even a claim to meet it, there is no break with the Communists, who continue to be the necessary allies. Only when the Hitler-Stalin pact made them Malraux's allies no longer did the final split come. But even in *Man's Hope* Magnin and Garcia are no Communists, and Manuel is "saved" not through ideology or discipline but through music.

The issues of *Man's Hope* were mostly the issues of political victory. Hence all were destined to be put aside by the ultimate defeat in Spain. In Malraux's next work all these questions seem, not settled, but vanished. It is only much later that they reappear. But the issues raised by the decline of the Bolshevik hero and by Malraux's espousal of a general humanism are not of the same fragile order. When the menace of victory passes, Malraux turns to an examination of the fundamentals of his new position.

The Walnut Trees of Altenburg (1943) begins the examination of these fundamentals. Some potent suggestions, in fragmentary form, outline the direction of individual development of character and intellect which Malraux eventually idealized and sought to make possible for and attractive to all. The figure of the liberal hero, concerting action and intellect in a way neither Kyo nor Old Gisors, neither Alvear nor his son, could, begins to emerge in Vincent Berger and his son. But the main force of the book lies in its argument for a universal humanism, for a fraternity across time—with the dead, and with the dead of other cultures. An odd and trivial point, it would appear. But it is a point that will be revealed as basic to Malraux's whole position, once he begins writing on the meaning of the art of dead civilizations to living men.

The position that Malraux has reached in the undercurrents of *Man's Hope* has already been characterized as one of "humanism." In order to maintain any universally humanistic position, it is necessary to hold that all men are either essentially alike or can become so—to have a general philosophical conception of man—as Malraux plainly does. It is men believing in the existence of man as such, and in the purposive and positive nature even of imperfect action, who can and will make "l'homme total." If man does not exist today, it is "man's hope" that he will exist tomorrow. The problem posed originally in "D'une jeunesse européenne," that of the destruction of the Western notion of man and thus of Western man himself, begins to find a complete positive answer at last: the creation of a new idea of man, and of man himself (as so conceived) through the active realization of the idea.

But this philosophical statement calls forth a contradiction and an argument on a high level of metaphysical and cultural-anthropological discourse. Is it, after all, possible to subsume all men *through all historical time* under a single idea? The question might also arise: "Can we speak of one human nature transcending national societies and class boundaries?" Malraux treats this question as less central than the other in *Altenburg,* but it is answered in the same way. Vincent Berger reaches emotional certainty of the unity of historical man through seeing the walnut trees of Altenburg. A single experience wipes away national lines for him (the gas attack) and class lines for his son (the tank trap). Intellectually, both the questions and the experiences are unanswerable because they are, as Ling declared, fundamentally arbitrary, resting on and requiring an act of faith men are free to give or withhold, based on valuation and not on observation. The "general philosophical conception" of man—solitary, pitted against the force of his destiny—must apply either to all men or only to some men—those who are near to creating the idea, or to being created by it. How can it include *both* the men of the past and those of Malraux's present? It must include both to remain general; but in remaining general, it begins to appear chimerical. What can the present possibly have to do with the past? The most glaring discrepancy seems to be in the roof which the general concept tries to put over all the separate cultures in which men have lived. Can one idea embrace not only the entirety of mankind, but the whole aggregate of alien and often extremely hostile—and sometimes, worse, apparently incomprehensible—cultural existences? There is a counterpossibility: that the human race is not actually one race at all, that there is no "essence" of man that will make him the same being no matter what his surroundings, that so-called man is actually a completely plastic character and "mankind" a completely plastic term. If that boldly used word, "man," denotes anything and everything, or even if it denotes only a biological species whose members have a resemblance which in no way rises above the biological, what is the point to using it? Complete plasticity implies that the notion of man is incapable of bearing any metaphysical meaning whatever.

This is the question Malraux faces in *Altenburg,* the last of his novels. The questioner who raises it most directly is the anthropologist Möllberg, one of a group of intellectuals who have gathered at the old priory of Altenburg for a colloquy upon the subject of "The Permanence and Metamorphosis of Man."

Möllberg is an ethnologist who has just returned from a journey to Mesopotamia and Africa. He sculpts small, sad, half-human half-gargoyle figurines which all look like him; he in turn looks like a "fairy-tale vampire." He has been a German nationalist and, in the face of the popularity of ideas concerning the pluralism of civilizations, has pursued in ethnology the "official"

German Hegelian synthesis, the idea of man as a strict continuity and a historically enduring "framework for the human adventure." But Africa has been deadly to his ideas: Africa, "The endless succession of days under the dusty firmament of Libya or the heavy leaden sky of the Congo, the tracks of invisible animals converging on the water points, the exodus of starving dogs under the empty sky, the time of day when every thought becomes a blank, the giant trees gloomily soaring up in the prehistoric void" (p. 113). His manuscript, *Civilization as Conquest and Destiny*, is scattered over Africa, its leaves draped across trees from Sahara to Zanzibar. "In accordance with tradition, the victorious carry off the spoils of the defeated" (p. 82).

Möllberg begins with the central question: "Is there any meaning to the idea of man?" Can one dig down under the masses of varying myths and beliefs, through the different mental structures, and "isolate a single permanent factor which is valid throughout the world, valid throughout history, on which to build one's conception of man" (p. 98) before arriving at the merely biological? There are societies which are ignorant of the Western concept of fate, living like ants rather than men; societies which know nothing of the connection between the sexual act and birth; those which have no conception of trade, and those which know nothing of our ideas of death. "Between the men we have just mentioned, and the Greek, or the Gothic man—or anybody else—and ourselves, what is there in common?" (P. 104) Men's variant mental structures possess men, not the reverse, and the variation is perhaps most clearly revealed in their conception of fate: the West's seems to be country or revolution; behind that, history; behind that, perhaps, time. Each such conception must try to give meaning to human life, the human adventure: "We must have a world that we can understand. . . . If humanity's fate is a story with a point, then death is a part of life: but if not, then life is a part of death" (p. 107). And what meaning can there be in history? "If mental structures disappear forever like the plesiosaurus, if civilizations succeed one another only in order to cast man into the bottomless pit of nothingness, if the human adventure only subsists at the price of a merciless metamorphosis," then unity within a single civilization, the communication of a few Western artists, is of small import, "for man is a chance element, and, fundamentally speaking, the world consists of oblivion . . . . Oblivion" (p. 107).

Each of the other intellectuals has been deeply hit by this argument, for they realize that it proclaims "the absurdity . . . of the world" (p. 108). There is no need to insist upon the importance of this theme. The Absurd has suffered a long series of mutations: its generic title has changed to death, to destiny, to history; it has been found in dreams, in the acts of stuffed dummies, in the myths of civilization, in the impositions of the social order, in crowds, in torture, isolation, the elements, in extreme situations, fire, war, and now in the relations of cultures. Whatever its name or location, we still discover in it the primitive and permanent foe to all mankind.

Vincent Berger has been struck by the reference to time because he has seen a culture which seems to ignore it, and he and the others raise a series of protests which only call forth a clearer statement from Möllberg. Thirard proposes that the psychic realm of one who is not completely steeped in his own culture, a workman for example, may resemble that of a workman in another culture. Möllberg answers that the more men partake of their civilization, the more they tend to resemble others of its members, the less they resemble members of others; "but the less they partake of it, the more they fade away. The everlastingness of man can be conceived, but it's an everlastingness in nothingness" (p. 110). Berger suggests that, on the contrary, the enduring peasant or workman may be "fundamental man." Möllberg: " 'Will you have it that for the peasant the world is not made of oblivion? Those who have learnt nothing have nothing to forget . . . . There is no such thing as fundamental man, developed, according to the age he lives in, by what he thinks and believes: there is man who thinks and believes, or nothing' " (p. 111). Under the structure, the mask imposed by a particular civilization, there is only the animal, having in common only dreamless sleep—and death. "Whether nothingness is everlasting or not, what does it matter to us, if the very thing that gives man his dignity is forever condemned?" Rabaud contends that one eternal thing there is, at least, and that is the thinker's knowledge of his separateness from the world and his ability "to call the world into question"; and Möllberg, for Malraux, points out the terrible meaninglessness of this struggle if it is forever without victory: "Sisyphus too was eternal" (pp. 111-12). And at last Stieglitz demands to know why the German concept of history should not be able to perform the unification of mankind by integrating all its meanings into one world history culminating with Germany, and drives Möllberg to his final sweeping statement of the gulf between cultures in space and time and the meaninglessness of nations and histories.

"Humanity's successive psychic states are invariably different, because they do not affect, do not exploit, do not involve the same quality of man . . . . A Christian king and a prehistoric king whose life is dictated by the stars have not got two *ideas* of destiny: for the Christian king to be aware of destiny, for him to conceive it, the other king's psychic world must first disappear. I doubt if there's any communication between the caterpillar and the butterfly. Even between the Hindu who believes in the absolute and the transmigration of souls, and the Westerner who believes in the fatherland and death, any communication is artificial . . . . If the human adventure had any meaning, then Germany would be chosen to give it expression." [Pp. 112-13]

But it has none, to talk of it makes no sense at all, and no sense can be made of it or of anything.

Möllberg is the central and compelling devil's advocate, the leader of an opposition which goes to the root of what Malraux believes, affects him deeply, compels him eventually to reformulate his ideas in terms of an answer, but does not fundamentally change him. Argument can be answered with argument; it can be surpassed, be overcome, only by the most direct route of experience. In the book there is no complete intellectual theory constructed as a response to Möllberg. But immediately following the account of Möllberg's encounter with Africa, Vincent Berger receives a directly contrary insight, linked to the walnut trees of the title. Through the chapter there have been occasional references to wood and woodcutting: logs are being tipped out of wheelbarrows in the village square nearby; "outside, men were loading tree-trunks like the ones my grandfather had stacked for forty years in front of the Town Hall at Reichbach, like the ones stacked by the foresters of the Holy Forest in the sun of the Middle Ages" (p. 107). In the library of the discussion, there are three walnut wood statues, a pretentious ship's figurehead of Atlas and two Gothic saints. Stieglitz, attacking the idea of similarities between modern and Gothic man, uses the statues as objects which make his point; but Vincent sees another side to them: "Greek marbles have an inward look, my father thought, but good Gothic ones always look like blind men trying to see . . . like these men around him, at the mercy of the devil of an intelligible world" (p. 109). And Möllberg uses them to demonstrate the nonsensicality of ideas of "fundamental man": "Those two Gothic sculptures and that figurehead are of the same wood, as you know. But those forms are not shaped from fundamental walnut, but from logs of wood"; and likewise the structures of civilizations are imposed over no "fundamental" man but the biological (p. 111).

Now, the discussion over, Vincent has gone out over the fields near the priory and, under the drifting clouds and dusty twilight, is lost in thought as before:

The sun was setting kindling the red apples on the apple-trees. Idle thoughts of orchards eternally reborn, which the same fears always kindle like this evening's sun. Thoughts of long ago, thoughts of Asia, thoughts of this rainy, sunny summer day, so accidental, so rare—

like the white race of men in the Marseilles evening, like the race of men outside the window of the dead man's room, the overwhelming, commonplace mystery of life in the restless light of dawn . . . ." [Pp. 114-15]

He reaches the big trees and is struck by two great old walnuts:

the strength with which the twisted branches sprang from their enormous trunks, the bursting into dark leaves of this wood which was so heavy and so old that it seemed to be digging down into the earth and not sprouting from it [P. 115]

give him at once an intuition of permanence, of freedom, and of ceaseless metamorphosis (an intuition which will become most important for Malraux in a few more years) which touches humanity and directly contradicts Möllberg's Spenglerian view of it.

Between them the hills rolled down to the Rhine; they framed Strasbourg Cathedral far off in the smiling twilight, as so many other trunks framed other cathedrals in the meadows of the West. And that tower standing erect like a cripple at prayer, all the human patience and labor transformed into waves of vines reaching right down to the river, were only an evening decoration round the venerable thrust of the living wood, the two sturdy, gnarled growths which dragged their strength out of the earth to display it in their boughs. The setting sun cast their shadows across to the other side of the valley, like two broad furrows. My father was thinking of the two saints, and of the Atlas. Instead of supporting the weight of the world, the tortured wood of these walnut trees flourished with life everlasting in their polished leaves under the sky and in their nuts that were almost ripe, in all their venerable bulk above the wide circle of young shoots and the dead nuts of winter. "Civilizations or the animal, like statues or logs . . . ." Between the statues and the logs there were the trees, and their design which was as mysterious as that of life itself. And the Atlas, and St. Mark's face consumed with Gothic passion, were lost in it like the culture, like the intellect, like everything my father had just been listening to—all buried in the shadow of this kindly statue which the strength of the earth carved for itself, and which the sun at the level of the hills spread across the sufferings of humanity as far as the horizon. [Pp. 115-16]

Möllberg is answered as much as he will be in the novel. The rest of *Altenburg* consists of a set of experiences each in one way or another verifying Vincent Berger's intuition. Yet the characteristic of those experiences, as of Möllberg's experience, is their momentariness: they are complete for and in an instant; then they pass away, and no permanent proof remains. To leave the reader confronted by a mystery is to invalidate Möllberg's experience for him, but not his argument. The original question—is there a fundamental man?—thus remains unanswered on the level on which it was asked, and it remains so until *The Voices of Silence,* in which Malraux perfects and completes his philosophy with as explicit an expression as he has ever reached.

But already it is perhaps possible to understand the cryptic words of Garcia in *Man's Hope,* unconnected seemingly either to Garcia or to the action, in answer to Scali's question, " 'Tell me, Major, how can one make the best of one's life, in your opinion?' . . . 'By converting as wide a range of experience as possible into conscious thought, my friend' " (p. 396). There is also a new understanding both of the link to Communism and of the force which breaks it in Malraux's speech to the Congress of Soviet Writers in the less cheerless days of 1934, entitled "Every man endeavors to think his life": "The cultural password that Communism opposes to those of the greatest individualist epochs and which, in Marx, links the first pages of his *German Ideology* with the last rough drafts of *Das Kapital,* this password is: 'More consciousness.' "[2] It is not surprising to hear the artist referred to in works to come as the man whose mission it is to transform destiny into consciousness. The intuition of fatality and of meaninglessness is balanced by an intuition of permanence and freedom in

Altenburg: the art of the novelist transforms both into consciousness. If one or the other wins a victory, it is won in the mind of the reader, by an elective affinity. But Malraux does not leave the matter at that, for the novel itself is the story of the defense provided by the experience of Vincent Berger, transformed into consciousness in his notes, and transmitted to his son.

The theme of the transmission of experience reaches full expression in *Altenburg* and in the works on art, but it begins in the earlier novels. Already there existed the crucial relationship called "fraternity," the feeling of communion among individuals who struggle and suffer together. Side by side with it now, redeeming men equally from isolation, there appears communion between individuals, one of whom is defended in an encounter with the Absurd by the other's previous torment rendered into art.[3]

Vincent Berger's son, captured at the beginning of the Second World War by the Germans, is sustained as he remembers the notes in which his father had set down his own life. That life was a series of encounters with the same emptiness and absurdity that now grip his son's dreams. It was also a series of experiences, like that with the walnut trees of Altenburg—a series of affirmations that dispel the metaphysical dread known to us from Malraux's earliest grapplings with the world. It is between Vincent Berger and his son that we find the exemplary relation in its completest form; a just understanding of man's position in this world, its limits and possibilities, combined with a fellowship which "goes beyond the grave" by nature, are evoked for one man in an extremity by the recollection (or the representation) of another in such extremity and of what he was able to make of it.

The two Bergers, unlike Möllberg, are intellectuals who act as well as think: philosopher-adventurers, writer-soldiers. Where pure thought fails them (as it failed Möllberg), they have re-

[3] Frohock, *André Malraux and the Tragic Imagination*, pp. 143-144. Gerda Blumenthal, *André Malraux: The Conquest of Dread*, Baltimore, Johns Hopkins, 1960, pp. xiii, 164.

course to experience. When their action fails to construct and
enact their wills and dreams, they find their victory elsewhere. If
the lyric illusion is good, the victory of fraternity is better—so it is
recognized in *Man's Hope*. But when the illusion fades and the
political victory is denied, the old form of action—the political
enactment of a will—might leave only desperate memories and
renewed emptiness.

But there is another form of pure action—that is, of the transformation of destiny into consciousness—which the Bergers alone
among Malraux's heroes embody. The new style of action has the
new quality of never suffering defeat: no longer even completely
manichean because no longer thoroughly political, the only kind
of action which by and in itself completely justifies its agent is
creation. (Garine reached out to touch this point—and drew
back.) Young Berger receives what his father passes on in the
form of his unpublished notes, and in his turn adds to them and
gives his experience to the reader, who is inevitably, if blindly, led
to the idea of creative art as the form of communion across time
and despite defeat, as he was led to the idea of the common fight
as the instrument for communion in the moment. Nothing should
therefore surprise but the critical astonishment when Malraux
turns from the practice to the theory of art.[4]

As of 1943, then, Malraux's myths of the hero (intended to
justify emulation), of the good political order (intended to justify
engagement), and of the nature of man (intended to supply the
basis of a culture filled with defended rather than tormented men)
have reached another definable level of development.

The heroic individual—now the liberal hero—is in the human
predicament: he experiences the Absurd in many forms, but he
experiences it without permanent despair and with many defenses.
The general means of his defense are consciousness and action.
He recognizes the manichean, partly corrupt, character of action.

4 *Yale French Studies* 18, p. 29.

Nevertheless, when there is a struggle against some force that, in his view, represents the political Absurd (that is, more humiliation for the individual), he fights against it, leading, even organizing, and being elevated by that action. His consciousness is sentimental before it is analytical—he feels before and after he thinks —and his highest emotion is one of fraternity or of communion. Among the living, his partners in this communion are both those with whom he fights and those who have the character of "fundamental men"—who are struggling, before his eyes, with one of the old shapes of the Absurd. Because he strives to make experience into consciousness (because he creates art), and because he can reclaim from the art of others the experience it contains, he is also capable of communion with the past. The entire transition from the Bolshevik to the liberal hero has been demonstrated, but the explication of it remains; in the next years Malraux proceeds to expand what has here been extracted, and more.

The political utopia is still hazy, largely because it is less original. There are elements from many philosophies: anarchism (universal dignity, no oppression, no humiliation, no compulsion for the pleasure of compulsion); welfarism (betterment of the condition of the poor); Marxism (the end of the alienation of labor by giving work a meaning for the worker); moral and intellectual aristocracy (a social order safe for and permissive toward intellect, nobility of character, and Malrauvian heroes). Only the last segment of this utopia, which is his own, receives much further attention from Malraux.

The cultural myth holds, contrary to extreme individualism and to other theories, that man is of one nature, a nature capable of universal communion, across space and time. At whatever time, in whatever country and status, this man lives the same psychic life. He is placed in the same predicament despite its many shapes; he collapses before it or transcends it in many ways, but all of these many ways are recurrent. He can receive the experience of the past when it is made into art. Along with the figure of the hero, the myth of the single great human culture is extensively developed in Malraux's works on art.

The development is ending, but not ended; though the reader has moved through many stages with Malraux's heroes, and though the movement can be summed up well enough, the process is not yet finished. If Malraux had stopped writing in 1943, his political thought would still be impressive in its depth. Malraux does not stop. Between *The Walnut Trees of Altenburg* and *The Voices of Silence* there intervenes a period of transition in Malraux's political life, and another of new political thought on a more practical level; then he resumes his work and constructs for himself a monumental philosophy of history and of politics.

5. TRANSITION AND UNITY

DURING AND AFTER THE SECOND WORLD WAR, Malraux changed his political role from that of revolutionist to that of government official. Having been an ally of the Communists, he became a follower of Charles De Gaulle. He wrote no more novels; instead he wrote works on the history of art. Before interpreting his thought in and after this transition in the style of his life, it is necessary to ask whether these changes do not imply a discontinuity in the character of the man himself that in turn leaves the two phases of his thought fundamentally at odds.

For nine years now André Malraux has been Minister of State for Cultural Affairs in the Fifth Republic. In this capacity he has played a bureaucratic role, and a dramatic one: he administers culture to the French people; he is also a high priest of their history. To explain these posts to "Anglo-Saxons" is the intriguing task of one who might write on this particular ministry: to explain why Malraux fills them and to what end, the task of one who would write on "Malraux the Minister." But to one who knew vaguely of Malraux's activities (and even more vaguely of his writings) only up to 1939, the first question to occur would be not what Malraux does as minister, or why: but, how in the world he arrived there. What could prevail on a leftist cosmopolitan adventurer, a lover of action and revolution, to become a *minister*; a minister of *culture*; a Gaullist; and a French nationalist?

Of course these questions were asked, and in some measure answered, immediately after the Second World War, when Malraux first became a Gaullist minister and showed his change of front. The significance of his conversion as a topic of gossip is now fortunately gone; the light that this biographical episode can shed on Malraux's thought, and his thought on this change, is not.

Party schisms, the lure of office, an unsuspected and buried allegiance, all often explain why "leftwing" public figures have made surprising evolutions. But when the political liaisons of thinkers are concerned, these typical factors may have less application. The striking changes in the public lives of Sorel and Barrès, figures difficult to label as "left" but of importance nevertheless (and in more ways than this one) may have some relevance for an understanding of Malraux. Sorel seemed to pick up political attachments across the spectrum, from revolutionary syndicalism to reactionary royalism, from Mussolini to Lenin. Barrès began too nihilistically to have any political character, became a Boulangist without illusions, and ended as a voice of French nationalism and traditionalism, raising the memories of the dead even as does Malraux. Indeed, the analogies merit further pursuit.

Beginning with the first, it can be seen how Malraux the "Marxist" could become Malraux the "Gaullist"; returning to the second, it is clear what nationalism can mean to one who believes only in Man.

1.

Under all of Georges Sorel's inconstant allegiances there is a constant moral norm. Neither this norm, an image of the good life for man, nor Sorel's best-known political prescription—that of the *Reflections on Violence*—is as surprising as the fact and manner of their combination: capitalist virtue to be generated by class struggle.

Sorel as moralist envisages the good life as clearly as the bad: one is the bourgeois ideal, the other the bourgeois reality. The bad is the mediocre and decadent: repetition, routine, material fullness and emptiness of the spirit, parasitic nonproductivity or stupefied production followed by demoralized consumption, ultrarefined stupidity, timorous peacefulness. The good life, for the many, combines the ideals of capitalism and of religious enthusiasm: passionate individualism, hard and productive work done with zeal, vigorous energy, thrift, the rigid values of family life (chastity, fidelity, and devotion to the weak). For the few, the image of the captain of industry and the Homeric hero are merged: let them view life as a struggle, not a pleasure, and seek energy in action and victorious attack on moral evils; they are warlike creators of productive forces, bold captains, insatiable and pitiless conquerors, of indomitable energy.

If Sorel had been merely a moralist, he would have preached these lives to others and praised or blamed their free choice according to how it was exercised. As he was a political thinker, he asked how these virtues might be brought to birth, what mechanism might insure the preservation of the highest morality. His answer was always some form of social struggle, notably that of the revolutionary working people against the decadent exploiters. Strikes and violence would be the key, perhaps to overturning the exploiters, perhaps to their awakening to their own class sentiment and struggle for survival; perhaps to the political power of the workers, perhaps to their secession from society, but surely to their morale, their new culture. Real violence (and the mythic martyrology that a Sorelian propaganda would take care to salvage from the casualty list) would support the myth of a future, apocalyptic general strike: accepting this myth (an expression of a determination to act), the revolutionaries would learn a patient apprenticeship, an extraordinary ardor, an "entirely epic state of mind." At that point, the general strike itself would have become unnecessary precisely because the "state of mind" and not the strike was the true objective of the Sorelians and because their new morality, not some economic advantage, would be the true reward of the revolutionary proletariat.[1]

[1] Georges Sorel, *Reflections on Violence,* trans. T. E. Hulme, New York, Peter Smith, 1941, p. 294.

But it did not have to be the proletariat which was thus regenerated by myth, struggle, and violence. Any political movement, provided it was a mass-based movement, might in its struggles for power (if not after its victory) be the source of virtue. For Sorel, therefore, attachment to syndicalism, or to some other philosophy, was not a matter of principle. The question was, at any moment, what force's struggle might (even unintentionally) produce the desired effect. Hence his seeming faithlessness to causes whose stated goals were to him not goods in themselves, but instrumental energizing myths which might or might not do the job in hand; whose struggles were means, not to ultimate victory, but to immediate virtue.

At the most general level there is an identity between these thoughts of Sorel's and Malraux's attitude toward political forces —a sort of philosophical opportunism. The goal is the creation of a certain state of feeling and action in men; the method is to attach such men to a force in conflict, whose impact will make them become as they ought to be. But Malraux's choice of forces, seemingly more simple than Sorel's, is more complex in fact. For the political struggles of revolutionaries (and others) seldom lead to Sorel's frozen and balanced tableau wherein "a united and revolutionary proletariat confronts a rich middle class eager for conquest"—and indefinitely sustains the confrontation.[2] Rather, they lead to defeat and to victory—classic problems to which the philosophers of action, conflict, and revolution are then forced to attend.

These problems are the real ones that underlie Malraux's move from apparent apologies for Communism in *Days of Wrath* to public denunciations of Communism at the side of De Gaulle, from "Marxist humanist"[3] in 1934 to Gaullist minister in 1945, agitator in 1948, minister again in 1958. This is the notorious change in his politics, which has given rise to the argument of a

[2] Ibid., p. 91.
[3] At the All-Union Congress of Soviet Writers in Moscow, August, 1934.

discontinuity in his thought, beneath which lie all too often the emotional accusations of "sellout" and "fascist."[4]

Since Gaullism as a movement has shown itself to have no recognizable doctrine of race or class, indeed to be situational and pragmatic almost beyond comprehension, the cry of fascist politics has faded. But its exciting quality served to obscure Malraux's elucidations. It has also served to make the explainers forget that Malraux has repeatedly said that, had Leon Trotsky won his battle with Stalin, he himself would have become a Trotskyist Communist,[5] and that, while De Gaulle was in the wilderness after the failure of the RPF, Malraux was not unwilling to associate himself with Mendès-France.[6] These episodes hint that Malraux has never put his total allegiance anywhere, not in official Communism, not in nationalism, not in the person of De Gaulle. If Malraux's alliance with Communism is seen as essentially tactical, dictated by a philosophy which was his own and which,

---

[4] A variation on this theme finds a deeper continuity in Malraux—he was always a spiritual fascist, or at least a nihilist: he has never surpassed his initial perception of the world's absurdity, for all his principal characters are nihilists and all their lives are empty cycles of struggle and death; they engage in struggles of the will, which are demoniac, and this delights him, which is fascistic. (See "Malraux Man," *Times Literary Supplement,* November 26, 1964, pp. 1049 ff., and H. A. Mason in *Scrutiny,* Spring 1947, pp. 162-171.) Seeking in Malraux's novels the representative hero-figures who win arguments (if there are any), and attributing their views to Malraux, the reader may find (with some difficulty) a consistent character from Perken's straight-out nihilism and action in *The Royal Way* to Möllberg's intellectual rejection of action, intellect, and meaning. From the man of total action to the man of sheer intellect, from unthinking superman to passive intellectual, there is a straight line: do they not show the same belief in the meaninglessness of human existence, the same incompleteness as persons, at last the same defeat in life? Indeed; but what matters is that Malraux, too, understands this and, through Claude Vannec and Vincent Berger, passes judgment upon these figures, who stand for an attitude toward human life which Malraux in the beginning and the end rejects.

[5] This did not prevent him (according to Natalya Sedova-Trotsky) from suppressing the Trotskyite press in France while he was Minister of Information: *The New York Times,* March 10, 1948, p. 26.

[6] *The New York Times,* February 14, 1948 (column by C. L. Sulzberger), p. 26; *L'Express,* December 25, 1954, p. 10, and January 29, 1955, pp. 8-10.

despite appearances, Communism never shared, his lack of total devotion can more easily be understood. The proper terms of this understanding are not those of self-advancement, but of tactics: at one point the goals of the parties to an alliance coincide, and the alliance increases their chances of success; at another, this is not so, and tactics dictate the replacement of the old alliance with a new one. "I have not changed. It is the world, and most of all the Communists, who have changed."[7]

Malraux has sought in his political career a political force which will, knowingly or not, yield certain ethical and political goods; but the goods he has sought have altered over the years as his thought has developed. A successful revolutionary movement can yield power to its leaders; this power Garine of *The Conquerors* sought, and received, by attaching himself to the Canton Communists; as Malraux judged, it was not enough. Even an unsuccessful revolution can break the existential isolation of the revolutionaries at the level of sentiment; this is the discovery and the victory of Kyo Gisors in *Man's Fate*. No Marxist, he finds his fraternal bond with revolutionaries who happen to be Communists, that is all. But for a leader it is not sufficient to fail gloriously: having animated others with a mythic future where their dignity will be assured, and having, as it were, gained one's own freedom by imbibing their hope, it is no longer satisfying to be a defeated hero fraternally joined to others equally doomed. One must live instead to create the future, to build the social order that will insure the brotherhood of man: this is the understanding that emerges from the complex dialectic of *Man's Hope*.[8]

[7] Quoted by T. S. White, "The Three Lives of André Malraux," *The New York Times Magazine,* February 15, 1953, pp. 13 ff.

[8] Already in the lives of Old Gisors and Hemmelrich (*Man's Fate*) and in the preface of *Days of Wrath* Malraux had affirmed that such an order was possible. Thus the ethical goal of momentary fraternity was subjected to a higher goal of lasting fraternity. And the search for a presently satisfying political struggle, which demanded of an ally only competence and violence, became a search for a permanently satisfying political order, which required a political force capable of victory and committed to the creation of such an order. The

On the one hand, one must accept the conditions of organization and authoritarian discipline that are required if a revolution is to be more than a presently absorbing struggle with a doomed future —the anarchists are therefore no longer a politically valid force; on the other hand, the chance of victory attracts sadists and racketeers to the movement, and one must ask if the movement truly can and will make good the myth of hope on which it has operated when victory is won—the Communists therefore become thoroughly suspect as allies. *Man's Hope* was still able to distinguish between the Pradases and Kurtzes of the Communist Party on the one hand—the dogmatists, factionalists and spies—and on the other the Manuels, men who were not wholly in opposition to what Malraux stood for. The Hitler-Stalin pact made it somewhat clearer which types were in control and marked the final parting in what was never more than a match of convenience.

For Malraux the Second World War was a continuation of the Spanish Civil War, offering the same personal rewards when there was no hope and the same opportunity for institutionalizing fraternity when victory came in sight. In France, where he fought, the war was at first and became again more a national than a civil war. In the Resistance, as with the Spanish Republic, a tenacious and desperate struggle offered at its darkest moments the intense emotional bond that the same society at peace could not provide.

In *Altenburg* victory is no longer in sight, and the goal of fraternity is returned from the future to the present; but those who share it are no longer revolutionaries. This is characteristic: wherever the real world seems to resist and reject all attempts to

Communist ally was subjected to a more stringent judgment in *Days of Wrath* and passed it; again so subjected in *Man's Hope* and failed it. It is incidental to this period, but not to Malraux's later role, that the better order was seen by him less as a certain set of ideal relations between men and economy than as a certain set of ideal attitudes of men toward other men. That the ideal order is psychopolitical rather than politico-economic should be no surprise, since the virtue that order is intended to create is a sentimental and not a material well-being. Again, Sorel is in point here.

transform it, there appears in Malraux the figure of the defeated hero, for whom the justification of action is internal rather than external to himself. When men are defeated, dying, or in prison, when their struggle has become hopeless, an experience or a sentiment overshadows the failure to achieve concrete results. In *Altenburg* the attainable human good is fellowship; the force that supplies it is first fighting France, then defeated France.

But the Resistance was ultimately successful, and Malraux, at the head of the Alsace-Lorraine Brigade, shared the victory. In the struggle, as he puts it, "I married France." What this meant, however, was that Malraux demanded that France possess herself of the "universal humanism" he still advocated. France ought to take advantage of her moment of unity to make herself over, to create the social order in which the dignity and the brotherhood of man would be insured. This demand was in line with the myth of national regeneration that had animated the Resistance. That myth was, in turn, in line with the mystique of De Gaulle: toward the end of the war Malraux sought to achieve his goals through exploiting the spirit of the Resistance and the prestige and leadership of De Gaulle.

No doubt something beyond tactics drew Malraux to the side of this figure. It might be a form of Pygmalionism: De Gaulle is an ideal type of Malraux's devising made real but enlarged. He is the active intelligence, the hero combining mind and will. But he was, and was again to become, the hero without the morbid touch of inner and outer failure that afflicts most of Malraux's own literary creations. Even in real history Saint-Just, Trotsky, T. E. Lawrence are the men of action over whom Malraux reflects; all welded fragmented nations into victorious armies; all, of course, tasted defeat after victory. De Gaulle resembled them; now he has gone them one better. There is a psychological as well as a tactical reason for Malraux's adherence to his cause. But the tactics predominated.

Factionalism, the parties, and the old order combined to

frustrate De Gaulle and the Resistance mystique alike. The latter dissolved into impotence; Malraux took part in founding a party, the RPF, for the benefit of the former. De Gaulle could not win at the polls and would not cross the Rubicon of revolution; Malraux drifted away and thought that Mendès-France might do the job. But it was De Gaulle whom the death of the Fourth Republic called back to power; and with him, but not as one of his chief servants, came Malraux. He is irreplaceable in a sense: he fills a role no one else of any stature could. But the role is more necessary to Malraux than to De Gaulle. The incantatory part of that role may be understood by contrast to Barrès, to whose idea of history (as to Sorel's tactical ethics) Malraux is profoundly in debt.

2.

Again, however, the comparison must be kept within limits. Unfortunately Barrès journeyed from egoism to nationalism, and Malraux made the same journey. This parallel lends itself to over-statement. The two ends of Barrès' evolution are indeed close and relevant to Malraux's; the path is entirely dissimilar.

Barrès begins (in *Le Culte du Moi*) with a Cartesian isolation of the ego and a non-Cartesian devotion to it. Among all false gods and spurious religions, the self is the one tangible reality. Therefore defend this sole value and nourish it. Defend it against the others, the non-ego, who would "constrain or impede or distort"[9] its development; nourish it on self-exploration, and employ study and travel and action to create new and obscure emotions to be explored.

The next step is taken when novelties no longer seduce but pall, when the self dries up under its own microscope. To save its life, to unplug the spring of emotion, the ego must find a love and a purpose, concludes Barrès. And these are achieved through a different sort of self-knowledge: this ego must ask: what made

---

[9] F. Y. Eccles, "Maurice Barrès," *Dublin Review*, 143 (1908), pp. 244-263.

me, what determined what I am? Barrès' answer, in general, is, "Your roots"—race, surroundings and time. The land and the dead created you—your land and its dead. To survive and flourish, then, return to your roots (which you share with *some* others). You cannot be nourished by a universal civilization: you have a specific moral patrimony from your country, your province, your community, and your family. Take the inheritance that is yours, see yourself as one of a series, look at the lives of your forebears to determine what you ought to do: follow in the footsteps of the fathers. Construct your life, then, deliberately, as a work of art to be worthy of the past and productive for the future: find your narrow social sphere, or create a situation for yourself, and rooted there, persevere doing the service that discharges the example and the duty inherent in your rank, place, and ancestry. The inheritance is all that sustains your ego; those who threaten the inheritance—innovators, revolutionaries, foreign and hostile communities—are your sworn enemies. Whoever would undo the work of the dead would destroy the only means of life. He who is destined for political service ought, then, energetically to sustain the noblest traditions, uphold the old national mission, renew the national strength, and repel the enemies of them all.

Malraux's novels are explorations of the means of defending the self against the pall of sterility that frustrated Barrès' individualism. But the defenses that satisfy Malraux do not lead to a landed proprietor's conservative ideal and do not include the search for roots. Rather, the individual can break his ultimately deadly isolation through political action, the fraternal bond of common struggle, the myth of human dignity that ennobles a conflict of power, and the possibility of a future social order yielding actual dignity—dignity being a sort of negative freedom, the absence of oppression and of humiliation. Or he may do so through artistic creation, the transmutation of destiny into tragedy. For through the creation and contemplation of works of art,

Malraux claims (or rather, deeply believes), men can be made aware both of their isolation and destiny, and of the great human ideals by means of which they can come to terms with their predicament. He is as pragmatic about the ethical contents of art as he is about political allegiance: whatever ideals will produce the desired psychological changes are those which the artist is obliged to transmit: if he has a sense of history, he will know whether the appropriate myths are religious or humanistic, revolutionary or nationalistic. Such ideals and myths have their fitting uses and appropriate moments, but only the predicament against which they defend endures. When action fails, the artist can redeem the failure by shaping the memory of action and preserving the ethic for future dreams.

This ideology of art and action diverges from Barrès significantly enough, but it offers no readily apparent justification for the appearance of Malraux in the thoroughly Barrèsian role of high priest of history for France and intellectual aide-de-camp to a general more discreet and more fortunate than Boulanger. Nationalism and Gaullism are opportune means and instruments for Malraux where both are absolutes and ends for De Gaulle, while Barrès' nationalism was a commitment deduced from, rather than instrumental to, prior principles, and only his Boulangism was a momentary instrument. Not only the source of attachment to France is unlike for Malraux and Barrès, but also the function of nationalist propaganda: Barrès wrote to evoke a will to action, to defend France (or rather, to defend men's roots there) against her inward and outward enemies as he understood them. Malraux, in a manner less magnificent than that of De Gaulle but no less magniloquent, seems to have been trying to create France.

This is essential: for Barrès the nationalist, there is a France, which is threatened and needs to be preserved. For Malraux the nationalist, the France that would be worthy of defense does not yet exist: it is still to be born. For De Gaulle, France exists—

occasionally. Barrès means by "France" the traditions of a nation. De Gaulle means, primarily, its unity (and consequent pride). Malraux means its unity and its humanism. France since the Revolution has had a disunity of spirit far larger than that between the American North and South since the Civil War. As between right and left (and, less violently, as among many fragments of each) there have been few experiences of common struggle and many of mutual hatred; few mutual heroes, many figures idolized on the one hand and detested on the other. Those nationalists, however, whose myth of France includes all Frenchmen without regard to class or party have sought to evoke figures and episodes of the French past that do not involve the retrospective humiliation of some living and historically conscious Frenchmen. The American secular cults of Washington and Lincoln, popular sentimental symbols of national unity, display equivalents of the common memories these French nationalists seek. De Gaulle is such a nationalist. For him, the full existence of France, its unity in pride, requires a charismatic leader who is such a sentimental symbol and who evokes the symbols of the past. For him, the key figure of French history is Joan of Arc: restorer of national unity, strength, territory, leadership, and honor.

For Malraux the unity of France need not pass with De Gaulle, nor indeed depend upon him, so long as the symbols of the past are evoked by someone. These symbols are the land and the dead, interpreted so as to yield unity and not division. Malraux's speeches display and promote the intention of unifying a nation— or some of them do. Those about Frenchmen and French places are directed at national unity; those about foreign lands and about policy, however, go beyond the goal of unity to the uniquely Malrauvian goal of national humanism.

The youth of France are to receive from the Republic not only the myths of France, but also the myth of man. As the voice of French history, Malraux evokes the past, vividly and passionately: at Orleans, Joan of Arc; at the Parthenon, Jean Moulin, Resistance leader; at Metz, the Alsace-Lorraine Brigade; at Rennes, the first meeting of Free French and Resistance leaders, and the liberation of Paris. The dead must not be forgotten, they must be called up to create common memories for the young people. The memories of a mystical national unity and fraternity, past action transformed by the orator's art into present consciousness, become the basis for present unity even in the absence of a great common struggle. "The history of a people is made of illustrious deeds, but its soul is made of forgotten deeds which would disappear as a cloud drifts, if they were not mysteriously brought together again."[10] Places contain a file of such memories: "Chateaus, cathedrals, museums, are the fraternal and successive landmarks of the immense and lively dream pursued by France for nearly one thousand years. . . . Our monuments are the greatest dream of France. That is why we want to preserve them . . . for the emotional response of the children. . . . It is for them that the battles, the hatreds and the fervors which make up our history unite, transfigured, on the fraternal ground of the dead."[11]

In 1924, when he was no nationalist, in *The Temptation of the West* Malraux analyzed the concept of the nation: "The mind supplies the idea of a nation, but what gives this idea its sentimental force is a community of dreams. Our brothers are those whose childhood develops according to the rhythm of epics and legends which dominate our own. We have all felt the freshness and the haze of the morning of Austerlitz . . . . What images white men need to give them a national spirit!" (P. 96) It is these images Malraux now resurrects; for, having analyzed the nation, he now espouses it.

Where Barrès invoked French history to remind Frenchmen

[10] Speech, Metz, May 14, 1961 (France, Ministry for Cultural Affairs; mimeographed copy).
[11] Debate, National Assembly, December 14, 1961. France, *Journal officiel, Dèbats parliamentaires, Assemblée nationale* (hereafter cited as DPAN), 1961, p. 5637.

both of the limits beyond which they must not go if they were to have the only identity they could ever attain and of the enemies whom being French required them to defy, Malraux awakens history to let Frenchmen feel that their isolation as men is broken by the fraternity that being French permits them to share with the dead and with the living to whom the same dead belong. Nevertheless, the construction of men's identities by an appeal to men and places, to the land and the dead, is the same enterprise for Barrès and Malraux. What sets Malraux apart from Barrès (as from De Gaulle) is simply his refusal to declare that the national tie is the primary or the ultimate bond among men.

This retention of humanism atop nationalism is expressed by Malraux's willingness to evoke equally the spirit of French and non-French places and to discuss the "meaning" of Athens or of Brasilia to man as well as to Frenchmen: Brasilia, where man's struggle against the land is given worthy forms; Athens, which (like Malraux himself) unites the spear and the intellect in the statues of Pallas and the person of the citizen-soldier-poet. But the humanist Malraux is better represented by his official ministerial role as overseer of French cultural affairs than by his rhetorical preservation of the spirit of history. Neither Barrès nor Malraux, after all, has written a history of France, as would be required by full devotion to their antiquarian and monumental approaches to history. But Barrès was satisfied with his limited role as mediator between Frenchmen and their past, for he believed that the order of society was basically sound: if only men did not uproot themselves and did not let others cut off the past, little urging would be needed to keep them faithful to the land and the dead; if they did their duty, they would keep their healthy egos. Malraux has consistently considered most established means of defending the ego fruitless and unsound (*Man's Fate* is the catalogue of unsound methods): the old human virtues are not available in normal life but only to unusual individuals, in extreme situations, or in a new order of things. His program as Minister for Cultural

Affairs reflects an extremely gradual approach to such a new order, which is really more an order of thoughts than of things, of culture than of society.

3.

Besides the supposed "discontinuities" in Malraux's political alignment (Communism to Gaullism) and philosophy (humanism to nationalism), other disunities have been suggested: Malraux abandons the political novel for esthetic theory; Malraux abandons action for art. It would be wrong, however, to assume that the approach to esthetics in *The Voices of Silence* is entirely new in Malraux's thought. Just the reverse is true: Malraux as a student was concerned with art before he became involved in politics in Indochina (and he would not have gone to Indochina had he not been interested in Oriental art). The analysis of Western culture in *La tentation de l'occident* rested first of all on Western art. Through the years of political novels, Malraux's esthetic concern continued alongside his politics. Claude Vannec of *The Royal Way* makes a short speech for which a setting has practically to be concocted and which prefigures several essential ideas of *The Voices of Silence*.

My view is . . . that the personal value we set on an artist may blind us to one of the main factors affecting the vitality of his work. I refer to the cultural status of the successive generations appraising it. It looks as if, in matters of art, the time-factor were deliberately ignored. What interests me . . . is the slow disintegration, the gradual change which comes over such works—their secret life which battens on men's deaths. Every work of art, in fact, tends to develop into a myth . . . . For me museums are places where the works of an earlier epoch which have developed into myths lie sleeping—surviving on the historical plane alone—waiting for the day to come when artists will wake them to an active existence. . . . In the last analysis, of course, no civilization is ever understood by another one. But its creations remain—only we are blind to them until our myths come into line with theirs. [Pp. 61-62]

Kama of *Man's Fate,* Scali and Alvear of *Man's Hope,* continue the preoccupation with visual arts, Kassner and young Berger with writing as art.

And the demand for action to be creative,[12] contained in *The Walnut Trees of Altenburg,* is the obverse of the conclusion at which Malraux early arrived, that art was a form of action, fulfilling the same role as action does in human life, and indeed action's highest and purest form. "Art lives by virtue of its function, which is to make it possible for men to escape from their lot as men, not by evasion but by an act of possession. All art is a means of possessing our destiny" by transforming it into conciousness, he said in 1936.[13] Garcia in *Man's Hope* believes that one can makes the best of one's life "by converting as wide a range of experience as possible into conscious thought" (p. 309). And Malraux asserts, in his own voice, that art and action are complementary forms of the attempt to "translate the widest experience possible into consciousness."[14] Art, like action, is therefore throughout Malraux's thought a revolt against man's fate. The demand for creativity in action is the signal for a merger of esthetic and political acts in a general theory of history and human action.

Thus *The Voices of Silence,* far from being discontinuous with Malraux's prior work, could almost be said to replace the missing volumes that were to follow *The Walnut Trees of Altenburg.* It contains Malraux's humanistic response to Spengler and Möllberg, picking up Vincent Berger's idea of the permanence of the walnut trees through change and applying it to the history of a unified humankind. Vincent's experience is transformed into a theory. Like the expressionist art critics of the twenties, Malraux

12 That is: the action which defends me is creative if I then make it, by means of some art, accessible to another for his defense.
13 "The Cultural Heritage," *The New Republic,* October 21, 1936, pp. 315-317.
14 André Malraux and James Burnham, *The Case for De Gaulle,* New York, Random House, 1948, p. 70.

in this theory sees the world of art as composed of art works which are primarily the personal style that an artist achieves only through first imitating and then challenging and breaking with the styles of previous artists. The artist achieves his style by trying to recreate the world in a form acceptable to himself. The expressionists added that all the styles that flourish within a given civilization express the myths of that civilization. Spengler raised the crucial point: if each style mirrors the group mind of its period, there must be as many radically different types of men as there are styles, and therefore no single humanity. Malraux replies by first of all rejecting the implied ascendancy of the group or culture over the stylistic revolts of individuals. If there were to be a total lack of communication, it would mean not the isolation of cultures one from another, but the total isolation of individuals, since the primary perception of each individual is of his own oneness. But in fact, communication through history exists: the artist can and does annex elements of style coming from other cultures and is therefore not caught in a closed and separate cycle; he can and does take or reject the styles of other individuals and so joins them in a common and universally human defiance of the force of destiny.[15] Thus the idea of a discontinuity within Malraux's work, and that of a flight from action, must be cast aside along with that of a dissonant new politics; and it becomes reasonable to insist on Malraux's permanence through change.

Along with the political attachments which he has not since deserted, Malraux from 1940 to 1947 attained a point in his philosophical evolution from which he has not been moved.

---

[15] *La psychologie de l'art*, Geneva, Skira, 1947-50; revised and published as *Les voix du silence*, Paris, Gallimard, 1951; translated by Stuart Gilbert as *The Voices of Silence*, New York, Doubleday, 1953: cited as V.S.; see pp. 272, 324, 334, 348, 359, 520, 543, 630-634, 639, 642. See also Frohock, *André Malraux and the Tragic Imagination*, pp. 150-160; H. Tint, "Voices and Novels," *Yale French Studies*, October 1957, pp. 323-332; and E. Gombrich, "André Malraux and the Crisis of Expressionism," *Burlington Review*, December 1954, pp. 374-378.

Unlike all his previous engagements, the Resistance ended successfully. With defeat no longer inevitable, Malraux shed the pessimism about action which cast a shadow over *Altenburg*. Now he is free to express a positive theory of history: he finishes *The Psychology of Art,* on which he has been working intermittently since 1935, capping the development which has been continuous for Malraux since 1921. What follows it is an expansion, the exploration of the deeper ramifications of a philosophy in which the artist joins with the political hero to struggle with and to overcome the old obsessions of destiny, death, and the absurdity of human life. Malraux's thought can now be treated analytically rather than chronologically: the evolution ends; the transition is also a completion.

PART II
MALRAUX'S POLITICS AS A WHOLE

6. ESTHETICS AND POLITICS

MALRAUX'S POSTWAR WORK on esthetics details, extends and exemplifies his ideas about culture and its relation to the human condition. The art of all cultures expresses men's defense against the Absurd because the relation among the artist, his style, and his work make art into a form of revolt against destiny. To secure the fullest extent of defense, a civilization needs an artistic style of its own: the West has not yet attained such a culture style. One answer to the needs of the West would be the free and deliberate creation by artists of a humanistic style; but there is another, more manageable answer: the revival of the great art of the past.

1.

The origin of the problem of man is in his nature: we must therefore begin with Malraux's sketch of human psychology. Biologically, the mind is a set of sensations. By uncertain processes a man attains some consciousness, some idea of identity. This self may be well-integrated or it may be disintegrated; that is, it may be a relatively stable image or innumerable images none of which has any consistency or fixity. Morally (for this is an ethical psychology) the images of the self, which become the driving and motivating elements of action, may represent either the "divine" or the "diabolical" elements within man.[1] Such definitions as

---

[1] The sources of this distinction may be the Freudian division of Eros and Thanatos, and the Nietzschean "human, all-too-human" as against the "human, superhuman." Before one criticizes this psychology for the unscientific and simplistic dualism it displays, it would be well to recall that Malraux *means* by

reside in these conflicting elements are either ethical or meta-phoric. The divine is all within man that tends to enable him, to drive him, to self-transcendence; the diabolical is whatever tends to animalize or destroy him. "The demons of Babylon, of the early church, and of the Freudian subconscious have the same visage" (V.S., p. 541). These human virtues and vices are classical, not novel: to define them, it would be necessary to follow Malraux's suggestion and examine the characters of the angels and demons of the religious periods, for these are men's projections of the best and worst within them.

Biology has provided psychology with its key problems: present solitude and future nonexistence. Whatever implies and recalls to a man his dependence and insignificance—the marks of aging, the power of the forces of nature, his subjection to incomprehensible coercion from his rulers—can make his existence a constant torment. Against this anguish the self-image of the individual, created around his values, may offer a bulwark. But if he has no stable self, his experience is meaningless and he waits in pain for a senseless death. And if his identity is organized around "diabolical" values, he is cheated in life, repeatedly surprised by anguish, and eventually hurried toward a miserable, isolated death. A man can hold his own against the Absurd of destiny only by ordering his being around a chosen and a divine part of man.[2]

This necessity is the deepest structure in what is considered human culture. From the beginning the human mind has faced the same need to escape from the Absurd. Each culture confronts the same problem, and each supplies its own answers, its selected part of man, the values which it chooses to promote. These values

psychology, not a scientific appraisal of human nature, but an artistic creation, a mythology which changes with cultures and artists.

[2] "Man and Artistic Culture," in *Reflections on Our Age*, New York, Columbia University Press, 1949, p. 87.

relate man to action and being, to life and death, to himself, his fellows and his gods, to duration and to eternity. Often the highest values are expressed in myths about individuals: "each hero, saint or sage, stands for a victory over the human situation" (V.S., p. 633). If a culture cannot deliver man from death, "the great cultures have sometimes managed to transform his outlook on it, and almost always to justify its existence" (V.S., p. 540). All cultural values are in the last analysis contributions to the common cause of humanity against history and destiny.

A culture is defined for Malraux less as a particular heritage of knowledge, legend, and art, than as a "world-view," a set of values and a conception of man contained within this heritage. Culture is the soul of a civilization and is composed of "all that which permits man to maintain, to enrich or to transform without weakening the ideal image of himself" sponsored by the builders of the culture and inherited by each of its members (V.S., pp. 631-33).

Of all the media of culture, art is the most significant. The relationship between art and its historical or social context is intrinsic: the work of art is part of the culture in which it is created; art history is part of the history of civilization. The statues of a Gothic cathedral are works of art, created by individual artists: but they are not independent of the cathedral, nor of the Gothic style, nor of Western civilization (V.S., pp. 13-14). And art is the most vivid expression of the civilization to which it belongs. To probe the mind of Greece, we must go to the Acropolis; we find Rome in the Forum, and Europe in its museums (T.O., Letters III, V, VI, X-XII). Every great work of art expresses or suggests its time, for the artist cannot belong to any other; he cannot will away the contemporary present and its special vision of the past (V.S., p. 407).

At this point two items become clear in this movement from psychology to art. First, Malraux's psychology is of an introspective character not too unusual at the beginnings of schools of thought. It is grounded upon an insightful but not too explicit judgment of what constitutes "mental health." Psychological moralists might well debate Malraux's definition against others: adjustment, display of normal (customary) behavior, and the like. And, considering the vogue of concepts of alienation, there ought to be some techniques of measurement that could be applied to discover how much of any population is actually suffering from the syndromes described by Malraux and others. (Perhaps the millions could be induced to write their autobiographies?) For Malraux has little to say about causal factors at the psychological level, though the lives of his characters often suggest that it is the family structure—especially the relation to father and grandfather figures—that is decisive. There is much room for systematic exploration, to follow up intuitive insight.

Second, Malraux does not explain or argue why art should be the most significant value expression of a culture. What of the philosophies, laws, social theories, actual arrangements of the social order, and historical (not legendary) individual actions that take place within a civilization? Are these not expressions of value? If so, any discussion of Malraux's programs will raise the question of whether they ought not to be considerably broadened in their scope.

2.

For Malraux, however, art is the key bearer of values, and the connection between art and culture is made by style. Both the artist and his culture have a style of their own. Style is a feature which all art possesses and must possess: one " 'paints Byzantine' as one might 'speak Latin' " (V.S., p. 106), and there is no such thing as a styleless art. Style is not simply a set of characteristics common to a given group or period: it is the object of the artist's activity, and art is precisely that whereby living forms are trans-

lated into style. The particular style of a period conveys to us its
cultural values. All great styles are special interpretations of the
world, and every one implies a certain significance and orientation of man.

Changes in style are dialectical. A new order of forms arises to
pit itself against an older order out of which it arises and against
which it reacts. Certainly a more conventional notion of the birth
of style can be seen to have much truth in it: individual artists
have their own themes or programs, which they define as they
work; "when those of several great artists have proved themselves
so effective as to give rise to a style, the programs of individual
artists are adjusted to this style—until new modalities emerge and
it becomes obsolete" (V.S., pp. 335-37). But this interpretation
does not pay enough attention to the factor of conflict: "Never
do we find an epoch-making form built up without a struggle with
other forms" (V.S., p. 271). A style as such is not consciously
created where nothing existed before. First the artist must accept
the forms of a predecessor, then he must rebel against the limitations he finds in them, then overturn them by introducing a large
or small number of new forms and a new mode. "The masters who
imposed on Byzantium its first distinctive accent did not begin by
thinking up an abstraction—the Byzantine style—to which they
proceeded to adjust their art"; they began with a consciousness of
the discrepancy between classical forms and their Christian
world, and they responded by destroying the style inherent in
those classical forms and works, because the world order these
implied was in their eyes rooted in a lie (V.S., p. 339). The relation of stylistic to historical change becomes as clear as that of
culture to history: artistic "ruptures with the past . . . are multiplied and sometimes amplified by the great turning-points in
history" (V.S., p. 415). "As deliberately as Byzantium wrested
from the figures of Imperial Rome the immobility of the Torcelli
Virgin, Europe wrested from Byzantine majesty the tenuous smile
that was to make an end of it. Like the Sassanian Renaissance,

like all rebirths, the Italian Renaissance made haste to modify the forms which it had taken for its models because they supplied it with the means of overcoming its immediate predecessors . . ." (V.S., p. 272).

The means by which an artist achieves his personal style makes his work into an enterprise against destiny. The work of the artist has for him the same general characteristics it has for the world: those of struggle and victory. But for him destiny, history, takes a particular form: it is past style, past art, which tends to force him into its patterns and from which he must break away if he is to be free and himself.

An artist begins his career by copying his master's forms, his master's schema for ordering the world; but he soon comes to understand (if he is in fact an artist, and not merely a craftsman: "I call that man an artist who *creates* forms . . ." [V.S., p. 310]) that he must have his own language to interpret the world, that to use another's involves his own servitude; to win his artistic freedom he must break away from his forebears. "Every great artist's achievement of a style synchronizes with his achievement of his freedom, of which that style is at once the sole proof and the sole instrument" (V.S., p. 359). If he is to build his own style, the artist cannot start from nothing, he must begin with certain forms which he inherits: "Not one problem of the artist's vision but is conditioned by the past" (V.S., p. 271). He can only master the world "by a victory over the forms of an immediate predecessor, that he has taken over and transmuted in the crucible of genius" (V.S., p. 334). Goya, for example, began his work in the Italian style: and it took him forty years, in which he repudiated all that he had learned and substituted for it his own forms, for him to become himself, to become Goya (*Sat.*, p. 9). This path all artists must follow in order to reach significance: they must constantly renew art, constantly bring in new forms to replace the old; otherwise their art, and the style of their culture if they should happen to dominate it, will become retrograde, mere signs and ideograms copied and recopied without significance, expressing nothing at all, eventually not even art (V.S., p. 132). Therefore it is correct to say that art strikes a blow for man's freedom from absurdity. "All art is a revolt against man's fate" (V.S., p. 639). Every feature of art combines in the assault. Style: "Every great style of the past impresses us as being a special interpretation of the world . . . ; this collective conquest is obviously a sum total of the individual conquests that have gone to its making" (V.S., p. 334). The artist: "Every artist of genius . . . becomes a transformer of the meaning of the world, which he masters by reducing it to the forms which he has selected or invented" (V.S., p. 334). The work of art: "Every work that makes us feel its esthetic value . . . testifies to a victorious element in man, even though he be a man possessed" (V.S., p. 576). The rest of the conquest is for each artist a victory, "and this victory over his destiny as a man joins, in an immense exhibition, that of art over the fate of humanity."[3]

It is agreed that the artist's victory is the result of his own revolt against the influences of previous artists. There is, to be sure, a constructive element in art: "Art is always the response to an inner voice" even though "the true personality of the artist takes form . . . in his work in ways that vary greatly" (V.S., p. 417). To be haunted by an inner voice means also to be driven to impose an ideal schema or pattern upon the world: "Sculptors and painters try to adapt lines, masses and colors to an architectonic (or destructive) schema that fully reveals itself only in their output viewed as an entirety" (V.S., p. 335). "All art is the expression, slowly come by, of the artist's deepest emotions vis-à-vis the universe of which he is a part" (V.S., p. 424). But in revolt what matters is the destructive, even demoniacal, quality of art, "the artist's impulse to destroy the forms

[3] "A Universal Humanism," *Liberté de l'esprit,* June-July 1950, pp. 97-100. (Cited as H.U.)

that gave him birth" (V.S., p. 89). "Every artist starts off with the pastiche" (V.S., p. 312); "the artist is born prisoner of a style" (V.S., p. 316) and then revolts against it, destroying it in the process of forcing his own birth. And to some extent the destructive aspect of art predominates over the constructive.[4] "The artist's break with the forms that were his starting-off point forces him to break with their significance, and since no neutral forms exist (in other words no no-man's-land in which the artist, freed from his masters, can bide his time until he finds himself), his creative process is directed, its orientation being neither unconscious nor deliberate, but specific to his personality" (V.S., p. 414).

Art speaks, then, for all men: it provides in small scale a replica of the struggle, and possible victory, of all humanity. The artist thus becomes a supreme culture-hero, and the legendary "deed" which speaks for all men is the masterpiece.[5] The masterpiece therefore assumes in Malraux's esthetic a place as important as that assigned to it by traditional views, but for new reasons. Like all myths (of which it is certainly one), the notion of the masterpiece has evolved along with culture. From the sixteenth to the nineteenth centuries it was the unique approximation to an ideal Platonic beauty. Later, when works were first exhibited together, it became any painting which possessed the same surface qualities as the group of already recognized masterpieces. Now, when an anthology of an artist's work is possible, we know that "an artist's supreme work is not the one in best accord with any tradition—nor even his most complete and 'finished' work—but his most personal work, the one from which he has stripped all that is not his very own, and in which his style reaches a climax" (V.S., p. 19). And

---

4 This constitutes the answer to those nihilists who, rejecting art for action, claimed that art, being "merely" creative, could not contribute to the destruction of an existing order.
5 See V.S., pp. 416, 632; *Sat.* pp. 112-119.

the roster of masterpieces will also include the most significant works of each great style.

This definition satisfies the sociological concept of art, but plainly not the metaphysical one. That is not neglected: a masterpiece is also, for the artist who creates it, "a fragment of the world he has annexed and which belongs to him alone . . . a fragment of the world of which Man has taken charge" (V.S., pp. 17-19). "Every masterpiece, implicitly or openly, tells of a human victory over the blind forces of destiny" (V.S., p. 461). Thus, and by means of no better criterion, is art to be set apart from the antiarts: "We begin to distinguish that which un-equivocally separates these works from the creations which glut the most avid and acute sensibilities: the artist is there so powerfully liberated from destiny that they carry the echo of his liberation to all who understand their language. Posterity is the recognition men give to those victories which seem to promise them their own" (V.S., p. 630). The victory of each artist over the world becomes one in which all humanity can participate. "Each of the masterpieces is a purification of the world, but their common message is that of their existence, and the victory of each individual artist over his servitude, spreading like ripples on the sea of time, implements art's eternal victory over the human situation" (H.U.).

Great art conveys the example of a struggle with the Absurd, the promise of a victory in the struggle, and the values which can make up the sound identity of the man who has been more than a match for his fate. Thus art is a defense against the Absurd for the sensitive spectator as well as for the creator, because of the nature of creativity.

The question arises of how the eye of the spectator is to be trained so that he will perceive this essential element in a mute work of art. How particularly does one derive the values that a work of art conveys? Malraux, unfortunately, does not dwell on either the psychology or the method of connoisseurship.

This neglect of a central matter bore its fruit later, in the form of what might be called a materialistic or laissez-faire program of cultural action.

3.

If it is style that conveys the values of a culture, it would seem that a civilization must have a style that conforms to some aspect of "the divine" in men if it is to possess usable ideal images of man. And this is true. But it might also appear that any contemporary culture will automatically have such a style and such images, simply through gradual accretion and growth. But, according to Malraux's theory of style, there is no progressive building up of style from lower to higher. "The Hellenistic forms in the Gandhara region were forms from which art deliberately broke free" (V.S., p. 639). Wherever past influences persist unmodified, wherever predecessor styles are not rejected, "we find art wasting away in a kind of slow consumption" that signalizes the death of culture, for creation has been replaced by production. Art, to be creative (that is to say, to be art), must be dialectical, it must revolt. The very idea of style implies a refusal to accept earlier "learning" as valid and earlier values as real. But such revolts and refusals mean that human history cannot be a simple accumulation of style or of values or of human images.

Despite this negative relation among styles, there are important resemblances among styles besides the morphological ones (the similar manner of birth and death of individual styles). In fact, examination discloses a dualism of stylistic types, two poles about which styles cluster: the religious and the humanistic. The one dominated Egypt, India, and Christianity; the other ruled only in Greece—and rules potentially in the modern world (V.S., p. 169). Parallel to the types of artistic style are types of cultural values. "One civilization seems to defend itself against destiny in binding itself to cosmic rhythms and another in blotting them out" (V.S., pp. 74-75; H.U.). As between the two types, Malraux prefers the humanistic because the fellowship created by religion is limited to one's coreligionists even though the human predicament to which religion is a response is universal and part of the lives of all men. And therefore Malraux finds no fault with the modern waning of religious values.

For religious values, along with the religious style, have indeed reached the vanishing point today. Not since the fifteenth century has the artist's most fertile emotion been the sense of man's reconciliation with God. Our civilization is incapable of binding itself to cosmic rhythm, for this is the civilization of the conquest of the earth. Man is no longer allied to the world, he is its adversary. Religion today is one of the false defenses. Like love, opium, and power, it is an "absolute." Certainly a man may immerse himself in such an absolute: thereby "the profound feeling of dependence, the remorse of being oneself, is utterly consumed, along with the entire man" (H.U.). An ironic "solution" to the problems of man—self-annihilation! And the absolute is never found after all: Perken and Ferral, searching for love and power, in the end find nothing but defeat and death.

Yet if our modern Western culture cannot be religious, it is not yet humanistic but still in an elaborate and painful process of transition. Our civilization is that of the machine age, of the conquest of the earth: if for the Greeks fire put the gods in question, for us the machine has killed them. Our art and science are not affirmative, they are interrogative: our art proclaims the least subdued and most virulent interrogation of the world that has ever existed. But it affirms nothing; it interrogates man and his culture as thoroughly as it interrogates the world. Western culture has lost not only the Christian faith in God, but also the secular optimism and faith in man of the last century.

The intellectual ancestor of modernism in this respect is Goya: for him the European idea of man has already collapsed, to be replaced at best by a question mark, a new variety of the Absurd. Worse—in Malraux's eyes, Goya practically succeeded in recreating the devil by transmitting the streak of the diabolical in his psyche. And Goya is not the only one; there becomes apparent "a curiously persistent affinity between the obscure side of certain great works of art and the dark places of man's heart . . . intimations of the dark, demonic side of man's nature."[6] For as Western culture loses faith in itself, questions its own philosophical bases, and begins to tear itself apart, the diabolical principle and "the *negative values* which bulk as large in our civilization as in our art come to the fore" (V.S., p. 590).

This emergence is not necessarily conscious. The artists of the modern style, divorced from religion, have developed to replace it, not an image of man, but an ideology of art: "the modern artist's supreme aim is to subordinate all things to his style" (V.S., p. 603). The diabolical principle takes root beneath this style which in itself is nonhumanistic because it is arcane, elitist; it may express the artist's experience, but it does not communicate to the people. For the first time the masses exist: people not nourished by the art of their culture but cut off from it. A civilization needs a style that speaks to all and for all, or it is defenseless. Our civilization has none.

Several points in this analysis of the use of styles deserve at least an inquiry or a comment. What are the external signs that art belongs to the religious or humanistic category? Is this particular dualism of styles and cultures truly usable? Believers exist today, and the absolute of religion seems to defend Chen-Dai (of *The Conquerors*) and Ximenes (of *Man's Hope*) adequately enough. It may well be that a factual inquiry into the emotional states of many men would show that some are protected from anguish precisely by those values of the absolute or of the diabolical that Malraux finds not only

6 "N'était-ce donc que ça?" *Liberté de l'esprit,* April-June 1949, pp. 49-51, 86-87, 117-118. (Cited as "N'était-ce . . .")

morally repugnant but actually unsuccessful. In such a case the entire appeal of his humanism would have to be made simply on ethical and emotive grounds. At this point, too, the consequences of Malraux's concentration upon one aspect of culture to the neglect of all others become somewhat clearer: if as a student he had chosen to study political philosophy (for instance) rather than esthetics, he might have discovered more humanism in the contemporary world and in his subject matter. It would hardly have been enough to satisfy him, however, and he might well have been forced to broaden considerably the scope of his ultimate cultural policy. That in itself would have been valuable.

4.

Modern art is therefore not all that art ought to be. But it can be, or can become, true defense. If past art could and did speak to all, so can the art of the present. The crowds carried Cimabue's *Madonna* through the streets: art was not meaningless for them. Art was for every man, and could reveal at once (like the *Oedipus*) man's servitude and his ability to transcend it, to hold his own among the blind forces, to escape from a destiny-ridden world into one controlled by human minds. But to regain this power the artist must become a prophet, speaking to others in language they can understand, so as to open their eyes, to turn them from a world of appearances to one of "Truth"—that is, of fruitful myth. A new style is then required, bound up with some struggle in which artists and masses alike all may be engaged, a style prepared—like that of the great sermons of the Middle Ages—to go directly to the inner selves of all the people. Such an art must be representative as well as prophetic: it must repeat and duplicate the struggle of all humanity. The artist must speak in the name of all the participants in his culture against their common ontological predicament. When he does so, he will attain the status of the supreme culture-hero: the poet will replace the Prometheus myth with the *Prometheus Bound* and, in so doing, will usurp for himself the place of Prometheus. With this formulation of a program for a new style and a new art Malraux promotes art over revolution as a liberating way of life and makes artistic consciousness, if not artistic creation, part and parcel of the myth of the liberal hero. The balancing of art against action is something which Malraux has applied in his analysis of T. E. Lawrence: "Now that all action was closed for him, he felt himself more engaged once again in this intellectual adventure than he had ever been in the Arabian adventure" (V.S., p. 119). For Lawrence as for Malraux, the reason for the partial estrangement from action is the discovery of the "manichean" nature of action. "Art insensibly supplanted action in his most profound struggle . . . . What had in fact separated him from the revolt . . . was that every human action was soiled by its very nature" (N'était-ce . . .). This conception of the manicheanism of the world and action within it was first expressed by Garcia, in *Man's Hope*. A compromise was reached there and later renewed; Malraux has not become a monk, nor has he accepted any of the forms of passivity analyzed in his novels. But, as *The Walnut Trees of Altenburg* indicated, only action which is finally creative can be justified, and not all political action—certainly not all violent action—can be called "creative." Art is an equivalent of political action ("Politically, an indictment of the social situation leads to the destruction of the forms that countenance it; in art, an indictment of the human situation leads to the destruction of the art forms that take it for granted" [N'était-ce . . .]), but one which is not soiled as action is, and one that is invariably constructive in some measure. Yet action is not put aside. There is De Gaulle; and there is the fact that art, too, may be manichean—may pay service to diabolical values and may degrade man.

Nevertheless Malraux makes his greatest appeal to the artists.

This appeal to take the lead in reconstructing human history could only be based upon a theory of artistic creation which, as Malraux's does, rejects the dominance of historical conditioning and influence: which intends, in other words, to adopt a view of art as free rather than as determined, and searches not for its objective causes but for its proper ends. Insofar as he is a creator, the artist is independent of history; he belongs not to a social group molded by a culture, but to a culture which he is in the process of building up (V.S., p. 540). The artist frees himself not by receiving but by wresting and making his own forms which express and let him possess his autonomous, coherent, significant universe. And in this way Malraux can call upon the artist to create heroes who free themselves and thereby to liberate men as he liberates himself.

There is no doubt that such a call is a political one, though it omits a role for the instruments of the state. But it may be observed that once we abandon the "modern style" and its ideology of art as the artist's business, once there is again a social goal for art, a more conventional politics may be apposite. Its inspiration need not come from the regulated art of "socialist realism" in its Zhdanovite era; it can stem from the memory that great religious art, linked to a hierocratic state, was often commissioned by such a state from professional artists or made the project of an entire community over generations.[7] If appeals to artists do not work—and they may not—we may ask if the selection and commissioning of humanist works might not here and there educe humanist masterpieces.

5.

The altering of the modern style is not a matter with which Malraux himself has been deeply concerned, except in so far as

[7] Malraux notes that the Church set the subject of Gothic statuary, but not the style, which was determined by the faith and the creativity of the artisan (or his want of either).

his work might alter it by example. His real preoccupation since the war has been with a more easily manageable employment of art as a defense for the masses and for all men. It is not art yet to be created, but the great art of the past, that he intends to use —and for that matter, is using.

For art is the expression of the value of a culture, and cultures are all, in the Malrauvian school, styles of response to the enduring human problems. The ideal images of man of the past, the classic virtues, are not necessarily invalid today: man has not improved so much that he has no more to learn from his history. And if the men who partook of the sculpture of Greece or ancient Egypt have died, their art has not: their statues are in our museums; therefore their culture has survived them.

The modern style of art is largely responsible for our being able to appreciate and to exploit this heritage. We look at the painting qua painting, at the work of art as just that. But "a Romanesque crucifix was not regarded by its contemporaries as a work of sculpture"; the Chinese painting was meant to be contemplated in order to enhance the viewer's communion with the universe (V.S., p. 416). In order to become conscious of the fact of differing styles and to be forced into making a theory of stylistic change, it was necessary for us to become aware of these objects as members of a single species, "art."

This awareness has been a consequence of the museum, a material attribute of our civilization and of its refinement, the "museum without walls," the photographic collection of reproductions of all great art. For this collection to be made it was necessary for the works to lose both their original significance as objects and their value-bearing function, so that they appeared merely as art works displaying more or less of talent.

Because of the museum, our culture possesses a tremendous inheritance. The works of art of the whole past are for the first time collectively available to a civilization—all past arts are available to us to draw on, all is resurrected. Modern art drew

upon the inheritance in its quest for forms to utilize in its battle
with its predecessor, the "illusionist-realism" of nineteenth-century bourgeois art. But the effort must go further, to resurrect the
function as well as the forms; then we can possess, even if altered
by our active and myth-creating reception of them, all the values
and the ideal images of man with which the past defended itself.
And this is available to the educated spectator: one need not be
an artist to act to annex the great and to defend oneself (V.S., pp.
13-15).

Still cultivation is required. One must be habituated to the
presence of works of art and to contemplation of them; no doubt
one must also shed the esthetics of the modern style in order to
become accustomed to seeking in art a communion through time
and an image of man. This cultivation entails, in effect, a social
decision for a liberal mass education, more theoretical and purposive than any country's universities are accustomed to give the
national elite. But Malraux is not prepared to go so far; if he did,
he would face problems even more enormous than those raised
by his own program for reclaiming the universal heritage for
the masses, a program which goes under the title of "cultural
democracy."

It is to his actual policies, then, that attention must now be
paid. In them the advocacy of a new and humanistic attitude and
style is outweighed by the determination to turn the old values to
account. And in considering his idea of cultural democracy, Malraux's final definition of culture, the product and sign of all his
esthetics, and of his intent to annex the entirety of the cultural
heritage must be reflected on.

"Culture would seem then, first and foremost, *to be the knowledge of what makes man something other than an accident of the
universe,* be it by deepening his harmony with the world, or by the
lucid consciousness of his revolt from it. . . . Culture is the sum
of all the forms of art, of love, and of thought, which in the course
of centuries have enabled men *to be less enslaved.* . . . Thus art

and culture appear to us as expressions of the most fundamental liberty."⁸ Thus, in political terms, the struggle of the West against Communism is the struggle to substitute a real democratic culture for the false appeal of totalitarian culture. Malraux's idea of democracy thus has little to do with traditional Western liberalism, insofar as that has always preferred to define the institutional forms which will bring about freedom, or in which freedom consists. Political liberty, like cultural liberty, is the freedom to destroy old forms and to create new ones: permanent institutions are only impediments to such a program, and could not count for less. If Malraux chose to follow out this reasoning about political liberty, he would arrive either at anarchism (with respect to institutions) or at a program for permanent revolution. Instead, he follows the less slippery path of discussing the formula for allocating the cultural heritage so as to bring the maximum of liberty to all.

6.

It is possible to illuminate Malraux's political route to his present stance by reference to Sorel and his rhetorical role in De Gaulle's Republic by allusion to Barrès. Malraux's cultural policy affords no such parallel. This policy is expressed in the development of the institutions through which the French government has traditionally patronized the various arts. If there is a discrepancy between Malraux's vision and the concrete progress of his policy, that is not to be wondered at; nevertheless, in practice, the administrator has dominated the cultural revolutionary, and in a way this shift is regrettable. France is not the only state to have a cultural policy, but it is perhaps the first to have an "existentialist" cultural policy that proceeds deductively from the principles of an ethical thinker. The full expression of those principles, more than merely interesting, could have been, for good or

⁸ "What Stand Will You Take?" *Confluence*, September 1952, pp. 3-11.

bad, exemplary for the rising number of contemporary thinkers who concern themselves less with the attainment of general opulence than with the quality of life in the prosperous society. But Malraux's experiments retain some interest, for their motivation and theory more than for their gradualist and reformist scale.

The theory can be briefly summarized—it is the last stop on Malraux's philosophical journey. Every man is in the same "human predicament" (a premise by now familiar). For the few, violent political action or artistic creation may serve to break the isolation of the ego and to create "communion." The only means of defense in principle available to all is the consumption[9] of culture. Whether an individual is or is not able to employ this means depends on two social conditions: his access to the contemporary culture and its quality. Both of these conditions are in turn, according to Malraux, subject in part to conscious control by the state.

The cultural distribution system of modern industrial societies is, says Malraux, doubly faulty. To an intellectual elite ample access is provided to cultural objects of the highest quality. The rest get little access to the best, and a deluge of shoddy trash. This situation holds true for bourgeois society, such as the United States, where there is no political leadership in the cultural field, and where culture is largely accessible to a man in proportion to his wealth. It holds true also for totalitarian society. Soviet Marxism declares that art is nothing but the expression of the political orientation of the artist (reactionary or progressive) and

9 Malraux avoids economic metaphors in this context. I shall employ them, even though they suggest a crude approach that Malraux does not take, because they also suggest a parallel to certain programs of economic reform through welfare-state action. This parallel will in turn suggest standard criticisms of the competence of men of intellect and men of affairs to deliberate upon and to control the consumption of other members of their society. The fact that Malraux is discussing art raises added questions of the competence of such men in matters of taste and questions of the relative propriety of moral education under the surveillance of the state vs. character formation by an ethical free market.

that the dominant art of a society is nothing but its reflection. No distinction can, then, be drawn between artistic creation and artistic production, between the masterpiece and the fourth-rate. This ideology conceals the fact that in modern culture, East or West, the *creator* of art is not in harmony with his world, and "art is opposed in its profoundest sense to the society within which it is born." Once this is denied, a totalitarian state can conscientiously suppress creativity and promote production: rubbish for all, when in the West it is rubbish for some.[10] But it is with the reform of the Western system that Malraux is concerned, and the rest of his analysis relates to it alone.

In the West limited access to true culture has turned the majority into a cultural proletariat, a situation concealed by the general access to so-called mass art—novels and paintings and films which indeed command a mass audience, but which constitute antiart. Formerly there was a "popular art," truly of and for the people, as well as for the few, intimately bound to the central values of the contemporary society. But modern society has no stable values; the people have dissolved into the rootless urban mass. Authentic art serves some chosen part of man, relates him to time or to eternity or to some ethic of human nobility. Authentic art, in a civilization united by an ethic, a goal, or a myth, transmits that vision to all and makes them not masses but brothers. Where such a civilization is absent, antiart flourishes. Antiart is a nonexpressive phenomenon whose purpose is to sell itself for profit and which concerns itself therefore not with transmitting values but with catering to pleasures. It creates in men not profound emotions, but superficial and puerile ones: "the sentimentalities of love or religion, the taste for violence, a touch of cruelty, collective vanity and sensuality" (H.U.).

Antiart distracts mass taste; it obscures the cultural im-

---

[10] Official totalitarian culture is not culture at all, therefore, but psychotechnical propaganda in favor of the ruling class. The passage in quotation marks is from "What Stand Will You Take?"

poverishment of the majority. The uncontrolled proliferation of an imagination not grounded upon values, through pop fiction, radio, records, cinema, and television, does worse. The mechanization of dreams for the tastes of a free market composed of men out of communion with values and with one another reinforces what is least human and most animal in men: sex and death instincts in their most primitive form—the urge to dominate, to exploit (Ferral and Valérie in *Man's Fate*), and to kill—even if only in the imagination.[11]

Culture influences human nature. According to the manichean psychology that appears marginally throughout Malraux's works on art, there are available in human nature elements that tend to ennoble man, to lead him to self-transcendence and communion, and elements which tend to animalize, isolate, and destroy him. The antiart of mass "culture" appeals to and encourages the demonic in human nature.

A reform in access might amend this state: authentic art cannot be mass-produced, but it can be mass-distributed; let the masses have access, then, to modern artistic creation, and they can be liberated. But here the question of quality again enters in; even authentic art in a civilization where the artist is not in harmony with society, where it is a matter of chance what values he inherits, may be a source of corruption rather than of regeneration. "Every authentic work of art devotes its means (even the most brutal) to the service of some essential part of man passionately or obscurely sponsored by the artist" (V.S., p. 524). But the dark, demonic side of man's nature is as elemental as the divine. Western civilization is displaying a disturbing tendency to interrogate and to rend the divine, to advance the diabolical, even at the highest levels of authentic art. Modern artistic creation is,

11 Others besides Malraux often take this line, of course. Often, because they generally speak from a socially conservative and religiously traditionalist position, their program is not like Malraux's: they propose a return to "the sentimentalities of love or religion" which, in Malraux's view, are equally elements of antiart.

consciously, following in part the same damaging line as that unconsciously pursued by mass antiart. Mass distribution of modern authentic art cannot, then, provide men with the defense they need. Men must receive art of a certain quality.

Malraux's vision of the (cultural-reformist) future politics of art has, consequently, three phases, which may be called the new human type, the systematic resurrection of the past, and cultural democracy. The artist-politician must strive to humanize the art of the present, revive the "divine" art of the past, and make the one and the other available to all.

1. *Building tragic humanism.* Humanism, Malraux's title for his own final philosophical position, is to him at once an ideology and the name of a type of cultural style that expresses the ideology. The nineteenth century was the zenith of optimistic humanism: God was dead, but the kingdom of man had replaced Him; the world was the sphere of progress in manners and morals, customs and arts, under the guidance of reason and of science. Two wars and war science displayed such suffering, such horrors, and such human degradation that that happy world was slaughtered along with its inhabitants. In the face of the world, the best that can be found in man, the maximum value that we and our culture can possess, is a tragic humanism: this is the alternative to demonism in art—or to antiart and totalitarian "art," which peddle themselves or the will to dominate of the ruling class (*Reflections* . . . , pp. 84-89). Tragic humanism combines the belief that no change in the material or political conditions of life can substantially alter the terrible isolation of every man with the belief that under certain political conditions men can choose to make political and ethical commitments, which will in turn produce emotions and memories by means of which their predicament will be from moment to moment mitigated or abated.

In his own view Malraux is not the lonely advocate of the philosophy he calls "tragic humanism": this humanism is a new culture, struggling to be born. It will be born when the West reconstructs for itself the idea of man. Every great *politique* creates its new human type,[12] a myth around which human ideals orient themselves; the next great human type is the liberal hero. "Symbolic types of this sort are born from the merging, at certain moments of history, of attitudes which seemed up to that time irreconcilable."[13] Such a type provides the individual with a clear understanding of what his civilization expects from him. But Malraux has never delineated the liberal-hero type. In all probability, however, this character reflects the best of an earlier Malrauvian hero type, the Bolshevik, a combination of "tremendous energy, of violence, and of humanitarian ideology," to which is added a new reflectiveness, a new intimacy with art, in consonance with Malraux's postwar views.[14]

The emergence of such a "positive" hero—and accordingly a liberating rather than a corrupting effect, a humanist rather than a negative style—in authentic modern art is necessary if that art is to bring men the rewards that Malraux's esthetics considers possible. But having rejected the idea of an official style, Malraux allows no decisive role to the state in "reforming" artistic creation: all that it can do is to promote and support art which it must not closely control. His own works and rhetoric, however, preach his gospel; no doubt this is the most radical political action he conceives as tolerable in the creation of the new human type. It cannot satisfy the impatient and threatens to be ineffectual.

2. *The resurrection of the past.* It is, however, possible to

---

[12] On such types, see Nicolas Berdyaev: "The War . . . produced a new spiritual type inclined to transfer wartime measures to the ordering of life in general, prepared to put the theory of violence into practice, and with a love of power and a great respect for force . . . a new anthropological type, a new facial expression . . . a different gait, different gestures . . . . This is a world-wide phenomenon; it is seen equally in communism and in fascism." *The Origins of Russian Communism* (London, 1937, Geoffrey Bles), pp. 122-123.

[13] André Malraux and James Burnham, *The Case for De Gaulle* (New York, Random, 1948), p. 62.

[14] Thus Malraux offered as a slogan for French youth, "culture and courage," a purely natural outgrowth of his own concern with reconciling esthetic perception with political activism. This liberal hero resembles none of his fictional heroes, not even Vincent Berger, so much as he resembles Malraux himself—or the Malraux myth.

affect the minds and the style of the artists of tomorrow while ignoring or short-circuiting those contemporary creators who are not humanists. A main premise of Malraux's esthetics is that art feeds on art, that each artist develops his unique style first by imitation of, then by revolt against, some predecessor or predecessors. (These need not be men of the last generation, or even men of his own culture.) A second main premise holds that for men in the twentieth century all previous styles of all previous artists and cultures have become potential predecessors—thanks to anthropological and esthetic research, to the attitude of cultural relativism, and to the large-scale technology of artistic collection and distribution represented by museums, photography, and the ethnological cinema. Since the preservation and distribution of past culture is a large-scale organized operation, it is suitable for state action in a way individual creativity is not.

Hence the key themes, in Malraux's political speeches, of the young and the dead: "We intend" to form the taste of the young by systematically giving them the chance to know the great films of the past; we shall recapture all of the human past, we shall render accessible the largest possible number of *capital* objects-of-art; true culture requires a communion, a *"presence,* in our lives, of what should belong to the dead" and an emotion in that presence—our job, therefore, is to make the genius of humanity not merely known but loved; to create our exemplary men and to shape our new past, we must "conquer" all forms of love, art, personal greatness, and thought that, during the millennia, have allowed men to become less enslaved; let our culture be the resurrection of the *noblesse* of the world. In political terms, let the state undertake not only a promotion of uncontrollable creativity, but also a selective preservation of the creations of the past.[15]

---

15 Debate, Senate, November 23, 1960. France: *Journal officiel, Débats parliamentaires,* Sénat (hereafter cited as DPS), 1960, p. 1844. Debate, National Assembly, July 23, 1962. DPAN 1962, p. 2776. Speech, Brasilia, August 23, 1959. (France: Ministry for Cultural Affairs; mimeographed copy.)

3. *Cultural democracy.* It is not enough, however, to shape the tastes of tomorrow's creators. To them, and to the past, a mass public must be restored. The cultural distribution system must be reformed so that every man has access to authentic and defensive art as well as to antiart. To Soviet totalitarian culture and American bourgeois culture, France can counterpose a democratic culture. This was impossible in the nineteenth century, not simply because culture was synonymous with refinement, but because twentieth-century economic technology has invented mass reproduction and mass distribution techniques. The works of humanity will be rendered accessible to all; even the poorest man must be able to know art, and every child of sixteen is to have a real contact with the glory of the human spirit. "From the university level down to places that are quite defenseless today, within thirty years . . . any human being must have the means to defend himself, and we must afford him those means." In the past the museums won the elite away from the antiarts; in the future the general distribution of works of art and photographic reproductions will win back the masses. And this process is totally democratic in the sense that a facility is created that anyone may use, but the masses are not forced "through another political rolling mill." Again, state intervention is required to break the cash nexus and the class discrimination of the cultural distribution system.[16]

At the theoretical level, then, the state is justified in assuming a major or even a dominant role in the promotion, preservation, and distribution of culture. Since Malraux found the French state already so involved, he was able to move piecemeal to turn that involvement to the service of his theories.

More state action in a given area normally translates itself into

[16] Debate, National Assembly, October 6, 1961. DPAN 1961, p. 3148. Debate, Senate, December 8, 1959. DPS 1959, p. 1569. Debate, National Assembly, November 17, 1959. DPAN 1959, p. 2500. Debate, National Assembly, November 9, 1963. DPAN 1963, p. 7091. *The Case for De Gaulle,* p. 69.

a bureaucratic demand for more appropriations and higher priority. Under Malraux, expenditures for culture have been increased, and the budgetary priority of cultural affairs has been raised; the cultural affairs budget has been given autonomy, instead of being the least important item in the education budget, and episodic appropriations have been regularized by means of a "cultural Five-Year plan"—or rather, a place in the fourth national plan of modernization.

The various areas of French cultural life have been unevenly organized by the state. Where intervention has been lacking, Malraux has initiated it on a small scale: thus, a commission of officials and specialists in music has been created to consider the needs of music; money has been sought to commission representative contemporary artists to create prototypes in the decorative arts (especially furniture), to revive that industry.

France's promotion of contemporary artistic creation encompasses measures to foster the physical well-being of artists (projects of relief and social security for writers, painters, sculptors, decorators, of construction of housing-and-studios for artists) and to increase their numbers (more scholarships and endowments for the national and regional schools of music, drama, architecture, art, and decorative arts), as well as more direct approaches. In each of the arts, and for all, there are special measures for the preservation of masterpieces, for production support and quality control, and for "decentralization."

In the realm of the film France has organized an international film festival at Cannes; a cinémathèque, or library of great films of the past; a commission for research into technical improvement; an institute for advanced filmic studies; federations of cine-clubs; and special programs in scientific and ethnological cinema. Malraux has worked to reduce taxes on the industry, to subsidize the modernization of studios, and to get the national film-distribution organization to favor "quality films" by handling the prize-winning films from international festivals. Automatic state support to film production has been replaced by selective aid, in the form of advances and guarantees of receipts, to productions judged by an advisory commission, on the basis of scenarios or previews, to be of high artistic merit—a system which has supported many international prize-winning films.

In the national theater, Malraux has sought to alter the repertory and enlarge the audience. The national theater, in his view, was suppressing the national and human patrimony —Racine, Shakespeare, Greek tragedy—in favor of popular comedy: a classic, traditional, and tragic repertory has been reinstated. For private theaters Malraux has sought tax relief; those that reduce their prices for students and members of cultural groups are aided; particularly, productions are subsidized (on consideration of the value of the work, author, direction and actors) by repayable advances. State aid has been afforded directly to permanent, itinerant, and "young provincial" troupes, and new ones have been encouraged and developed into permanence; the attempts of provincial towns to subsidize tours by Parisian troupes have been seconded; aid to the provincial dramatic festivals has been increased and made more selective.

In architecture, a national inventory has already classified at least 20,000 structures of historical, artistic, or archeologic interest which it is desirable to preserve. The next step in the inventory is to compile and make public photographs of all these structures. Meanwhile the repair and restoration of the neglected "monuments" is under way, with a vast dirt-removal campaign to restore their original appearance and full restoration for a few great structures. Not only have individual structures received attention: the preservation of entire streets and quarters, through external restorations and internal modernization, is also under way.

Distribution has largely been equated in practice with decentralization; that is to say, the problem is seen not as getting culture from the elite to the masses so much as getting it from Paris to the provinces. A cultural diffusion center catalogues all the "manifestations" (dramatic, musical, filmic, literary, and sporting events, artistic expositions, conferences, and the like) that can be put on tour; the center affords further aid to mayors and cultural leaders for their procurement. A special project of Malraux's own devising is the organization of fixed and mobile "maisons de la culture" in the provinces, for the deposit of collections of reproductions of phonographic, cinematic, and other artistic masterpieces.[17]

The impressiveness of this practical program and its superiority to that of other nations may be conceded. It seems better to aid the arts than to talk about aiding them; the French approach is probably superior to either pure free enterprise or pure state control. This concession does not mean that political analysis must not raise the pertinent questions of unintended effects, of the corruptions of power, and of the adequacy of means to ends. Judgments of quality in a work of art contain the danger of political flattery or of cliques or of academicism, depending upon whether politicians, artists, or critics make the selection: who is to judge? Regulation of private enterprises is often reversed; under a less forceful successor, may not its wider audience appeal lead to pressures, in the name of profits and of democracy, for the subsidization of "antiart"? How does one make certain that statistics showing an increased audience reflect the awakening of masses, rather than an increased interest on the part of the extant consumers? And if the object of all this activity is to bring about a change in men's attitudes and consciousness, how can success or failure be measured when statistics reflect only a physical presence? Malraux has evaded the first problem by referring most selections to committees of "experts": he has not, to my knowledge, dealt seriously with the rest either. But eventually they must and will be forcibly raised, and he, or his successors, will have to

[17] *The Case for De Gaulle*, p. 68.

confront them. There is no need to confront them at this juncture
except to note that while they remain unanswered, Malraux's
practical achievements cannot be considered either to have attained or to have validated his cultural utopia and theory, which
must still be judged as provisional hopes, not as established facts.
We do not know whether all Frenchmen will become Malrauxs;
we are permitted to wonder whether they can.

Malraux has returned to the dilemmas of victory. In the old
days a losing political struggle was the good fight even so, if only
it could break the parallel solitudes of the fighters. To win was
more dangerous; victory could be justified only by the intention
to experiment with the social order, so that it might increase the
availability of the spiritual and artistic means of feeling human
fraternity. Otherwise a stable social order would be an evil one
though that result had never been planned. For war and revolution, the normal opportunities for men to step outside themselves,
would be banished without a substitute.

Since the victory of De Gaulle, Malraux has tried, in a Cabinet
composed of men not particularly sympathetic to his style of
thought, to justify that victory—or rather, to make it justifiable.
His attempt has had a rhetorical mode, which justly recalls the
rhetoric of Barrès by its evocation of historic places and dead
heroes and its intention to induce in men by an intensely emotional appeal the state of mind which only violent action could
previously permit. And his attempt has had a bureaucratic mode:
the Minister of Culture seeks by administrative action to insure
the exposure of all of France to those masterpieces which, he
believes, will permit those who perceive art rightly to experience
that same psychological escape from and "conquest" of the
human predicament that the grosser instrument of political
struggle surely allows.

It would be a bold man who would presume to judge the
validity of Malraux's diagnosis of the psychological malady of

modern humanity or who would care to forecast with much certainty the eventual outcome of his policy. All that needs to be said at this point is that André Malraux, after a varied but internally consistent and comprehensible career, has obtained an enviable opportunity. Unlike most political thinkers, he has secured the power to test his theories and to realize, if they can be realized, his dreams. He has tried. Now we must wait on the outcomes of the experiment.

7. MALRAUX IN PERSPECTIVE

THERE CAN BE SAID TO EXIST a "classical" Western tradition, historically centered upon the Enlightenment, habitually describing itself as "liberal" in philosophy, secularly based, valuing science for itself and for the presumed progress it brings, and generally believing in and valuing reason, progress, individualism, democracy, and human rights and liberty. Malraux stands in a large gallery of figures who are outside this tradition. Yet Malraux too thinks of himself as speaking for liberty and for human values, and it is as such a speaker that he questions the other beliefs in this classical liberal tradition. He contends with them on their own grounds, ranging cultural against political liberalism, economic against political democracy. Not simply a stranger to liberalism, he is one of those who challenge its programs in terms of its own values. It is among such challengers that he deserves to be placed: by locating him among such others, we can comprehend better his ideas, his roots, and his significance.

Many names come to mind as potential subjects of individual comparison with Malraux; if his thoughts are new, his problems are not. There are certain evident parallels, among authors of earlier, the same, and later generations, as well as some not so evident. One thinks in connection with ideas of the extreme impact of fate, of necessity, of isolation and the desire for fraternity, and of action as providing illusions of victory, of Joseph Conrad, though Conrad was a far more gloomy figure, who, accepting the hopelessness of political action, found (Malraux might add "not surprisingly") a doubtful refuge in the other life of art. The deranged world of Franz Kafka and the self-destroying revolution of George Orwell are not unfamiliar to Malraux: but the distortion which Kafka presents as a feature of reality is for Malraux an aspect of the perception or misperception of those who experience it because of their particular situations—Manuel because of the treachery of his soldiers, Ch'en during and after his crime, Kassner in prison, Hernandez in submission to death; and the political understanding of Orwell that it is those lifted up by their skill in making revolutions who will destroy the goals of revolutions leads for Malraux to a rejection of a particular group and their revolution, but not also to a desolation of hope for the future. It has been shown how much Malraux derives from Sorel with his ideas on the myth, and how his political evolutions resemble those of Barrès. But there are even more fruitful comparisons to be drawn. Nietzsche, Hegel, Camus; two are predecessors; the contemporary tills the same field. The comparison provides insight; it also brings up intellectual reinforcements to several of the points where Malraux can be most strongly attacked by the defenders of classical liberalism.

NIETZSCHE: CULTURE AND OVERMAN

Friedrich Nietzsche, all his life an outsider to politics and action, deliberately apolitical in his philosophy, does not represent Malraux's whole past; nor is Malraux his sole heir. Yet Malraux acknowledges him as a direct philosophical ancestor; it is Nietzsche, also, on whom Vincent Berger lectures. And Malraux is commonly enough cited, by those who intend both praise and dispraise, as the Frenchman who has absorbed the most from that German philosopher.

We have found in *The Royal Way* and elsewhere a figure whom some might name "the Superman" rather than the Conqueror. But Perken is not Malraux's fulfillment of the prophecies of *Zarathustra*. Nietzsche spoke of a being, "humanly superhuman," and this is exactly what Perken is not. He is and displays himself as the very contrary, as "all-too-human." "Man is a thing that must be overcome. . . . 'My ego is something which is to be surpassed,' " says Zarathustra.[1] Perken, again and again brought crudely face to face with his human and ontological predicament, overcomes it only once, when he walks out to the Mois. Throughout the later Protean changes of his fate, in his engagements with disease, with the prostitute, with the Siamese, he never recovers the condition he achieved then, when for the first and only time he surpassed himself.

Perken's figure bears only a false relation to that of the "over-man" whom Zarathustra teaches. He resembles rather those "weak" men who, for Nietzsche, happen to be embodiments of the will to power which is in all men but who, unlike the truly strong, apply themselves to the domination of others and not to self-domination and the overcoming of self. For this reason the character of Perken is made into a type by shading it into Garine's, and Garine's into that of Ferral: all will their power in some form of external victory or domination, and sometimes achieve it "without content." Hence emerges the adventurer-type, the Conqueror-type. He is also a play-actor, drawn (like the more complex and equally futile Clappique) to turn his life into a set of sterile histrionics. Thus Perken destroys himself in trying to correspond with his own legend.

Nietzsche opposes himself to the histrionic spirit in the name of another and a greater metamorphosis of the universal will to power: the spirit of creation that belongs to the true, self-over-coming overman. "Little do the people understand that which is great—that which creates. . . . Around the devisers of new values the world invisibly revolves. But around the actors revolve the people and the glory: such is the course of things."[2]

That other Nietzschean metaphor of the spirit figured as lion,

---

[1] Friedrich Nietzsche, *The Philosophy of Nietzsche*, New York, Modern Library, 1954: *Ecce Homo*, p. 896; *Thus Spake Zarathustra*, p. 86.
[2] *Zarathustra*, pp. 54-55.

camel, and child, recalls Malraux's idea of the two lives men may fitly lead, of the liberations through political action or artistic fabrication.

To create new values—that, even the lion cannot yet accomplish: but to create itself freedom for new creating—that can the might of the lion do. . . . To assume the ride to new values—that is the most formidable assumption for a load-bearing and reverent spirit. . . . Innocence is the child, and forgetfulness, a new beginning, a game, a self-rolling wheel, a first movement, a holy Yea. Aye for the game of creating, my brethren, there is needed a holy Yea unto life: *its own* will, willeth now the spirit; *his own* world winneth the world's outcast.[3]

There exists a representation of the Übermensch that is quite alien to this metaphor, a false representation current among some Nietzscheans and anti-Nietzscheans: Malraux draws it in order to contend with it. Claude Vannec witnesses the single moment of self-transcendence that Perken finds (and loses); he witnesses the destruction of the dreams and power of Grabot and Perken, who had loomed superhuman. His witness and realization embody Malraux's first—but final—rejection of this proud beast and false hero. Even the false, the would-be supermen of Nietzsche are conceded more of a modicum of glory than Malraux's Conquerors achieve, with their sometime glorious illusions that shatter with an inevitable necessity. If to build a surpassing illusion seems the closest human approach to the sublime, even so an ecstasy such as Perken's moment, the moment when the world is conquered by a man's mind, must be repeated in the face of every repetitious confrontation with the predicament, if its victory is not to dissolve and be forgotten.

The real overman for Malraux is also a creator, a man who repeats his triumphs and preserves them, one who understands the meaning of Nietzsche's juxtaposition of creativity and freedom, in the symbol of the lion, again in the psychology of the will to

[3] Ibid., pp. 24-25.

power (when he speaks of that will as the "instinct of freedom").
Malraux's creative hero is finally constrained to understand that
his highest goal is not the domination of others, but power over
himself and—adding a point to the Nietzschean understanding of
true power as self-transcendence—power over his world. That
word may be capitalized, written as World, and generalized, for
through its intrusion into men's lives it may assume the face of the
earth and land, or any of a hundred other masks. The artistic-
creative struggle against the world in Malraux thus harks back to
the Baconian-scientific notion of man's conquest of nature
through scientific knowledge and power; struggle, conquest,
power here are none of them Nietzschean, for in Nietzsche the
object to be overcome by power does not lie outside oneself.[4]

PSYCHOLOGY

Nietzsche's psychology is monistic although monism is not internally necessary to it. It depends upon a single will-to-power to
explain human actions multiple and divergent in direction. But
this monism is, as Walter Kaufmann points out, "dialectical,"[5]
and in this way capable of absorbing the Apollonian-Dionysian
dualism: the will to power gives itself form and destroys it,
struggles against itself by assuming mutually opposed and
mutually destructive forms. Freudian psychology and psychoanalysis, in all its phases, seems to tend more to "dialectical"
dualisms (which become dualistic human typologies in Jung),
and this facet of psychoanalysis seems to have impressed or influenced Malraux most. It would not have been outrageously
inconsistent for the man who made "good" and "evil" attributes
of a psychology both social and subjective, who could speak,
dialectically as well as oracularly, of an "orderly chaos," and who
developed the idea of a cultural cleavage between the Apollonian

---

[4] *The Philosophy of Nietzsche: The Genealogy of Morals*, pp. 704-05.
[5] Walter Kaufmann, *Nietzsche*, New York, Meridian, 1958, p. 204.

illusion of order and the Dionysian vision of chaos, to have postulated a parallel cleavage within the human individual psyche.
Malraux's manicheanism does postulate that, and claims Freudian
psychology as its predecessor. It is Freud's early "discovery" or
delineation of the unconscious to which Malraux's idea of the
reintegration of the "demonic" within man refers. There is an
even closer resemblance between the Freudian Eros and Thanatos
and Malraux's vaguer opposition of human creative powers to
those forces within man which tend to destroy him.[6]

One wonders, however, (to linger over Freud rather than
Nietzsche for a moment) whether Malraux or a like-minded
political philosopher might not feel justified in objecting to the
appellation of Eros for the principle opposed to the death wish.
It seems too narrow a title; it points toward sex, not politics. And
yet the name of Eros has a long tradition, not exactly calculated
to oppose Malraux's meaning of the generally creative powers
of humanity. Plato's Eros, "the love of generation and of birth
in beauty," universal because "to the mortal creature, generation
is a sort of eternity and immortality"[7] is the perfect beginning
for that tradition, and an evidence of how persistent a single
thought-motif can be. And the Freudian Eros combines creativity
with the web of libidinal ties that bring about social cohesion and
solidarity. A certain political conservatism is, however, implicit
in the Freudian interpretation of ties among human persons that
Malraux's "fraternity" does not tolerate. Is it because authoritarianism as well as heroic leadership, the "physiological" as well
as the creative features of the exercise of power, rest on an Eros
(rest also on a perverse species of the will to power) that Malraux
has not chosen to make use of this term or to align himself more
closely with its theory? Such a conclusion is speculation. The
mainstream of psychoanalytic practice attempts to adjust men,

6 V.S., p. 642.
7 *The Works of Plato*, ed. Irwin Edman, New York, The Modern Library,
1928: *Symposium*, p. 374.

taken one by one, to their particular situations rather than to foster common rebellion against a common and imposed condition of domination by human or natural forces. Malraux is not enamored of the illusion-piercing process, to which psychologies are prone, of interpreting man's acts not in their own terms, but in terms of their secret and often sordid causes. In psychology Malraux is thus not so close to Freud as he might seem. He might be placed closer to Nietzsche if the thought of both on these points had more precision.

But in explaining these imprecise dualisms, let it be noted that these concepts, like all philosophical concepts, are renewed rather than entirely new in each author. Any age that does not believe in an independent God is likely to find a way to transfer the struggle between God and the Devil into the human realm. When Giovanni Pico della Mirandola's *Oration on the Dignity of Man* speaks of men who have the unhindered power to make themselves more in the semblance of angels or more like beasts, we know that we are not far from the opinion of Nietzsche when he spoke of the philosophers, artists and saints who had made themselves truly human and *"no-longer-animals."* We are equally close to Malraux's humanism, which "does not consist in saying, 'No animal could have done what we have done,' but in declaring: 'We have refused to do what the beast within us willed to do, and we wish to rediscover Man wherever we discover that which seeks to crush him in the dust' . . . for a man becomes truly Man only when in quest of what is most exalted in him."[8]

REASON, HISTORY, CREATION

Both Nietzsche (despite his declarations against romantics and in praise of the Enlightenment) and Malraux are in reaction against the Enlightenment and its rationalistic and optimistic

---

[8] Nietzsche, *The Use and Abuse of History,* New York, The Liberal Arts Press, 1949, pp. 40, 63 et passim. *Reflections on Our Age,* p. 84.

ideals; both thus qualify as "romantics" in one sense of the word. Nietzsche attacked the idea of a universal dissemination of knowledge as "dangerous": the spread of scientific values would degrade society by their encouragement of skepticism, objectivism, and moral relativism; skepticism devitalizes the necessary myths and life-giving illusions of a society, objectivism subverts independent (therefore subjective) moral judgment of the present and the past (*"You can explain the past only by what is most powerful in the present"*), thereby demeaning independent action, and moral relativism debases all moralities, bringing them down to the level of the meanest egoism. Malraux regards the humanist optimism that is the heritage of the Enlightenment as blind, deceptive, and unjustified, its objectivism as a tool for falsifying history by killing off its significant personages with a penstroke, and its science unleashed as the final human menace; "Science," he says, "means Bikini." And before it meant Bikini, it meant the gas attack of *Altenburg,* or perhaps the psycho-conditioning of Pavlov; all denials of the Baconian and Enlightenment dreams of nature-conquest by a tool which has taken on a life and movement of its own and has become an instrument of fate's conquest of man.[9]

In both cases Enlightenment ideals are rejected in favor of a philosophy which puts a high value on action. "Measure the height of what thou knowest by the depths of thy power to *do.*" Nietzsche's ideas of history, action, and art enter in combination when, rejecting the movement of German historicism, he adopts as a motto Goethe's phrase, "I hate everything that merely instructs me without increasing or directly quickening my activity." All past history is most properly viewed as a conflict between the creators of art and value and the sometime consumers of art. In the present, history (now considered as history writing and history reading, a process of education for historical greatness

[9] "Man and Artistic Culture," in *Reflections on Our Age,* passim.

through the interpretation of past and history-making acts) must be made to serve the creators of the moment (always an esthetically, if not always socially, superior few) by inciting them to undertake great actions, to *make* history in the act. The written record or myth of the past available to the present is put to service to spur the inhabitants of the present to action. Malraux seems to espouse this sort of account when he talks (infrequently) of history writing; but generally he means by history a form of "destiny"—those conditions and tendencies inherited from the human past which tend to circumscribe man, and against which his action must be directed: the value—action, creative action in the present—is the same.

Both men are in opposition to the historicists of their time while assimilating from the opposition certain historical values useful for present life; one rejected Hegel's conservative influence in favor of a command in history to be a creator, to rise above the mediocrities of everyday life, to produce a masterwork; the other opposed Spengler's extreme pessimism in favor of an engagement in all forms of historical action. Both agree that action in history involves the extensive use of myths to incite to action, in place of an "objective" (equated to academic and quietist) interpretation of "reality"; but Malraux, in a time filled with history writers with objectivist ideals and training, has fewer hopes for the mythical potential of the discipline of history writing. For both Nietzsche and Malraux, creative action in history involves and must be tied to a destruction of the old reality, the old forms of life and society. "How dear a payment has the setting up of *every* ideal in the world exacted? . . . To enable a sanctuary to be set up, *a sanctuary has got to be destroyed:* that is a law—show me an instance where it has not been fulfilled!"[10]

Nietzsche developed his idea of history further than Malraux

---

[10] Nietzsche, *Use and Abuse*, pp. 3, 86; *Genealogy of Morals*, pp. 714-715.

does his; but most of what Nietzsche had to say could quite easily and without confusion be assimilated to what Malraux does say. "Man is always resisting the great and continually increasing weight of the past; it presses him down and bows his shoulders": would these words be inappropriate as an introduction to the figure of Malraux's artist, in revolt against the burden of the forms of the past that stand in the way of his own creation? The load of the past is the same; so is the service it may be forced to render. "Historical study is only fruitful for the future if it follows a powerful, life-giving influence, for example, a new system of culture. . . . History is necessary to the living man . . . in relation to his action and his struggle" (*Use and Abuse*, pp. 5, 12).

The categories of antiquarian, critical and monumental history are worth noting as methods and styles of making the past do service to the present. Abused, antiquarianism ceases to inspire, turns into mad learning-collection, a "raking over all the dust-heaps of the past"; criticism deceives its users into believing that they have escaped the situation, influence, and error of the past; monumentalism degrades the work of the present by too much worshiping at the shrines of old gods or, turned into rootless myth, drives egoists to frenzies of violence in attempts at mad emulation of fantasies of great conquerors whose lives never resembled their myths and images. Used rightly, in the service of life (the true and legitimate will-to-power) all is altered. Antiquarian history teaches us our roots, and how to revere what has been accomplished by those who preceded us. This history that teaches us to know our past is complemented by critical history, which teaches us to destroy it, so that it will not limit and inhibit the present. An objective statement of old fact will not do: "Man must have the strength to break up the past. . . . He must bring the past to the bar of judgment, interrogate it remorselessly, and finally condemn it. Every past is worth condemning. . . . 'For everything that is born is *worthy* of being destroyed' " *(Use and*

Abuse, pp. 20, 21). Monumental history fixes on the great figures of the past, to hearten the present, to give comfort by example in the face of contemporary mediocrity, to inspire imitation and emulation, to set up archetypal images that give a powerful spirit the impulse it needs to quicken it. "The man of action and power who fights a great fight . . . needs examples, teachers, and comforters: he cannot find them among his contemporaries" *(Use and Abuse,* p. 12). One thinks of Malraux's "On Saint-Just," of his own preoccupation with monumental figures, heroes of adventure or politics or art: Lawrence, De Gaulle, Goya; and of Malraux's created figures.

For Nietzsche, in order to live our lives we must possess all these three varieties of history, to provide us with examples, with a continuing bond to our past, and at the same time with a way to criticize and destroy the past and drop its burden. Think of *The Voices of Silence:* the exemplars, the great painters who have overcome their own condition as men; the persistent connection with the past, which we make *our* past through our constant resurrections of its art; the recurrent rebellion against the past imposed upon us, the break with inherited tradition, destruction of former innovations that have now become bars to new creation—all are there. And then think of what Nietzsche means by the "life" history is to be utilized to serve: action; and by "action," creation. Malraux creates art, creates a history, guided by an esthetic philosophy of history; Nietzsche is in the process of expounding just such an esthetics of history. For Nietzsche historical action may itself be termed "art," then, in the same sense that it may be explicitly creative and to the extent that it is. Malraux has not gone quite so far in suggesting that art and action are indistinguishable, but he has found them to be highly compatible and both to involve the quest to "translate the widest possible experience into consciousness." And this means, equally well: to change one's attitude toward one's experience of the world from passive reception and habitual response to mental activism, organizing and interpreting experience into knowledge and voluntary myth by a conscious act; to make the experience one has of human life into art; to organize the exterior world in terms of one's own ideas, by application of the conscious will, by action.[11]

All the uses of history belong to a variety of consciousness which Nietzsche calls the "historical." As the memory to the mind of the individual, this segment, functional to consciousness considered as a whole and in general, does not stand alone. It coexists with and is opposed to elements Nietzsche calls "unhistorical" and "superhistorical." "The unhistorical and the historical are equally necessary to the health of an individual, a community, and a system of culture." A surfeit of history such as Nietzsche finds to characterize modern men, too much awareness of the reality of the past, of the status of events as part of a gross historic flux, is a weakness accentuating the distinction men tend to make between an inner and an outer world, a self-controlled realm and a domain of necessity, when on the contrary health ("life"; creation) requires that the distinction be effaced and the sphere of power extended. Excessive historical consciousness weakens the personality by tending to make men into the spectators at a free-flowing chaos of events, leads them to think of themselves as either the culmination or the tail end of history, destroys the life-giving illusions that men and nations must have, and sets an age to looking at itself in ironic and eventually cynical terms or to demanding that men submit themselves to the processes of history that do not depend on men. The unhistorical consciousness contends with these processes, as is fitting: presented with the limitations of history, it *forgets* them in order to disencumber action.[12]

The "superhistorical" view, too, sees history within its own limitations, sees it as in no way evolving from lower to higher,

11 See *The Case for De Gaulle*, p. 70.
12 See *Use and Abuse*, pp. 8, 22-65, 69.

sees no finality in it; if a man holds this view, and yet does not divorce himself from life, he will return from the endless becomings of the world to "that which gives existence an eternal and stable character—to art and religion." Supplied with the antidotes of the unhistorical and the superhistorical, as well as with all functions of the historical to a poisonous degree, men may serve their health and life by transforming all three ideas into a doctrine for their own personal use. Let them become the highest specimens of humanity: for in these, and not in the end of history, lies the goal of the human race. The Greeks point the way; for once their culture was but a swarming chaos of foreign and past forms, and yet, taking Apollo's advice, they learned to "organize the chaos," and they became "the masters and models for all the cultured nations of the future." Today, in the face of a system of decorative culture, says Nietzsche (as Malraux says), in which "we crumble and fall asunder, our whole being is divided, half mechanically, into an inner and outer side; we are sown with ideas as with dragons' teeth . . . we suffer from the malady of words," each man of us may organize the chaos within himself and discover "the idea of culture as a new and finer nature, without distinction of inner and outer, without convention or disguise, as a unity of thought and will, life and appearance." The Greek split of *physis* and *nomos,* nature and social culture, along with the Cartesian split of inner and outer, is to be seen and, like man's all-too-human and almost-animal character, to be overcome. And from the potential overcoming there is postulated the being who overcomes himself—the overman.[13]

ELITISM, RELATIVITY

Despite indicated differences, the discussion has until now been dealing with similar minds taking parallel courses. But when the philosopher becomes open advocate, it is certain that not all

[13] See *ibid.,* pp. 9-11, 68-69, 72-73.

will listen; some will follow and most will not; and a complete philosophy must have some conception of both groups. Here the two thinkers most plainly diverge. Nietzsche believes that the many, subjects of the will to power, who act for pleasure, who do not "sublimate" their will into an expressive act, are dross and nothing more. Nothing can be done to raise them in the future: it is the present, and the highest types of the present, who are to be valued; in history there is no progress and no end, only the eternal recurrence of symbolically identical events. There will always be the overman and the others, and that is all that can be said. There are creators of art and consumers of art, "Dionysian" men (the term is used so as to include the Greek tragedians who worshiped in the temple of both gods, who fused Apollonian and Dionysian modes) and the spectators, critics and crowds; and they are and ought to be opposed to one another. The masses are necessarily inferior to and against the superior men, and because these "superiors" may have no political power, they may be drowned out: such is the problem of the present, for Nietzsche. On the other side, the few will remain few: but their relation with the many ought not to remain dominated by the moral rules of the age. The world is justified only as an esthetic phenomenon, there exists in thought only artist-thought, and the artist is bound to recognize only himself:

a "God," if you wish, but assuredly only a quite thoughtless and unmoral artist-God, who, in creation as in destruction, in good as in evil, desires to become conscious of his own equable joy and mastery; who, in creating worlds, frees himself from the *anguish* of . . . *over-fullness,* from the *suffering* of the contradictions concentrated within him. The world is conceived as the continuous redemption of God, as the ever-changing, ever-new vision of the most suffering, most discordant, most contradictory being, who can redeem himself only in *appearance*. . . . He who would be a creator in good and evil must first be a destroyer, and break values into pieces. Thus the greatest evil belongeth unto the greatest good; but this is the creative good. [*Ecce Homo,* pp. 924, 940]

Nietzsche's elitism, close to a religious belief in this sketch of the artist-redeemers of God and self, derives then directly from the psychology of creativity as the highest form of the will to power, as a form forever closed to the majority. It extends the diagnosis of the sickness of "modern" times begun in *The Use and Abuse of History* and develops itself most fully in *Beyond Good and Evil* and *The Genealogy of Morals,* where it is accompanied by an idea of the social and psychological relativity of moral sentiments that permits what elitism justifies, a passing beyond conventions of good and evil, of truth and lie, a revaluation of all accepted human values.

The falseness of an opinion is not for us any objection to it. . . . The question is, how far an opinion is life-furthering, life-preserving, species-preserving, perhaps species-rearing; and we are fundamentally inclined to maintain that the falsest opinions . . . are the most indispensable to us; that without a recognition of logical fictions, without a comparison of reality with the purely *imagined* world of the absolute and immutable, without a constant counterfeiting of the world . . . men could not live. [*Beyond Good and Evil,* p. 384]

A religion is to be judged by a standard which makes it at best a disciplining and educative tool with which philosophers control the people and free themselves from them—an idea Platonic in its inspiration and in the sudden *conservatism* apparent in it but devoid, for moral reasons, of any noblesse oblige. Democratic philosophy and herd morality exist to be flouted and transvalued by the philosophers of the future. Their work is dialectical: no matter what value predominates, they are obliged to transcend it. That it is the value of the mass that is in this case to be passed over is convenient and appropriate, since the philosophers of logic, politics, morality, and art are necessarily in a minority, necessarily transvaluing with their value creation, their lawgiving and commands, the received truths, the former values. It is the business of the healthy not to cure the sick, but to surpass themselves; the sick, the majority, are to be controlled by their sick priests and their own religions. Moral relativism may be theoretically correct; it is not, however, to replace religion for the masses; it does not disintegrate Nietzsche's own ideals, since "relativism" has no particular force against a creator of values. A similar relativism, similarly limited, pervades Malraux's consideration of *artistic* forms; it is not for its "beauty" that a work of art is significant, but for the content of new forms that it carries, for the new values that it expresses. This relativism, which Nietzsche's apolitical tendency permitted to subsist alongside his condemnation of relativism in the name of believed illusion, does not prevail for Malraux's politics: for there he has *chosen,* and to choose one (any) political form (as need not be true, though it may be, with the choice of expressive artistic form) is, almost inevitably, to choose it against all the others that compete with it.[14]

Because of a political choice Malraux's idea of elites differs even more strikingly than his "relativism" from the corresponding Nietzschean notion. Granted that his artists are patently and explicitly set apart from the masses, granted that more of his fictional heroes do seem to belong to a specially perceptive few than, say, to a democratized elite group or to a Leninist elite vanguard of the proletariat, Malraux still advocates no aristocracy, political or otherwise, espouses no aristocratic morality designed to justify and deepen the gap of elite and mass. At the same time that he attacks political liberalism, he proposes a democracy of culture which Nietzsche did not believe capable of existing, let alone worth supporting. To the extent that Malraux might rightly be called an elitist, he is an unwilling one, driven by a realistic assessment of the world and its existing divisions, not by a feeling of necessary and irrevocable estrangement from the many. Nietzsche sees the division between the creative few and the multitude as necessary, permanent, and at

14 See *Beyond Good and Evil,* pp. 446-448, 493-497, 514-517; *Genealogy of Morals,* pp. 752-757.

base valuable. Malraux has nothing at all to say in favor of the divorce of the artist from the masses (not even what might cautiously be said, that at least a differentiation is necessary at a time when creative ethics do not prevail, in order to let the potentially creative personality have an identity of its own not seen as governed by a hostile ethos): it is not "permanent" because, historically speaking, it has not always existed; it is therefore not necessary for all society; it is a characteristic and unpleasant phenomenon of a dying social order that will be superseded, and that ought to be deliberately replaced, not necessarily as a whole, but certainly in its more diseased and temporary portions. He finds that the sense of separation—psychologically the most important component of the actual separation—can be erased by political and state action, and in his career he has done his best to encourage its eradication. Nietzsche the antipolitical ("The man with the *furor philosophicus* in him will no longer have time for the *furor politicus,* and will wisely keep from reading the newspapers or serving a party"), even in his esthetic elitism the enemy of all existing political elites, critic of the state as innate inferior and opponent of civilization, seems to match our modern fears of indoctrination and of the all-absorbing state; Malraux, the political man par excellence, seems to complement our own fewer modern hopes.[15]

EDUCATION

Despite all these differences, education is a vital element in the schemes of both. Education as cultivation is an essential element in any philosophy which insists on a nongenetic distinction—which, however, in a few cases or many, may be overcome or is to be overcome—between the majority of men and the best of men. Nietzsche's man is commanded to "become

15 "Schopenhauer as Educator," in *Thoughts Out of Season II, The Complete Works of Friedrich Nietzsche,* v. 5, London, Fowlie, 1910, p. 181.

what he is," to realize his true nature, to set himself apart from the herd by attaining to a culture which is second and higher nature. Fear and laziness conspire to bring him down, ignorance may prevent his realization: he will be liberated only by an education—or rather, by an educator, through understanding whom he comes to understand his own being. Having made use of such educators as Schopenhauer and Wagner, having had contact with monumental history, one may give a certain personal style to his existence, in the face of what surrounds him, in opposition to his age. To become educated, to acquire culture, means always to part company with one's age—in that sense, with the culture that is in existence—to become, oneself, "super-historical," and to join the "philosophers, artists, and saints," the high human types who complete, justify, and redeem nature, who fight inwardly the blind beast, who cut down the barrier between inner and outer life, and who outwardly fight for true culture and against its parasites. The enemies of culture are its false friends—the state, the businessman, the culture-Philistine, the institutions of education and their operators—all those who try to purvey, deform, and make use of culture. Without an educational revolution one can be transfigured only in solitude and isolation, and only in opposition to whatever exists.[16]

Malraux's heroes learn in various schools, from individual "educators" as well as from the experiences of their actions and lives. His artists make use of their predecessors in order to attain their own styles; his actors-in-the-world find a communion across space and across time with those they make their exemplars; and those who are able to do so become themselves or are made educators. The "educator" has his experience and his life turned into art, and his art into something that can be passed on to others, a heritage. The educative relation is the only means of resolving the conflict between hero worship and antiauthoritarian

16 See ibid., passim.

sentiment, between the democratic virtue of fraternity and the aristocratic virtue of dignity, between the will to follow and imitate greatness and the will to fight, overcome, and destroy outstanding others. But because there must be some means of assuring this relation, of disseminating this art of the educator—which is culture—the state, whatever its weaknesses, becomes an instrument. There is no such entity as a cultured state; but there is a state which is handmaiden to culture. With respect to the state, as with respect to elites, Malraux diverges from Nietzsche. But in judging the relations between these two—between what Nietzsche tells the world and what Malraux assumes thenceforth, between what Nietzsche theorizes upon and what Malraux attempts to put into effect—the ties and the similarities are decisive. Nietzsche commented in the third of his "Thoughts Out of Season" that "at bottom, it is not 'Schopenhauer as Educator,' but his opposite, 'Nietzsche as Educator,' who is speaking." Malraux has heard him; in his own works we find as constant narrator Malraux as Educator.[17]

HEGEL: ART AS CONQUEST AND FREEDOM

Nietzsche and Hegel: quite different men, quite different philosophies. But Hegel was, like Nietzsche and like Malraux, a critic of the Enlightenment tradition, of classical rationalism and abstract individualism. Like Malraux, after an early sympathy with revolution Hegel took a critical turn and ended within the body of the state without apology. A passage from one of his early writings, "On Classical Studies," may begin to dispel the air of absolute uniqueness which sometimes seems to surround him.

The progress of culture must not be regarded as the quiet continuation of a chain in which the newer links, though attached to the older ones

[17] *Ecce Homo*, p. 877.

without incongruity, are made of fresh material, and the work of forging them is not directed by what has been done before. On the contrary, culture must have earlier material on which it works and which it changes and modifies. It is necessary that we appropriate the world of antiquity not only to possess it, but even more to digest and transform it.[18]

Here begins the sense of history and of conflict within the organized culture of mankind; here, with art, enters the historical and history-transcending revolt that Hegelian parlance has named "dialectic."

Hegel's later *Philosophy of Fine Art,* despite a series of vigorous attacks on foes who subsequently fall victim to Malraux's partisan esthetic (delectation, the reduction of creation to rote production, the mimetic and naturalistic biases), seems to move off into the extreme attempt at complexity that parodies the most commonplace image of Hegelian thought. Art here proceeds from an absolute idea in order to achieve the sensuous representation of the absolute itself. "The level and excellency of art in attaining a realization adequate to its idea, must depend upon the grade of inwardness and unity with which Idea and Shape display themselves as fused into one." On the road to the artistic summit there is the celebrated evolution of the art-spirit, and of its subject matter—the conceptions of the world, the consciousness of nature, man and God—through a series of stages in which the various particular arts are realizing the self-unfolding Idea of beauty.[19]

Very nineteenth-century: but, without the certainty of upward evolution to a final perfection and of the absoluteness of the Idea, not so entirely far from the twentieth century either, as the discussion of the metaphysical ground and function of art once

18 G. W. F. Hegel, *Early Theological Writings,* trans. T. M. Knox, Chicago, U. Chicago Press, 1948, p. 327.
19 B. Bosanquet, *The Introduction to Hegel's Philosophy of Fine Art,* London, Kegan Paul, 1886, pp. 133-175.

more demonstrates. Art escapes the flux of being and transience that is nature: "Upon that which, in works of art, the mind honors from its own inner life, it is able, even on the side of eternal existence, to confer *permanence.*" It functions as a revelation of *"the truth,* in the form of sensuous artistic shape," of the very Hegelian truth of unity, of reconciliation of antithesis; of the truth also that man lives in two worlds, skewed and likewise in need of reconciliation, "inward freedom and natural necessity," man who is the "prisoner in common reality and earthly temporality, oppressed by want and by poverty, hard driven by nature, entangled in matter" and who yet "exalts himself to eternal ideas, to a realm of thought and freedom" (Bosanquet, pp. 55, 102, 105).

The ontological ground of art in human nature, its necessary origin, is for Hegel precisely the same as the basis of knowledge and of action. "The universal and absolute need out of which art . . . arises has its source in the fact that man is a *thinking* consciousness, *i.e.,* that he draws out of himself, and makes explicit *for himself,* that which he is, and, generally, whatever is." This is a species of self-realization, and simultaneously of self-discovery and self-creation, accomplished through all species of *"practical* activity" in the medium directly given to man, achieved, then, by man's "modification of external things upon which he impresses the seal of his inner being, and then finds repeated in them his own characteristics." Man's initial alienation from the outer world is the motive for the whole range and variety of phenomena that constitute human activity: art is but one "mode of self-production in the medium of external things" through which man acts "as a free subject to strip the outer world of its stubborn foreignness, and to enjoy in the shape and fashion of things a mere external reality of himself. . . . The universal need for expression in art lies, therefore, in man's rational impulse to exalt the inner and outer world into a spiritual consciousness for himself, as an object in which he recognizes his own self" (Bosanquet, pp. 58-60).

ALIENATION, TRAGEDY, AND ART

It is in his deprecation of rationalism and of the philosophies of history that progress to a high completion in favor of an assertion of the permanently tragic character of human existence that Malraux leaves Hegel behind. But tragic implications in Hegel's scheme suggest that he is not far to the rear.

Although he has antecedents (Goethe, St. Paul), Hegel is now held largely responsible for the newly respected idea of alienation (Entfremdung), of recent intellectual currency more probably because of interest in the early Marx. The comparability of a philosophically technical idea (Entfremdung) with a broad literary construct (la condition humaine) becomes rapidly evident. Hegel believes that the mind, setting up a concept of itself as a Self, an identity, necessarily sets up concepts of Others, over against it and separate: it can and must recapture them, recognize them as its own subjective constructions, reappropriate these products of its own activity with that activity. Man's alienation from other selves and his construct world, his feeling of his own estrangement, and his search for reconcilement, are quasi-religious conditions of a human tragedy. A persistent tragedy: after each recognition and reconciliation there comes necessarily, because of the conceptual structure of the subject, because of the enormous and irreducible complexity of the universe, a new alienation, a new opposition of mind to an other-thing. In Hegel, the new oppositions are structured as a hierarchical dialectic, as oppositions in higher categories, on new and higher logical planes. In Malraux, new oppositions, new conflicts, rise less on new levels than in new time, repeating and evolving and repeating. The difference is perhaps one of emphasis. It is surely one of teleology, for Hegel seems to believe, at least half the time, in an end to history, an end to time and tragedy, a conservative utopia. A dialectical philosopher should presumably be the last (but is often the first) to credit alienation with a potential end, since such an end would seem to imply the finish of man, mind, and the dialectic itself; perhaps only the poet, free of the need to draw logical conclusions from his premises, can equably envision eternal tragedy as the inescapable condition of being man.

Man is conceived by Hegel as naturally an art worker of sorts, even in his politics: he makes patterns, forms relations, constructs knowledges and ways of looking at the world, discards them to make new ones. Man is a many-sided enterprise, a complex struggle. To bridge the gap between himself and the alien world, he attempts to conceive that world, to define its particulars, to recognize them and distinguish them, to attain to consciousness by intellectual innovation, to visualize, rationalize, and organize his own separate life. But this attempt involves not only a long-drawn-out conflict with a universe of vague details: there is also an inner life and an inner battle against inferiority, against inertia, against animal resistance to staring at the brilliant light of self-consciousness, against painful and powerful reluctance; there is the struggle of the new pattern, in whatever realm, and its creators against the old pattern, which was the treasured creation of their ancestors and appears now only as a prison—the struggle, then, against this prison and its keepers, a conflict of generations which politically looks very much like attempted revolution. Human freedom consists in making nature yield to man, conquering the environment, building new patterns after breaking old: freedom is a moment in time, the passing moment when man is reconciled with himself, his fellows, his surroundings, his past, his state, his culture.

In politics as in art, this Hegel is very little antipathetic to Malraux. Had Hegel looked less at states and more at revolutions, less at cultures and more at political changes within cultures, the differences would have been fewer; had he believed less in political stability and teleology and more in the continuity of pathos as a staple of human life, they would have been practically nonexistent.

CAMUS: ABSURD, REVOLT, ART

Albert Camus, like Malraux, found in the hopelessness and absurdity of life and the finality of death the beginnings of his philosophy, not the end of thought. We can understand very well (because they have registered on us before) the convictions "that nature or the world is distinct from and foreign to the understanding and desires of man, but is at the same time his home where he is fascinated, surpassed, and finally conquered" and "that death is the final and inescapable destiny of all men, and that man must adjust his life and actions to this inescapable destiny."[20] The first idea, developed in Camus' early *Noces* (1938), recalls the strange vegetable world of *The Royal Way*, with its population of men like insects, to which Perken and Claude Vannec are so uncannily attracted and which finally destroys its two adventurer-kings. The inhuman wind which conquers the writer at Djémila in *Noces* blows from an underground, a cavern of the mind; in that same alien and subterranean universe hunches like a squatting spider that city of Ispahan which silently traps and inhumanly destroys an invading army in *Royaume farfelu*. As to the second conviction: both Camus and Malraux have counseled increasing awareness of and revolt against the futility death assigns to human existence. It is the fact of impending death that drives Perken back to be an adventurer. It is death that composes the destiny of man, determines his historical predicament, and eventually erases his significance in *The Voices of Silence*. But it would be impossible to say of Malraux that he favors "adjustment" to the inescapable; the acts

[20] Thomas Hanna, *The Thought and Art of Albert Camus,* Chicago, Regnery, 1958, p. 5.

of his heroes and of his artists alike become gestures that fly in the face of the inescapable. Nor is Camus a mere counselor of adjustment, of passive acceptance of inevitable futility, though he reacts less strongly than Malraux. Camus' adjustment to destiny is to become conscious of it and of the inutility of achievements and to stage an intellectual revolt: "I do not see that uselessness detracts from my revolt . . . , it adds to it."[21]

The human situation was styled "absurd" by Malraux in *La tentation de l'occident.* Camus in *The Myth of Sisyphus* makes the Absurd into a carefully analyzed philosophical problem.[22] Human life is absurd—that is, essentially meaningless: once this is known, is life livable any longer, in any style, for any purpose, or, on the contrary, does the philosophy of an absurd and empty universe demand suicide? The perception of the Absurd is the perception of a Hegelian Entfremdung, "a divorce between man and his life . . . an exile without remedy" in a universe divested of its comforting hopes and satisfying illusions.[23] If one honestly believes his existence absurd and irremediable, ought he not to put an end to it? Absurdity is the relation between the need of man and the offerings of his world, their confrontation, contradiction, and struggle: if this condition can no longer be escaped by the construction of pleasing illusions, ought it not to be destroyed entirely by terminating and disposing of the being around whom and for whom it exists?

The solution to existence is not faith. It is not an acceptance of the absurd relation, not a reconciliation with it, not evasion or elusion, not a false hope which pretends to transcend the Absurd, not a great idea which betrays life by trying to give it a meaning

[21] Albert Camus, *Noces,* Paris, Gallimard, 1950, p. 31.

[22] Malraux never gives the problem of the Absurd the analysis in depth that Camus devotes to it. Just as Camus' devotion to philosophical analysis is nothing like that of Sartre, Malraux's attention to that discipline cannot match that of Camus.

[23] *The Myth of Sisyphus and Other Essays,* New York, Vintage, 1960, p. 5.

beyond itself. Camus considers all such stratagems dishonest attempts to mask the evidence, to remedy the irremediable: "philosophical suicide." Suicide itself is only an acceptance of the decree of the Absurd for man.[24] The answer to the problem of how to live is consciousness without evasion and revolt without hope. Camus' "revolt," a form of the doctrine of permanent revolution adapted to individual life, consists simply in a day-to-day refusal to bow the *mind* to the absurdity of the world: living, and living consciously, is all that is required for human freedom.[25]

There are styles of living in constant refusal of the absurdity of the world, according to the rules of revolt, of freedom from the commonly accepted goals and illusions of existence, and of passionate living-in-the-present. Don Juan's is one such style, his liberation achieved by the repetition of short-lived and reborn love, opposite of the contradictory and self-destructive illusion of one permanent devotion. The actor's is another: he mimes the ephemeral of which he is a part, he acts and acts out day after day new characters, new lives. The conqueror's life is yet another illustration (and a thoroughly Malrauvian one): knowing that no victory is eternal, that action which does not remake man and world is useless, he chooses to repeat Promethean revolutions against the gods and world, believing that his liberation consists

[24] The deceptive hope which Camus has criticized as "philosophical suicide" is the same hope which Malraux treats with respect, but ultimately rejects, in the figure of Hernandez. For Kyo and for Katov (as for Perken, had he died in the act of saving Grabot from the Mois) choosing to die is not a response to philosophical anguish and would not fall under Camus' strictures. The self-immolations of the terrorist Ch'en and the anarchist Puig, and the refusal of Hernandez to escape his own murder, are done out of Angst and probably do constitute for Malraux submissions to the Absurd.

[25] Malraux too has seen in revolt the justification of man and the restoration of his dignity. But insofar as his revolt has been followed by a political revolution that proposes a social reconstruction, he would seem to have taken a position of hope untenable to Camus. Later Camus did propose various political changes, of a more systematic nature, in fact, than any Malraux ever advocated (including a replacement of national by international government); their relation to his philosophy of human life has not been fully clarified.

in mobilizing and being mobilized.[26] These are all continual and perceptible attempts at creating, repeating, and recreating particular and privileged realities; it should therefore not surprise that most illustrative of all should be the life and life style of the creator, whether artist or philosopher, the maker of his own world: in revolt, free, variegated, futile. Such lives restore dignity to man.

It should be noted briefly that the lives of revolt which Camus affirms have been touched on rather differently by Malraux. The character type of Don Juanism may be recognized in Perken, later in Ferral; that of the actor Malraux does not touch explicitly, but it appears in the figure of the mythomaniac Clappique; that of the conqueror is seen in Perken and Garine among others; and the creator, who receives some attention in *Man's Hope*, has of course been the subject of all Malraux's books since the war. But of these only the creator has not been sooner or later rejected by Malraux.

By the time of Camus' long study of revolt, *The Rebel* (1951), his idea of artistic creation has broadened into one of philosophical revolt that is quite Malrauvian; and, like Malraux, he had turned his attention from conquerors to social revolutionaries. A revolt, whether philosophical or historical, will, if it is faithful to its origins, affirm some common value and the solidarity of all men against some oppressor—the total human condition in the case of metaphysical revolt, the immediate political oppressor in

---

[26] Camus can accept the life of the conqueror as authentic because he rejects the implication of uncontrolled behavior and violence which Malraux draws from that image. In his play *Caligula* (1938) Camus portrays Caligula as having been destroyed because his uncontrolled behavior failed to recognize that, even if there is no transcendent absolute in the universe that can command men's actions, there are nevertheless limits which cannot be transgressed. Camus continued his analysis of violence in his play *Les justes* (1949), in which the idea of limits is directly applied to the problem of revolutionary murder (which had by then ceased to concern Malraux, whose politics, when they existed, were no longer revolutionary): we are permitted to kill only if we ourselves are prepared to die.

that of historical revolt.[27] But when Camus considers political revolutions as they have been, he finds that in only a few cases have they followed the pure spirit and bowed to the limits of *Les justes*. Mostly they have ended, when victorious, by placing the former victims in the position of being oppressors and have created new victims; the solidarity which they affirmed is replaced by solitude and cruelty. Revolution creates the same oppressive, totalitarian organization against which it struggles.

This is the same problem which Malraux observed in *Man's Hope* and which he titles there that of "the manichean nature of action." But the consequences have been different for the two men who found the same obstacle. Camus rejected the Communists and remained constantly outside the organized stream of French politics, a critic of all, in permanent revolt, refusing to recognize organization and elitism as legitimate. Malraux likewise rejected Communism; but he has at least sporadically affirmed and reaffirmed political action despite its manichean nature. Malraux has repudiated the politics of murder, but not those of organization. When the question of torture, which dogged French governments through the whole Algerian rebellion, arose to plague the government of the Fifth Republic, Camus was on the outside, on the attack; Malraux was on the inside, not because he approved of torture, which he also attacked obliquely, but because he was on the side of De Gaulle. An adherence to revolt has forced Camus to compromise with history through inaction—or rather, through unorganized action; a commitment to political action has forced Malraux to compromise with history through acceptance of the philosophical taintedness of all action. And thus at last the remarkably parallel lines of their development diverge.

[27] In Malraux, solidarity or "fraternity" becomes a value which his later revolutionaries and hero-figures attempt to establish: all his heroes are in revolt against the human condition, and the revolutionaries among them identify that revolt with their historical revolt against political regimes which are immediate representatives of this metaphysical oppression.

MALRAUX AS CHALLENGER AND MALRAUX AS EDUCATOR

The claim of a political thinker to a unique place can seldom be rested effectively upon his having a number of unique ideas. Malraux employs a dualistic, moralistic psychology: so did Nietzsche, and, at times, Freud. Malraux declares the psychological predicament of a man to be his estrangement from others and his world, as did Hegel. Camus, like Malraux, holds that certain styles of life and human solidarities are proof against the Absurd. Malraux believes that art feeds on the past and destroys it, that true creativity can liberate the artist and educate those who comprehend him in the ways of freedom; Nietzsche had taken the same stand. The uniqueness of a thinker such as Malraux can lie only in his particular synthesis of elements, which as elements he shares with others. As it happens, those whom Malraux most resembles were led politically either to secession from politics (on esthetic or ethical grounds) or to views that tended to authoritarian or conservative poles. The marriage of the virtues of art and action and democracy that Malraux has managed is indeed unique, and it is this singular marriage that gives Malraux his special claim to status among the challengers of classical liberalism.

But political criticism need not stop at an orderly contemplation and management of the past, at a search for what is unique in each thinker. We ought to draw out from the history of political thought what is sympathetic and profound, so as to extend our own ideas, or what is challenging and distasteful, so as to be forced to deepen our own understanding. If this is our intent, the meaning of a comparison among thinkers alters. We no longer search for the unique, we seek to synthesize. We reinforce Malraux's representation of alienation with Hegel's, his theory of the distinctive, liberating, and educative functions of art with

Nietzsche's, so as to strengthen ideas which either threaten or preserve us.

The whole past of political thought is available to us in the same way as the whole of past art. But the past of thought can be transformed in a manner that even the museum without walls cannot match. It is valueless to understand the history of thought as no more than the reflection of a set of changing historical circumstances, or as a deserted gallery of masterpieces, to be examined by specialists whose interest ends when they have defined and tagged the special style characteristic of each master. This past is not a set of persons but a set of values, problems, and alternatives. Political thinking today suffers even more from the diseases Malraux diagnosed in modern art than that art itself. Those who want ideas of their own could do worse than to turn to the ethical and political "masterpieces" of the past (and even of the present), both to draw upon them and to reject them. Ideally, we would be able to contemplate, not the ideas of this man and that, but all the thoughts that have been thought on, for instance, "alienation." But the implicit character of so much political thought prevents this and forces us to consider the past of thought as organized around persons rather than around ideas. Those men who have thought widely, deeply, or originally about things political, and who speak to us, are our educators. One educator is not enough: the ideas of each must be compared with those of others, not for the sake of comparison but to build and to have ideas against ideas. But among the educators who speak to the present, Malraux is surely one, and not the least.

Malraux began his career with a vision of man and the world which he has not lost. In his earliest works the real world is totally denied in favor of withdrawal into a fantasied universe. Later the world begins to appear as man's world, the inherited historical and social order of the past, and it is social order which is repudiated, society, in which man is left subject to death and "destiny." Then violent negation and revolution take the place of escape and isolation from the world, which is now equated with the forces behind the social order. At last the world, the opponent against which man is still pitted, takes on the appearance of the history which is created by the men of the past, and the conflict with this world becomes symbolic and artistic as much as it is real and political. Political action becomes one portion of the creative-and-destructive act of the heroic man, and the artist joins the revolutionary in the pantheon of human heroes.

At the end, and as a logical derivative of the original vision, Malraux provides a philosophy of history and of politics which so consistently places the human and subjective values above the historical and objective that there cannot be found in his work any complete logical analysis either of what the world and politics are or what they must or will become. Considered in his own terms, what Malraux has done is to create a network of myths a priori.

In response to the psychological disorder of man's nature, Malraux has sought to construct a myth of the hero. In response to the surplus oppression of political life in our times, Malraux has tried to construct a myth of the brotherly revolution and of cultural democracy. And in response to the breakdown of cultural certainties in our day, Malraux has built a myth of the tragic conflict of man and the world and of the forms of victory that men may enjoy in that struggle. These are new myths, which create and renew, with which to destroy those that stultify and kill: they are the elements of a universal humanism.

Malraux's myths can be compressed into a moral appeal. Only a system of values that relate a man to the conditions of his life will defend him from a miserable imprisonment in his own skull. His defense can only take the form of an extenuation, from moment to moment, of the fatality that oppresses him: the humiliations that the power of other men imposes upon him; the solitude that biology creates, and that the frigidity of the modern world enlarges; his insignificant transitoriness in the permanence of nature, the certainty of his own death. A man can never be preserved forever: he can gain his repose only from moment to moment. He is defended when feels the emotions of liberty and of communion. The feeling of exalted freedom belongs to the creator of values, the mythmaker and stylemaker, at those moments when he achieves his personal style. The feeling of communion belongs to those of the creator's audience who are able to feel at one with the hero or the artist in his moment of liberation; or to those who share a common struggle against a humiliating order, a common suffering, a common death. The way to live, then, is to create art, to know art, or to struggle against the common oppressions of the social order and in favor of the least oppressive of social orders. Or, perhaps, to live as fundamental man: as a worker who knows the purpose and the value of his work (which it must then have); or as a peasant, who always comprehends the meaning of his own struggle with the earth (but this is suspect, since Malraux's peasants are seen from quite a distance). For the most part Malraux is speaking to intellectuals—to those who endeavor to make their lives correspond to a reasoned-out image of what a man's life should be. The common prerequisite for such lives is consciousness and education: in the techniques and the past of art for the artist; in the past and the nature of art for the connoisseur; in the nature of oppression, the techniques of struggle, the corrupting influence of power, and the possibilities of minimally oppressive order for the rebel.

The power to create belongs to a few; the opportunity for a clear-cut political struggle is contingent on circumstances, as is the opportunity to make the state from a burden into a support of man. Any man can be uplifted by some form of art: this is the universal solvent, and educating oneself in culture is the universal moral task. Though no one can tell or prescribe what images of Man each will draw from the heritage to transcend his solitude, all men ought to share in that heritage; and those who can, ought also to take part in the lives of creativity and action. The ideal image, the liberal hero, has a share of all three lives, falling back upon contemplation when creativity deserts him and action cheats him.

There is no question that this ethical myth of the individual is a powerful and a worthy one. Only a full comparative or synthetic study of the images of all cultures and all times would permit each of us to say where it ranks for him. It is probable that with a closer examination of Nietzsche, of Freud and his successors, of Greek ethics, of Camus and Sartre, we could draw out other authentic and liberating styles of life, images equally worthy and living.

The prospect of moments of communion, of transcendence of solitude, within human associations not dominated by the Absurd, makes it possible to turn an individual ethic concerned with psychological healing into a political utopia intended to stimulate individual and collective action. Whether one ought to be a revolutionary or a reformist (or a quietist) is for Malraux a tactical question to be decided on the basis of a calculation of opportunities, of the complex of political forces and their oppressive and liberating tendencies. American readers of Malraux are not required to become Gaullists, no matter how much of Malraux's thought they choose to make their own. For every society, and for every social level up to the world level, the calculus of oppressive and humanistic tendencies has to be made, and for every individual political situation the choice exists.

Malraux's political utopia and his method of analyzing political forces are deficient even for those who sympathize with them as far as they go. Too much is left unsaid, perhaps because it is implicit, perhaps because it is nonexistent. Despite the importance of their family life and of world politics to almost all of Malraux's heroes, there is virtually nothing in his work that suggests what a well-ordered family or world would look like (though he describes the good life for the individual and for the national state), or how much responsibility for achieving such good order is to be placed upon persons, how much devolves upon states, and how much may be left to fatality. Is there a humanist foreign policy or world utopia? Malraux is not the man to stimulate our thought in these fields. One must (in America) make do with the varied conservative, liberal, and Marxist traditions whose ethics are selfish, sterile, primitive, or unsightly (whatever the technical skills they transmit, which are very considerable): these are not foundations, they are obstacles. The same insubstantiality pervades the ethics and technics of subnational human associations. The whole organizational, sexual, recreational, interactional, and instructional (and even economic) areas of life are treated inadequately by Malraux, as by society in general, as technical instruments of human well-being, whose different arrangements (from area to area and time to time) have perceptibly different psychological consequences, and which are therefore properly the subjects of consciousness, scrutiny, ethical prescription, and political action. Men in general do not think along these lines because they are accustomed to think of their whole culture as originally given, not as an instrument subject to experimental rebuilding with a view to seeing how all society can best be designed. The students of society (anthropologists, sociologists, social psychologists, even economists) have largely pursued purely scientific rather than practical-scientific goals and are even more reluctant on the whole to engage in moral debate, engineering technology, and political action on matters of sociocultural arrangements than are the political scientists and lawyers. Malraux is no help here because his persuasive definition of culture permits him to restrict his field of vision to art (broadly defined), excluding even such products of consciousness as physical and social science and philosophy (let alone social arrangements) from his purview. Here, then, a vast work awaits. Nevertheless, Malraux has ploughed the first trench in the virgin field of cultural politics by providing an analysis of the political meaning of art, and a program for influencing it, in the interest of freedom rather than of total control.

Political theory is the object of a creative process. Therefore Malraux is bound to seem an incomplete figure; or rather, his thought, which we can make part of our past, is bound to seem insufficient. What Malraux has to say about the good life, the good state, and the life-giving myth, and what he exemplifies in the style of his life and work, make him nevertheless by any standard a significant figure. By a standard which he could accept, he is also a successful one, a creator of political ideas and values. When we have named and considered those ideas and values and the points at which they stop, the work of political criticism is ended. We have defined Malraux as educator. The work of political thought is not ended. We must become our own prophets: no one else can substitute. In this realm of thought, too, we must create to live.

SELECTED BIBLIOGRAPHY

I. WORKS BY MALRAUX

A. Books (*English Title*)

1. Fiction

The Temptation of the West (T.O.), trans. Robert Hollander, New York, Vintage, 1961.

The Conquerors (C.), trans. Winifred Stephens Whale, Ed. with postface, Boston, Beacon, 1956. (Although it is not indicated in the text, this version has been altered in at least one place. I have not observed any other alterations; this does not necessarily prove their absence.)

The Royal Way (V.R.), trans. Stuart Gilbert, New York, Smith and Haas, 1935.

Man's Fate (C.H.), trans. Haakon M. Chevalier, New York, Smith and Haas, 1934.

Days of Wrath (T.M.), trans. Haakon M. Chevalier, New York, Random House, 1939.

Man's Hope (E.), trans. Stuart Gilbert and Alastair Macdonald, New York, Random House, 1938.

The Walnut Trees of Altenburg (N.A.), trans. A. W. Fielding, London, Lehmann, 1952.

2. Art

Goya Drawings from the Prado, trans. Edward Sackville-West, London, Horizon, 1947.

The Psychology of Art, trans. Stuart Gilbert, 3 vols., New York, Pantheon, 1949-1950.

Saturn (Sat.), trans. C. W. Chilton, New York, Phaidon, 1957.

The Voices of Silence (V.S.), trans. Stuart Gilbert, New York, Doubleday, 1953.

The Metamorphosis of the Gods (M.D.), trans. Stuart Gilbert, Garden City, N. Y., Doubleday, 1960.

3. Essays

(with James Burnham) *The Case for De Gaulle,* New York, Random House, 1948.

B. *Books (French title)*

ASTERISK INDICATES THAT AN ENGLISH TRANSLATION HAS BEEN PUBLISHED.

1. Fiction

Lunes en papier, Paris, Simon, 1921.

*La tentation de l'occident, Paris, Grasset, 1926.

Royaume farfelu, Paris, Gallimard, 1928.

*Les conquérants, Paris, Grasset, 1928. *Les conquérants, version définitive,* Paris, Grasset, 1949.

*La voie royale, Paris, Grasset, 1930.

*La condition humaine, Paris, Gallimard, 1933. *La condition humaine, édition revue et corigée,* Paris, Gallimard, 1946.

*Le temps du mépris, Paris, Gallimard, 1935.

*L'espoir, Paris, Gallimard, 1937.

*Les noyers de l'Altenburg, Paris, Gallimard, 1948.

2. Art

*Dessins du Goya au musée de Prado, Geneva, Skira, 1947.

*La psychologie de l'art, Geneva, Skira, 1947-1950.

   v. 1. *Le musée imaginaire,* 1947.

   v. 2. *La création artistique,* 1949.

   v. 3. *La monnaie de l'absolu,* 1950.

*Saturne, Paris, Gallimard, 1950.

*Les voix du silence, Paris, Gallimard, 1952.

Le musée imaginaire de la sculpture mondiale, Paris, Gallimard, 1952-1954.

   v. 1. *La statuaire,* 1952.

v. 2. *Des bas-reliefs aux grottes sacrées,* 1954.
v. 3. *Le monde chrétien,* 1954.
*La métamorphose des dieux, Paris, Gallimard, 1957.

3. Collections and Selections

Oeuvres complètes, Geneva, Skira, 1945.
Romans, Paris, Gallimard, 1947.
Scènes choisies, Paris, Gallimard, 1946.

4. Essays, pamphlets, etc.

*Esquisse d'un psychologie de cinéma, Paris, Gallimard, 1946.
Boukharine. Les problèmes fondamenteaux de la culture contemporaine, Paris, Association pour l'étude de la culture soviétique, n.d.
De Dimitrov à Thälmann. Echec au Fascisme, Paris, Bureau d'éditions, 4 rue Saint-Germaine-l'Auxerrois, n.d.
Ecrit pour une idole à trompe, ronéotypie, 1921.

C. *Articles and Fragments*

1. Articles

"D'une jeunesse européenne," *Ecrits, Les cahiers verts,* v. 70, Paris, Grasset, 1927, pp. 129-153.
"Ecrit pour un ours en peluche," *900,* summer 1927.
"Malraux nous parle de son oeuvre," *Monde,* Oct. 18, 1930.
"Réponse à Léon Trotsky," *Nouvelle Revue Française (NRF),* Apr. 1931, pp. 501-507, translated in *The Nation,* v. 144, p. 351.
"Jeune Chine," *NRF,* Jan. 1, 1932, pp. 5-7.
"L'art est un conquête," *Commune,* Sept.-Oct. 1934, pp. 68-71.
"L'attitude de l'artiste," *Commune,* Nov. 1934, pp. 166-175.
"Literature in Two Worlds," *Partisan Review,* Jan.-Feb. 1935, pp. 14-19.
"L'oeuvre d'art," *Commune,* July 1935, pp. 264-266, translated in *Partisan Review,* Oct.-Nov. 1935, pp. 41-43.
"Interview with Malraux," *New Republic,* June 24, 1936, p. 218.
"The Cultural Heritage," *New Republic,* Oct. 21, 1936, pp. 315-317.
"Forging Man's Fate in Spain," *The Nation,* March 20, 1937.

"Laclos," *Tableau de la littérature française,* pp. 417-428, Paris, Gallimard, 1939.

"Interview with Malraux," *Horizon,* Oct. 1945, pp. 236-242.

"Man's Death Is the Problem," *New Republic,* Nov. 15, 1948, pp. 11-13.

"Culture," *Liberté de l'esprit,* Feb. 1949, pp. 1-2.

"N'était-ce donc que ça?" *Liberté de l'esprit,* April-June 1949, pp. 49-51, 86-87, 117-118.

"Un humanisme universelle," *Liberté de l'esprit,* June-July 1950, pp. 97-100.

"Dix ans après," *Liberté de l'esprit,* June-July 1950, p. 103.

"De l'art et des masses," *Liberté de l'esprit,* June 1951, pp. 177-180.

"Barrès," in Pierre de Boisdeffre, ed., *Barrès parmi nous,* Paris, Dumont, 1952, pp. 189-190.

"Qu'est-ce que de musée?" *Arts,* June 8, 1954, p. 1.

"Nouvelle Gauche" articles, *L'express,* Dec. 25, 1954, p. 10; Jan. 29, 1955, pp. 8-10.

"The 'New Left' Can Succeed!" *Yale French Studies,* v. 15, pp. 49-60.

"Malraux Replies to 13 Questions," *Partisan Review,* Spring 1955, pp. 157-70.

An article on religion and tolerance, *L'express,* May 21, 1955.

"Lawrence and the Demon of the Absolute," *Hudson Review,* 1956, pp. 519-32.

"Sketch for a Psychology of the Moving Pictures," in S. K. Langer, ed., *Reflections on Art,* Baltimore, Johns Hopkins, 1958, pp. 317-27.

2. Fragments

"La genèse des chants de Maldoror," *Action,* April 1920, pp. 13-14.

"Mobilités," *Action,* July 1920, pp. 13-14.

"Prologue," *Action,* Oct. 1920, pp. 18-20.

"Journal d'un pompier du jeu de massacre," *Action,* Aug. 1921, pp. 16-18.

"Le voyage aux îles fortunées," *Commerce,* summer 1927, pp. 95-131.

"Les conquérants, fragment inédit," *Bifur,* Dec. 31, 1929.

"A l'hôtel des sensations inédités," *Marianne,* Dec. 13, 1933.

"War and Tyranny: two chapters from an unfinished novel," *Twice a Year*, no. 8-9, New York, 1942, pp. 24-53.

"Résurrections," *Liberté de l'esprit*, Jan. 1950, pp. 1-2.

D. Prefaces and Introductions

1. Prefaces

D. H. Lawrence, *L' amant de Lady Chatterley*, Paris, Gallimard, 1932 (trans. *Yale French Studies* 11).

William Faulkner, *Sanctuaire*, Paris, Gallimard, 1933 (trans. *Yale French Studies* 10, pp. 92-94).

Andrée Viollis, *Indochine S.O.S.*, Paris, Gallimard, 1935.

Bergeret and Gregoire, *Messages personnels*, Bordeaux, Bière, 1945.

Manès Sperber, ". . . qu'une larme dans l'océan," Paris, Calman-Lévy, 1952.

P. E. Jacquot, *Essai de stratégie occidentale*, Paris, Gallimard, 1953.

Jeanne Delhomme, *Temps et destin*, Paris, Gallimard, 1955.

Izis [Bidermanas], *Israël*, Lausanne, La guilde du livre, 1955.

Albert Ollivier, *Saint-Just et la force des choses*, Paris, Gallimard, 1954 (trans. *Partisan Review*, fall 1955, pp. 465-474.)

André Parrot, *Sumer*, Paris, Gallimard, 1960.

Les manuscrits à peintures en France du XIIIe siècle, Paris, Bibliothèque Nationale, 1955.

2. Introductions

Charles Maurras, *Mademoiselle Monk*, Paris, Stock, 1923.

Tout l'oeuvre peint de Léonard de Vinci, Paris, Gallimard, 1950.

Vermeer de Delft, Paris, Gallimard, 1952.

Van Gogh et les peintres d'Auvers chez le Docteur Gachet, Paris, L'amour de l'art, 1952.

E. Reviews in the NRF, 1922-1935

1. Major

M. Arland, *Où le coeur se partage*, Feb. 1928, p. 250.

G. Bernanos, *L'imposture*, Mar. 1928, p. 406.

208 BIBLIOGRAPHY

Marquis de Sade, *Contes, historiettes et fabliaux* and *Dialogue d'un prêtre et d'un moribund*, June 1928, p. 853.
Alexandre Violette, *Battling le ténébreux*, Dec. 1928, p. 869.
Hermann Keyserling, *Journal de voyage d'un philosophe*, June 1929, p. 884.
D. H. Lawrence, *L'amant de Lady Chatterley*, Jan. 1932, pp. 5 ff. (trans. *Yale French Studies* 11).
Franz Hellens, *Documents secrets*, Apr. 1932, pp. 815-16.
"Exposition Fautrier," Feb. 1933, p. 345.
M. Matveev, *Les traqués*, June 1934, p. 1014.
Jean Guéhenno, *Journal d'un homme de quarante ans*, Jan. 1935, p. 148.
Ilya Ehrenburg, *Sans reprendre haleine*, Nov. 1935, p. 770.
André Gide, *Les nouvelles nourritures*, Dec. 1935, p. 935.

2. Other

July 1922, p. 97.
Aug. 1922, p. 227.
May 1923, p. 836.
Apr. 1927, p. 550.
June 1927, p. 813.
Aug. 1927, p. 253.
Nov. 1927, p. 686.
Dec. 1929, p. 838.
Feb. 1931, p. 298.
Apr. 1931, p. 488.
Feb. 1932, pp. 345-46.
May 1932, p. 915.

F. Speeches

"Every man endeavors to think his life," Congress of Soviet Writers, Aug. 1934, in *Yale French Studies* 18, pp. 27-28.
"Rejoinder to the Sixty-Four," International Association of Writers for the Defense of Culture, Paris, Nov. 1935, in *Yale French Studies* 18, pp. 28-31.

"Our Cultural Heritage," International Association of Writers for the Defense of Culture, London 1936, in *Yale French Studies* 18, pp. 31-38.

"Man and Artistic Culture," UNESCO Conference, Sorbonne, Nov. 4, 1946, in *Reflections on Our Age,* New York, Columbia, 1949, pp. 84-97.

"Address to the Intellectuals," Paris, Salle Pleyel, March 5, 1948, postface to *The Conquerors,* Boston, Beacon, 1956.

"What Stand Will You Take?" Congress of Cultural Freedom, June 6, 1952, in *Confluence,* Sept. 1952, pp. 3-11.

Press Conference, Paris, June 24, 1958.
Speech at the Place de l'Hôtel de Ville, July 14, 1958.
Speech at Rennes, Aug. 24, 1958.
Speech at the Place de la République, Sept. 4, 1958.
Press Conference, Paris, Apr. 9, 1959.
Speech at Ouargla, May 1, 1959.
Speech at Athens, May 28, 1959.
Speech at Brasilia, Aug. 25, 1959.
Assembly Debate, Nov. 17, 1959.
Senate Debate, Dec. 8, 1959.
Response to UNESCO Appeal, March 8, 1960.
Assembly Debate, Apr. 29, 1960.
Assembly Debate, June 24, 1960.
Assembly Debate, Nov. 5, 1960.
Senate Debate, Nov. 23, 1960.
Assembly Debate, Dec. 2, 1960.
Speech at Orléans, May 8, 1961.
Speech at Metz, May 14, 1961.
Assembly Debate, Oct. 26, 1961.
Senate Debate, Nov. 21, 1961.
Assembly Debate, Dec. 14, 1961.
Speech at New York, May 15, 1962.
Assembly Debate, June 27, 1962.
Assembly Debate, July 23, 1962.
Speech at the Palais de Chaillot, Oct. 30, 1962.
Speech at Washington, D. C., Jan. 8, 1963.

Assembly Debate, Jan. 18, 1963.
Assembly Debate, Nov. 9, 1963.
Assembly Debate, Nov. 22, 1963.
Speech at Paris, Dec. 19, 1964.

II. WORKS CONCERNING MALRAUX

A. Critical works (English)

Blend, Charles D., *André Malraux, Tragic Humanist,* Columbus, Ohio, Ohio State, 1963.
Blumenthal, Gerda, *André Malraux: The Conquest of Dread,* Baltimore, Johns Hopkins, 1960.
Frohock, Wilbur Merrill, *André Malraux and the Tragic Imagination,* Stanford, Stanford, 1952.
Gannon, Edward, *The Honor of Being a Man,* Chicago, Loyola, 1957.
Hartman, Geoffrey H., *André Malraux,* London, Bowes and Bowes, 1960.
Lewis, R. W. B., ed., *Malraux,* Englewood Cliffs, N. J., Prentice-Hall, 1964.
Righter, William, *The Rhetorical Hero,* New York, Chilmark, 1964.

B. Critical Works (French and German)

Boisdeffre, Pierre de, *André Malraux,* Paris, Editions Universitaires, 1952.
Delhomme, Jeanne, *Temps et destin,* Paris, Gallimard, 1955.
Duthuit, Georges, *Le musée inimaginable,* Paris, Libraire Jose Corti, 1956.
Hoffmann, Joseph, *L'humanisme de Malraux,* Paris, Klincksieck, 1963.
Mauriac, Claude, *Malraux ou le mal du héros,* Paris, Grasset, 1946.
Kerndter, Fritz, *André Malraux,* München, Steinbauer, 1958.
Morny, Alois, *A la rencontre d'André Malraux,* Paris, La Sixaine, 1947.
Picon, Gaëtan, *André Malraux,* Paris, Gallimard, 1945.
————, ed., *Malraux par lui-même,* Paris, Editions du Seuil, 1953.

Savane, Marcel, *André Malraux,* Paris, Richard-Masse, 1946.

Vandegans, André, *La jeunesse littéraire d'André Malraux,* Paris, Pauvert, 1963.

C. Sections of Books

1. English

Brée, Germaine, *Age of Fiction,* New Brunswick, N. J., Rutgers, 1957, pp. 182-93.

Burgum, Edwin Berry, *The Novel and the World's Dilemma,* London, Oxford, 1947, pp. 322-49.

Flanner, Janet, *Men and Monuments,* New York, Harper, 1957.

Garaudy, Roger, *Literature of the Graveyard,* New York, International Publishers, 1957.

Gide, André, *Journal,* trans. Justin O'Brien, New York, Knopf, *passim* (e.g. Sept. 4, 1936).

Gray, J., *On Second Thought,* Minneapolis, Minnesota, 1946, pp. 222-45.

Howe, Irving, *Politics and the Novel,* New York, Horizon, 1957, pp. 202-34.

Knight, E. W., *Literature Considered as Philosophy,* New York, Macmillan, 1958, pp. 128-159.

Lewis, R. W. B., *The Picaresque Saint,* Philadelphia, Lippincott, 1959, pp. 275-95.

Levin, Harry, *James Joyce,* New Directions, 1941, p. 211 et passim.

Peyre, Henri, *The Contemporary French Novel,* New York, Oxford, 1955, pp. 182-215.

Shklar, Judith, *After Utopia,* Princeton, N. J., Princeton, 1957.

Slansbury, M. H., *French Novelists of Today,* Philadelphia, U. of Pennsylvania, 1935, pp. 209-20.

Slochower, Harry, *No Voice is Wholly Lost,* New York, Creative Age, 1945, pp. 319-31.

2. French

Albérès, R. M., *Portrait de notre héros,* Paris, Le Portulan, 1945.

————, *La révolte des écrivains d'aujourd'hui,* Paris, Corréa, 1949, pp. 11-16.

Bespaloff, Rachel, *Cheminements et carrefours,* Paris, J. Vries, 1938,
pp. 22-58.

Blanchot, Maurice, *La part du feu,* Paris, Gallimard, 1949, pp. 211-
15.

Boisdeffre, Pierre de, *Métamorphose de la littérature,* Paris, Editions
Alsatiens, 1953, pp. 390-477.

Ehrenburg, Ilya, *Duhamel, Gide etc.* . . . , Paris, Gallimard, 1934.

Emery, Léon, 7 *témoins,* Lyon, Les cahiers libres, n.d., pp. 89-93.

Magny, Claude-Edmonde, *Histoire du roman français depuis 1918,*
Paris, Editions du Seuil, 1958.

Mounier, Emmanuel, *L'espoir des désespérés,* Paris, Editions du Seuil,
1953, pp. 11-81.

Rideau, Emile, *Paganisme ou Christianisme,* Tournai, Casterman,
1953, pp. 137-42.

Rousseaux, André, *Littérature du vingtième siècle,* Paris, Albin
Michel, 1949, 1953, v. 3, pp. 47-92, v. 4, pp. 174-195.

Sachs, Maurice, *Au temps du boeuf* . . . , *Nouvelle revue critique.*

————, *Le Sabbat,* Paris, Corréa, 1946.

Saint-Claire, M., *Galerie privée,* Paris, Gallimard, 1947, pp. 133-48.

Simon, Pierre-Henri, *L'homme en procès,* Paris, À la Baconnière,
1950.

Stéphane, Roger, *Portrait de l'aventurier,* Paris, Sagittaire, 1950.

D. Reviews of Works

Groethuysen, Bernard, "Les conquérants; Royaume farfelu," *NRF,*
Apr. 1, 1929, pp. 558-63.

Trotsky, Léon, "La révolution étranglée," *NRF,* Apr. 1931, pp. 488-
501.

Arland, Marcel, "L'espoir," *NRF,* Feb. 1938, pp. 303-08.

Callois, Roger, "Powers of Life," *Commonweal,* Feb. 8, 1945, pp.
390-93.

Sackville-West, Edward, "La lutte avec l'ange," *Horizon,* Oct. 1945,
pp. 242-44.

Riése, Laura, "André Malraux," *Canadian Forum,* June 1948, pp.
62-63.

"Psychology of Creation," *Magazine Art,* Apr. 1949, pp. 122-27.

Hughes, S., "Culture in Fragments," *Commonweal,* May 4, 1951, pp. 92-94.

Kirstein, L., "Aspects of French Taste," *New Republic,* Sept. 10, 1951, pp. 18-19.

Modigliani, Jeanne, "S'il y avait une esthétique de l'impérialisme," *La nouvelle critique,* Dec. 1951, pp. 31-41.

Sigean, Louis, " 'Les voix du silence' . . . ," *Liberté de l'esprit,* Jan.-March 1952, pp. 19-22, 51-52, 83-88.

Merleau-Ponty, Maurice, "Le langage indirect et les voix du silence," *Les temps modernes,* June-July, 1952.

Czapski, Joseph, "Malraux and 'The Voices of Silence,' " *Encounter,* March 1954, pp. 60-64.

Douthat, Blossom, "Nietzschean Motifs in *Temptation of the Occident,*" *Yale French Studies (YFS)* 18, pp. 77-86.

Cordle, Thomas, "The Royal Way," *YFS* 18, pp. 20-26.

Picon, Gaëtan, "Man's Hope," *YFS* 18, pp. 3-6.

Hoog, Armand, "Malraux, Möllberg and Frobenius," *YFS* 18, pp. 87-96.

Lapique, Charles, "À propos des 'Voix du silence,' " Paris, Centre de documentation universitaire, 1959.

E. *Critical Articles*

Wilson, Edmund, "André Malraux," *New Republic,* Aug. 9, 1932, pp. 346-347.

Abel, Lionel, "Malraux and the Individual," *The Nation,* Oct. 17, 1934, pp. 443-45.

Bespaloff, R., "Notes sur André Malraux," *NRF,* Oct. 1935, p. 576.

Stone, G., "André Malraux: From Death to Revolution," *American Review,* 1936, no. 7, pp. 287-300.

Drieu la Rochelle, Pierre, "Malraux, the New Man," Justin O'Brien, ed., *From the NRF,* New York, Meridian, 1959, pp. 186-93.

Levin, Harry, "Tragedy and Revolution," *Sewanee Review,* July 1937.

Rice, Philip Blair, "Malraux and the Individual Will," *International Journal of Ethics,* Jan. 1938, pp. 182-91.

Dupee, F. W., "André Malraux," *Partisan Review,* Mar. 1938, pp. 24-35.

de Pontcharra, Jean, "André Malraux . . . ," *Etudes,* May 1938, pp. 451-65.

Chevalier, Haakon M., "André Malraux: The Return of the Hero," *Kenyon Review,* winter 1940, pp. 35-46.

Slochower, Harry, "André Malraux," *Quarterly Review of Literature,* no. 1, 1945, pp. 54-64.

Wilson, Edmund, "Two Survivors," *New Yorker,* Sept. 8, 1945, pp. 74-78.

Coliar, D. M., "The Importance of Malraux," *Horizon,* Oct. 1945, pp. 226-35.

Monnerot, Jules, "Sur André Malraux," *Confluences,* Apr. 1946.

Mason, H. A., "Malraux and His Critics," *Scrutiny,* spring 1947, pp. 162-71.

Murry, J. M., "Commentary," *Adelphi,* Apr.-June 1948, pp. 129-35.

Chiaromonte, Nicola, "Malraux and the Demons of Action," *Partisan Review,* July-Aug. 1948, pp. 776-89, 912-923.

"Interrogation à Malraux," *Esprit,* Oct. 1948.

Peyre, Henri, "La saison littéraire," *French Review,* Dec. 1948, pp. 97-102.

Blanchet, André, "La religion d'André Malraux," *Etudes,* June-Sept. 1949, pp. 45-65, 289-306.

Read, Herbert, "Malraux's World of Art," *The Hudson Review,* spring 1950, pp. 140-145.

Lansner, Kermit, "Malraux's Aesthetic," *Kenyon Review,* spring 1950, pp. 340-348.

Frohock, W. M., "Notes on Malraux's Symbols," *Romanic Review,* Dec. 1951, pp. 247-81.

Girard, René, "The Role of Eroticism in Malraux's Fiction," *YFS* 11, pp. 49-54.

Delmas, Claude, "André Malraux et le communisme," *L'âge nouveau,* Feb. 1953, pp. 51-62.

Chevalier, Haakon M., "André Malraux: The Legend and the Man," *Modern Language Quarterly,* summer 1953, pp. 199-208.

Onimus, Jean, "Malraux ou la religion de l'art," *Etudes,* Jan. 1954, pp. 3-16.

Frank, Joseph, "Malraux and the Image of Man," *New Republic,* Aug. 30, 1954, pp. 18-19.

Gombrich, Ernst, "André Malraux and the Crisis of Expressionism," *Burlington Review,* Dec. 1954, pp. 374-78.

Rees, G. O., "Animal Imagery," *French Studies,* Apr. 1955, pp. 129-42.

Harrington, M., "The Political Novel Today," *Commonweal,* Oct. 28, 1955, pp. 79-82.

Herz, Micheline, "Woman's Fate," *YFS* 18, pp. 7-19.

Roedig, Charles F., "Malraux on the Novel (1930-1945)," *YFS* 18, pp. 39-44.

Albérès, R. M., "André Malraux and the 'Abridged Abyss,' " *YFS* 18, pp. 45-54.

Girard, René, "Man, Myth and Malraux," *YFS* 18, pp. 55-62.

Brombert, Victor, "Malraux: Passion and Intellect," *YFS* 18, pp. 63-76.

Blend, Charles D., "The Rewards of Tragedy," *YFS* 18, pp. 97-106.

Darzins, John, "Malraux and the Destruction of Aesthetics," *YFS* 18, pp. 107-13.

Hartman, Geoffrey H., "The Taming of History," *YFS* 18, pp. 114-128.

Roedig, Charles F., "A Bibliographical Note on Malraux's Art Criticism," *YFS* 18, pp. 129-30.

Tint, H., "Voices and Novels," *French Studies,* Oct. 1957, pp. 323-332.

Frohock, W. M., "Notes for a Malraux Bibliography," *Modern Language Notes,* June 1958, pp. 292-95.

F. Sketches

Pierre-Quint, L., "Persons and Personages," *Living Age,* Feb. 1934, pp. 512-14.

"Writers in Politics," *New Republic,* Jan. 24, 1936, p. 218.

"Forging Man's Fate in Spain," *The Nation,* March 20, 1937, pp. 315-16.

"News from Spain," *Time,* Nov. 7, 1938, pp. 59-62.

Time, Oct. 30, 1939, p. 66.

"Courage," *Saturday Review of Literature,* Jan. 11, 1941, p. 24.

"Men's Fate," *Time,* January 13, 1941, p. 76.

Creel, G., "Heroes," *Collier's,* Dec. 23, 1944, p. 28.

Peyre, Henri, "The Resistance and Literary Revival in France," *Yale Review,* Sept. 1945, pp. 84-92.

Massane, P., "Le cas Malraux," *France Libre,* Apr. 1946, pp. 454-57.

"Malraux's Hope," *Time,* June 16, 1947, p. 35.

"Malraux and De Gaulle," *Adelphi,* Apr.-June 1948, pp. 129-35.

Wertenbaker, C. C., "De Gaulle's Idea Man," *Life,* June 7, 1948, pp. 120-24.

"Poet of Violent Defeat," *World Review,* Oct. 1949, pp. 57-66.

Cocking, J., "Malraux," *World Review,* March 1951, pp. 18-25.

"Hopeful Twilight," *Time,* March 19, 1951, p. 65.

White, T. H., "The Three Lives of André Malraux," *The New York Times Magazine,* Feb. 15, 1953.

Time, Nov. 23, 1953, p. 86.

Time, Dec. 21, 1953, p. 98.

"La grand aventure d'André Malraux," *Paris-Match,* June 26, 1954, pp. 34 ff.

Life, Oct. 4, 1954, p. 129.

Flanner, Janet, "Profiles," *New Yorker,* Nov. 6, 1954, pp. 45 ff., Nov. 13, 1954, pp. 46 ff.

Time, Jan. 10, 1955, p. 19.

"Man's Quest," *Time,* July 18, 1955, pp. 24-26.

"Black Sun," *Time,* Aug. 19, 1957, p. 65.

Gênet, "Letter from Paris," *New Yorker,* Jan. 18, 1958, pp. 80-83, June 14, 1958, pp. 100-103.

Mauriac, Claude, "Malraux: Again from Letters to Action," *The New York Times Magazine,* July 6, 1958.

"Vision of Victory," *Time,* July 7, 1958, p. 20.

Hauser, E. O., "De Gaulle's One-Man Braintrust," *Saturday Evening Post,* Sept. 13, 1958, pp. 32-33.

Cate, Curtis, "Malraux at the Bastilles of Culture," *The New York Times Magazine,* May 6, 1962.

APPENDIX

Systematic Table of Ideas
(with page references to the text)

A. HUMAN NATURE
  1. Basic, 104, 114-115, 137-138
     and cultures, 24-26; Kassner as prototype, 74; dualism of, 137-138, 157, 172
  2. Western, 20-21, 63, 147
     origin, 21; decay—in T.O., 22, 42, 62, in J.E., 26-28; future, 63

B. THE HUMAN CONDITION
  1. General: Absurdity, the Absurd, 21, 30, 36, 83, 107, 138, 191
     as meaningless experience, 16-19, 26, 30, 191; and Malraux's characters, 31-32, 37, 39, 41-43, 46-48; and Perken, 33; and Claude, 35; and Garine, 3, 38, 39-41; and Clappique, 55, 57; and Kyo, 66, 70; and Kassner, 74; and the Organization Men, 103; and the liberal hero, 113, 114; and art, 145; Malraux and Camus on, 190-192, 195; mentioned, viii, 23, 28, 29, 54, 64, 78, 112, 133, 148, 199
  2. Solitude (isolation, alienation), 20, 27, 158, 188-189
     acquired, 77, 97; contingent, 35, 41, 61, 71; transcended, 63, 70-72, 74-75, 121, 129, 158, 165, 197; Malraux and Hegel on, 188-189
  3. Death, anticipation of, 190, 197-198
     obsession with, 34, 50, 51; victory over, 61, 72, 190; Malraux and Camus on, 190; aging and, 29; suffering and, 38; disease and, 39-41; mentioned, 16, 17, 39, 46, 47, 74, 81, 133, 138
  4. Destiny (history), 175
     mentioned, viii, 21, 33, 46, 99, 133, 138, 139, 142, 143, 145
  5. The World (nature, the inhuman, the elements)
     as separate, 20; as menacing, 35, 39, 74, 138, 171, 190;

man's conflict with, 21, 63, 197-198; surrender to, 60; conquest of, 21, 171; mentioned, 81

6. The Social Order
   as absurd, 3, 33, 35, 36, 39-40, 48; and humiliation, 40, 43,
   47-48, 53-54, 60, 61, 69, 85; as oppression, 67, 74-75, 138,
   197, 198; rejected, 3, 33, 43, 61, 85, 197, 198

7. Anguish (Angst, existential anxiety), 37, 59, 138
   causes, 20, 47; and Christianity, 21, 47, 49; contingent,
   67, 68, 70, 138; liberation from, 65, 138; mentioned, 29, 32,
   50, 55-57, 58, 72, 81

C. DEFENSES AGAINST THE HUMAN CONDITION
   1. General, 22, 125, 160, 197-198
      culture as sum of defenses, 22, 153-154; mentioned, xiii, 36,
      41, 74, 78, 113, 137, 138
   2. Revolt, 33, 37, 131, 175
      failed, 34, 37, 72; Malraux and Camus on, 190-194; men-
      tioned, 28, 29, 39, 45, 72, 137, 143
   3. Myth—see D below.
   4. Unsound Defenses, 129
      The Demonic, 137-138, 148
      mentioned 16, 150, 157, 158
      Conquest (violence, power), 33, 40, 61, 100; see also Action
      (E below)
         illusion of, 36, 47, 52, 66, 121, 147; defeat of, 34, 41, 47,
         51-54, 100; mentioned, 17, 21, 31, 60
      Escape, 22, 52, 54-60, 100, 147
   5. Dignity, 61, 69, 100, 101, 114
      and work, 62, 63; and social order, 62, 101, 114; men-
      tioned, 48-49, 67, 70, 95
   6. Communion (fraternity, love) 36, 74-75, 112, 114, 155, 198
      in struggle, 70, 72, 74-75, 84, 100, 121, 123, 194, 198;
      ambiguity of, 77, 85, 88-91, 99, 103; in love, 68, 84, 153,
      160; beyond struggle, across time, 101, 102, 103-104, 112-
      113, 127-129, 160; mentioned, 35, 37, 41, 43, 68-69, 71, 74,
      94-95, 125, 147
   7. Consciousness, 111, 113, 126, 158, 177-178
      tragic consciousness, 83, 98, 100, 158; mentioned, 76, 86,
      89, 114, 125, 131

Self-construction, creative education, value-creation, 126, 138-139, 184-185, 198

Artistic creation, 114, 125-126, 131, 132, 145, 198
Malraux and Camus on, 193; mentioned, 41, 111, 142, 149-150, 155

Art consumption, 112-113, 125-126, 131, 155-156, 198
mentioned, 78, 83, 84, 102, 104, 114, 130, 132

D. MYTH AS A DEFENSE
  1. General, 29-30, 62, 113, 197
     mentioned, 23, 25, 31, 61, 125
  2. Cultural Myths, ("realities") 20, 24-26, 138-139
     Western, 20-28, 62; needed, 29-30, 42-43; Malraux's proposed, 63, 113, 114-115, 197-199; mentioned, 23, 106, 152
  3. Political Myths ("utopias"), 41, 61, 62, 119
     Sorelian, 30, 61, 63, 118-119; needed, 29-30; Malraux's, 61, 63, 77, 101-102, 114, 197, 199-200; mentioned, 23, 42, 113, 168
  4. Personal or Hero-Myths, 44, 62, 63, 137, 139, 158-159
     Malraux's, 31, 44, 113, 123, 197
     The Conqueror-type, 21, 31-43, 48-54, 101
       Perken as, 32-36, 37, 41-42, 168-170; Garine as, 37-42; König as, 48-49, 53-54; Ch'en as, 49-51, 54; Ferral as, 51-54; Malraux and Nietzsche on, 168-170; Malraux and Camus on, 192-193
     The Bolshevik hero, 42-43, 71, 75, 77-78, 101
       Kyo Gisors as, 61, 70; Kassner as, 74; mentioned, 31, 44, 79, 103, 114
     The liberal hero, 78, 102, 103, 113-114, 159, 170-171, 198-199
       no single character represents, 79; emergent in Bergers, 103, 113; education of, 184-185; mentioned, 31, 144, 150

E. DEFENSE THROUGH POLITICS: DOCTRINES AND PROBLEMS
  1. General, xiii, 62-63
     myth-creation as basis of political defense, 23, 29-30, 104, 126; mentioned, 41, 63
  2. Action, activism, 66, 71, 74, 175, 177-178
     creation as, 113, 126, 174-175, 177; Nietzsche and Malraux on, 174-175, 177-178; mentioned, 61, 83, 85, 100, 125, 155

Politics as a force-field, 40, 73
    choosing forces as allies, 73, 84, 102, 114, 119, 121-123
Manicheanism of action, 77-78, 85-89, 100, 113-114, 150
    and the intellectual, 86-90; mentioned, 81, 83, 93, 98, 114
3. Revolution, lyrical revolutionism, 72, 74, 90-91, 119, 121
    in C.H., 61, 63; and terrorism, 42, 49-51; mentioned, 37,
    99, 113, 122, 123
Present and future, the chance of victory, 77, 82-83, 98, 101,
    103, 122, 165; mentioned, 61, 63, 71, 75, 79, 81, 84, 88, 91
Organization, 194
    need of, 85, 88, 93-94, 98, 101, 122; cost of, 92, 94, 98-99
    Organization Men as heroes, 65-66, 72-74, 102; as absurd,
    65, 92, 94, 96-97, 103; mentioned, 42, 63, 71, 85
4. Anarchism (Malraux's), 61, 62, 114
    mentioned, 101, 125, 198
5. Humanism, 63, 100, 102, 158-159
    evolution of Malraux's, 31, 76-77; and nationalism, 123,
    126-130; and art, 137, 146; mentioned, 103, 104, 149, 197
6. Cultural Democracy, 153-158, 160-161, 183, 185
    mentioned, 101, 103, 122, 129-130
7. Nationalism, 116, 117, 120, 123-130

F. ESTHETIC THEORIES
1. Culture, 139, 152, 153-154
    unity of art and, 132, 152; art as expression of, 139, 140,
    146-147, 152
2. Style, 132, 140-141, 143, 146-147
    changes in, 141-143, 146
3. The Artist's Revolt, 137, 142-145
    his career, 132, 141-144, 160; his freedom, 151; his mas-
    terpiece, 144-145
4. The Cultural Predicament
    the modern style, 148, 149, 151, 152, 153, 157-158; anti-
    art, 156-157, 158; the masses as cultural proletariat, 156
5. Cultural Needs
    a revival, 137, 152, 153, 159-160; a style, 137, 146, 149,
    158-159

INDEX

Note: An analytical table of Malraux's ideas, systematically grouped, appears in the Appendix on page 217, with page references to the text. These concepts are also cited in the following alphabetical index, but with references to the appropriate section of the Appendix.

Absurd, The, *see* Appendix, B 1
Action, *see* Appendix, E 2
A.D., 21-22; mentioned, 19, 25, 29, 62
Aging, *see* Appendix, B 3
Alienation, *see* Appendix, B 2
Alvear, 81-84; mentioned, 86, 92-93, 103, 131
Anarchism, *see* Appendix, E 4
Angst, *see* Appendix, B 7
Anguish, *see* Appendix, B 7
Antiart, *see* Appendix, F 4
Art consumption, *see* Appendix, C 7
Artist, the, *see* Appendix, F 3
Artistic creation, *see* Appendix, C 7
Artistic style, *see* Appendix, F 2

Barrès, Maurice, 117, 124-129, 154, 165, 168
Berger, Vincent, 109-113; mentioned, 103-104, 107, 120, 131, 159, 168
Berger, young, 112-113; mentioned, 103, 131
Bolshevik hero, *see* Appendix, D 4

Camus, Albert, viii, 1, 168, 190-195, 199
Ch'en, 46-51; mentioned, 54, 58, 66, 168, 192
Clappique, 54-58; mentioned, 18, 47, 60, 193
Claude (Vannec), 34-36; mentioned, 42, 62, 71, 120, 130, 170, 190

Communion, *see* Appendix, C 6
Conqueror, The, *see* Appendix, D 4
Conquerors, The, 36-43; and *Man's Hope,* 78, 121; and *The Walnut Trees of Altenburg,* 78; and *The Voices of Silence,* 148; and *Man's Fate,* 78, 121, 148; and *Days of Wrath,* 39, 78, 121; and *Lunes en papier,* 16; and *Royaume farfelu,* 32; and *"D'une jeunesse européenne,"* 42-43; and *The Royal Way,* 36-37, 42; and *The Temptation of the West,* 42; mentioned, 3, 5, 19, 45
Conquest, *see* Appendix, C 4
Consciousness, *see* Appendix, C 7
Consumption, art, *see* Appendix, C 7
Creation, artistic, *see* Appendix, C 7
Creation of myths, *see* Appendix, E 1
Creative education, *see* Appendix, C 7
Criticism, political, vii-xi, 195-196
Critique of Malraux's thought, xi-xii, 139-140, 145-146, 148-149, 151, 153-155, 159, 164-165, 199-201
Cultural democracy, *see* Appendix, E 6
Cultural myths, *see* Appendix, D 2
Culture, *see* Appendix, F 1

Days of Wrath, 72-76; and *Man's Hope,* 74, 76, 78, 79, 102-103; and *The Walnut Trees of Altenburg,*

76, 77, 79, 102-103, 122; and *The Conquerors*, 39, 78, 121; and *Man's Fate*, 18, 44, 72-76, 78-79, 121; and *The Royal Way*, 76; and *Royaume farfelu*, 18; mentioned, 6, 7, 65, 119

Death, *see* Appendix, B 3

Defense (against the human condition), *see* Appendix, C, D, E

De Gaulle, Charles, and Malraux, 8-11, 119-127; mentioned, 2, 73, 150, 154, 165, 177, 194

Democracy, cultural, *see* Appendix, E 6

Demonic, the, *see* Appendix, C 4

Destiny, *see* Appendix, B 4

Dignity, *see* Appendix, C 5

Disease, *see* Appendix, B 3

"D'une jeunesse européenne," 23-30; and *The Conquerors*, 42-43; and *The Temptation of the West*, 23-24; and *The Royal Way*, 42; mentioned, 5, 104

Education, creative, *see* Appendix, C 4

Elements, the, *see* Appendix, B 5

Eros, 137, 172

Escape, *see* Appendix, C 4

Esthetics, Malraux's, *see* Appendix, F

Ferral, 46-48; mentioned 18, 51-54, 58, 61, 147, 157, 193

Fraternity, *see* Appendix, C 6

Freud, Sigmund, 137, 195, 199; dualistic psychology, 171-173

Future and present, *see* Appendix, E 3

Garcia, 84-93; and Manuel and Magnin, 78, 82, 85, 92, 95, 98, 99, 103; mentioned, 78, 82, 95, 98-99, 101, 103, 111, 131, 150

Garine, 37-42; and Perken, 37, 38, 41-42, 62, 71, 193; and Kyo, 61, 67, 71, 73, 75, 79, 121; and power, 73, 101, 121; mentioned, 3-4, 61, 62, 67, 71, 73, 74, 75, 79, 101, 113, 121, 169, 193

Gisors, Kyo, *see* Kyo Gisors

Gisors, Old, 57-63; mentioned 47, 52, 55, 67, 70, 78, 103, 121

Grabot, 34-35; mentioned, 62, 170, 192

Hegel, G. W. F., 185-191; cultural dialectic, 186; art, 187, 189; mentioned, 165, 175, 195

Hemmelrich, 61-65; mentioned, 47, 69, 121

Hernandez, 85-88; mentioned, 79, 81-82, 91, 168, 192

Hero, Bolshevik, *see* Appendix, D 4

Hero, liberal, *see* Appendix, D 4

Hero myths, *see* Appendix, D 4

History, *see* Appendix, B 4

Human condition, the, *see* Appendix, B

Human nature, *see* Appendix, A

Humanism, *see* Appendix, E 5

Inhuman, the, *see* Appendix, B 5

Isolation, *see* Appendix, B 2

Kassner, 72-75; and Kyo, 44, 65, 72-73, 75, 102; mentioned, 18, 44, 65, 102, 131, 168

Katov, 65-67; mentioned, 45-46, 51, 63, 69, 72, 75, 192

König, 47-49; mentioned, 53-54, 61, 63-64, 69

Kyo Gisors, 65-70; and Kassner, 44, 65, 72-73, 75, 102; and Garine, 61, 67, 71, 73, 75, 79, 121; mentioned, 40, 44-49, 51, 55-59, 61, 63, 72-73, 75, 79, 87, 99, 102, 103, 121, 192

Liberal hero, *see* Appendix, D 4

Ling, 19-22; mentioned, 31, 62-63, 104

Love, *see* Appendix, C 5

Lunes en papier, 16-17; and *Royaume farfelu*, 17; and *The Conquerors*, 16

Lyrical illusion, *see* Appendix, E 3

Magnin, 91-95; and Manuel and

Garcia, 78, 82, 85, 92, 95, 98, 99, 103; mentioned, 78, 82-83, 85, 88, 97-99, 101-103

Malraux, André
career, xii-xiii, 1-12, 115-117, 119-124
characters as moral prototypes, 32
and the Communists
  alliance with, 4-6, 44, 73, 102-103, 111, 120-122; breach with, 8, 103, 111, 122, 194
cultural policies, 11, 116, 127-130, 154, 161-165
and De Gaulle, 8-11, 119-127
esthetics, *see* Appendix, F
literary style
  argument, structure of the, 46-47, 76, 78-81; comic aspects of, 17, 38-39; in the early works, 15-19; plot, structure of the, 45-46, 72
originality, 195
politics, *see* Appendix, E
unity of his thought, Ch. 5

Malraux's thought, critique of, xi-xii, 139-149, 145-146, 148-149, 151, 153-155, 159, 164-165, 199-201

Man, Western, *see* Appendix, A 2

Manicheanism, *see* Appendix, E 2

Man's Fate, 71-76; and *Man's Hope*, 46, 74, 76, 78-80, 121, 131; and *The Walnut Trees of Altenburg*, 76, 78-79, 131; and *The Voices of Silence*, 131, 148, 157; and *The Conquerors*, 78, 121, 148; and *Days of Wrath*, 18, 44, 72-76, 78-79, 121; and *Royaume farfelu*, 18; and *The Royal Way*, 46, 76; and *The Voices of Silence*, 131, 148, 157; mentioned, 6, 40, 44, 129

Man's Hope, 76-104; and Camus, 193-194; and *Man's Fate*, 46, 74, 76, 78-80, 121, 131; and *Days of Wrath*, 74, 76, 78-79, 102-103; and *The Royal Way*, 76; and *The Walnut Trees of Altenburg*, 76-79, 81, 102-105, 111, 131, 150; and *The Conquerors*, 78, 121; and *The*

Voices of Silence, 111, 131; mentioned, 7

Manuel, 95-99; and Magnin and Garcia, 78, 82, 85, 92, 95, 98, 99, 103; mentioned, 78, 82, 85, 92, 102-103, 122, 168

Masses, The, *see* Appendix, F 4

May (Gisors), 68-69

Modern style, *see* Appendix, F 4

Möllberg, 103-112; mentioned, 120, 131

Myths, *see* Appendix, D

Myths, creation of, *see* Appendix, E

Myths, cultural, *see* Appendix, D 2

Myths, heroic, *see* Appendix, D 4

Myths, personal, *see* Appendix, D 4

Myths, political, *see* Appendix, D 3

Nationalism, *see* Appendix, E 7

Nature, *see* Appendix, B 5

Nature, human, *see* Appendix, A

Nietzsche, Friedrich, 168-185, 195-196, 199; overman, 169-171, 179-180; activism, 174-175; history, 175-179; elitism, 180-183; education, 183-185; mentioned, viii, xiii, 28, 137

Old Gisors, *see* Gisors, Old

Order, social, the, *see* Appendix, B 6

Organization, *see* Appendix, E 3

Perken, 32-38; and Garine, 37, 38, 41-42, 62, 71, 193; and the Mois, 34, 37, 168-170, 192; mentioned, 41-42, 47, 62, 71, 78, 120, 147, 190, 195

Personal myths, *see* Appendix, D 4

Political criticism, vii, xi, 195-196

Political myths, *see* Appendix, D 3

Politics, Malraux's, *see* Appendix, E

Power, *see* Appendix, C 4

Present and future, *see* Appendix, E 3

Problem of victory, *see* Appendix, E 3

Reality, *see* Appendix, D 2

Revolt, *see* Appendix, C 2

Revolution, *see* Appendix, E 3
Royal Way, The, 32-37; and *Man's Hope,* 76; and *The Walnut Trees of Altenburg,* 76; and *The Voices of Silence,* 130, 190; and *The Conquerors,* 36-37, 42; and *The Temptation of the West,* 32, 42, 130; and *Man's Fate,* 46, 76; and "D'une jeunesse européenne," 42; and *Royaume farfelu,* 32, 190; and *Days of Wrath,* 76; mentioned, 3, 6, 120, 168
Royaume farfelu, 17-18; and *Lunes en papier,* 17; and *The Voices of Silence,* 190; and *The Conquerors,* 32; and *The Temptation of the West,* 32; and *Man's Fate,* 18; and *The Royal Way,* 32, 190; and *Days of Wrath,* 18; mentioned, 5

Scali, 83-85; mentioned, 79, 92-93, 111, 131
Social order, the, *see* Appendix, B 6
Solitude, *see* Appendix, B 2
Sorel, Georges, 117-119; political allegiances, 117-119, 124; theories of myth, 30, 118-119; mentioned, 61, 63, 90, 122, 154, 168
Style, artistic, *see* Appendix, F 2
Style, modern, *see* Appendix, F 4
Suffering, *see* Appendix, B 3

Temptation of the West, The, 19-24; and *The Voices of Silence,* 130,

139; and *The Conquerors,* 42; and *The Royal Way,* 32, 42, 130; and *Royaume farfelu,* 32; and "D'une jeunesse européenne," 23-24, 42; mentioned, 4, 31, 128, 191

"Utopia," *see* Appendix, D 3

Victory, problem of, *see* Appendix, E 3
Violence, *see* Appendix, C 4
Voices of Silence, The, Ch. 6; and *The Conquerors,* 148; and *Man's Hope,* 111, 131, 150; and *The Walnut Trees of Altenburg,* 111, 115, 131, 150; and *The Temptation of the West,* 130, 139; and *The Royal Way,* 130, 190; and "D'une jeunesse européenne," 62; and *Royaume farfelu,* 190; and *Man's Fate,* 131, 148, 157; mentioned, 10, 177

Walnut Trees of Altenburg, The, 102-115; and *Man's Hope,* 76-79, 81, 102-105, 111, 131, 150; and *The Royal Way,* 76; and *Man's Fate,* 76, 78-79, 131; and *Days of Wrath,* 76, 78-79, 102-103, 122; and *The Conquerors,* 87; and *The Voices of Silence,* 111, 115, 131, 150; mentioned, 7, 123, 133, 174
Western man, *see* Appendix, A 2
World, the, *see* Appendix, B 5